P9-EJO-860

FIRE,
CHAPARRAL,
AND SURVIVAL
IN SOUTHERN CALIFORNIA

By Richard W. Halsey

Sunbelt Publications
San Diego, California
www.sunbeltbooks.com

Fire, Chaparral, and Survival in Southern California
Sunbelt Publications, Inc.
Copyright © 2005 by the author
All rights reserved. First edition 2005

Project management by The Marino Group
Edited by Krista Marino
Cover and book design by Eldon P. Slick

Printed in the United States of America

No part of this book may be reproduced in any form without permission from the publisher. Please direct comments and inquiries to:

Sunbelt Publications, Inc.
P.O. Box 191126
San Diego, CA 92159-1126
(619) 258-4911, fax: (619) 258-4916
www.sunbeltbooks.com

08 07 06 05 04   5 4 3 2 1

Adventures in the Natural History and Cultural Heritage of the Californias
A Series Edited by Lowell Lindsay

Library of Congress Cataloging-in-Publication Data

Halsey, Richard W.
  Fire, Chaparral, and Survival in Southern California / by Richard W. Halsey. – 1st ed.
     p. cm.
  Includes bibliographical references and index.
  ISBN 0-932653-69-3
  1. Wildfires – Prevention and control – California, Southern. 2. Fire ecology –
  California, Southern. 3. Chaparral ecology – California, Southern. I. Title.

SD421.32.C2H26 2005
634.9'618'097949 – dc22
                            2004023628

All photos by author unless otherwise credited

Dedicated to

Vicki, Nicholas, and Jake

All is black and green is gone,
after the fire-drake spit forth its thermal bomb,
but in its haste to guard its treasures,
scorching the ground with violent pleasure,
the flame's remains broke hibernation,
to bring forth the chaparral's resurrection.

– Jim Hart

Table of Contents

Author's Introduction vii
List of Figures xi
Chapter 1: Chaparral, the Unknown Wilderness 1
Chapter 2: When the Fire Comes 31
            With special contributions by:
            – Susan Conniry: Prepared 37
            – Michael Wangler: Reflection on a Firestorm . . . . , , 39
            – Michael Klein: Insects and Chaparral Fires 41
            – Bill Howell. Rebirth 43
Chapter 3: Fire and Firefighters 47
            With special contributions by:
            – Two Veteran Firefighters: How We Fight Brush Fires 55
            – Chris Blaylock: From the Ozarks to Marin 60
Photo Section
Chapter 4: Getting Ready for the Next One 65
            With special contributions by:
            – Kurt Schasker: A Contractor's Perspective 67
            – Klaus Radtke: Preparing for a Wildfire 72
            – Candysse Miller: A Wake Up Call for Homeowners 83
Chapter 5: After the Fire . . . . , , ... 85
            With special contributions by.
            – Wayne Spencer and Richard W. Halsey:
              Post-fire Recovery: Nature's Way or Our Way? 86
            – Klaus Radtke: Treating Newly Burned Slopes 88
Chapter 6: Learning From Fires 99
            With special contributions by:
            – Max A. Moritz: Rethinking How We Live with Fire 103
            – Marti Witter and Robert Taylor: Preserving the Future:
              A Case Study in Fire Management and Conservation from the
              Santa Monica Mountains 105
            – Jon E. Keeley and C.J. Fotheringham:
              Lessons Learned from the Wildfires 112
Chapter 7: The Next 100 Years 123
Chapter 8: The Essential 64 Plants and Animals of Southern California Chaparral 131
            Key to Photo Identification Guide 132
            Check list 134
            Photo Identification Guide 137
Appendix: Nature's Value, Anne S. Fege 169
Literature Cited 171
Contributors 181
Acknowledgements 185
Index 187

Author's Introduction

Since the southern California firestorms of October 2003, in which over 750,000 acres and 3,600 homes were burned, and 24 people were killed, chaparral has caught the attention of millions of residents; it's the place where fire happens. This is not news to our state's firefighters, but a risk factor the public has difficulty remembering. Fires have shaped the southern California lifestyle since humans first ventured here, and the flames have been increasing ever since, especially over the past century due to accidental ignition and arson.

Surprising to many, the size of the 2003 fires was not without precedent. In September 1889, an estimated one million acres burned in Orange and San Diego Counties. It was not front-page news because few people lived in what was then the backcountry. But now, as we push into the wilderness without adequately understanding the risks, every fire receives significant news coverage.

Many of the losses suffered in California wildfires are of our own making. It's neither the chaparral's fault nor the fault of firefighting agencies. Like earthquakes, fires are an unpreventable part of living in southern California. And like earthquakes, there are things we can do to avoid catastrophic loss of life and property before the next one: retrofitting existing communities to increase their chances of survival as the flames pass by and requiring new ones to incorporate rigorous fire safety designs. The most dangerous type of fire is structural because buildings are concentrated sources of fuel. Once one home ignites, the distance of separation between the next is so small that a domino effect quickly comes into play; entire neighborhoods are wiped out before anything can be done about it.

Under severe Santa Ana wind conditions wildfires often break out in groups or become so large so quickly that firefighting resources are overwhelmed and homes are left to survive on their own. Even homes far from the fire front are easy targets because flying embers can travel a mile or more from their source. Until the wind stops, the fires will continue. It is unrealistic to expect firefighters to stop fires under such conditions. During the 1991 Oakland Hills fire, a new home was ignited every 11 seconds (Jones 2004). By the end of the day, although only 1,600 acres burned, 25 people were killed and nearly 2,900 residences were destroyed. Many communities today, such as the Claremont Mesa community in San Diego, are equally vulnerable. Wildfire is not restricted to the back country. Suburban neighborhoods with streetlights, sidewalks, and even 100-foot defensible space zones can burn if homeowners fail to correct unsafe building designs.

Unfortunately, the politically expedient solution to wildfires has been to blame the CDF (California Department of Forestry and Fire Protection), environmental laws, or the "scrub-infested" chaparral. Representatives from fire fighting agencies are accused of incompetence during public meetings, ordinances are passed to "clear the brush," and burned hillsides are sprayed with shamrock green mulch, all quite visible to the public eye. The more difficult choices are pushed aside. To be fair, some cities and counties in California have been at the forefront of fire safety. They have strengthened building codes and implemented fire management plans. The Mountain Area Safety Taskforce (MAST) was organized in San Bernardino and Riverside Counties to address public safety and forest health issues in 2002. The evacuation plans MAST developed were instrumental in saving lives in the 2003 Grand Prix and Old fires. San Diego County has developed more stringent building standards within the wildland-urban interface zone (where communities connect with wild open space). Such standards were important factors in saving homes during the 2003 Cedar fire.

Still, much needs to be done. Although politically formidable, the decision to exclude building in high fire risk areas remains the single best way to avoid wildland fire casualties. For those who currently live in such areas, government leaders and agencies need to help them understand that they will most likely be left to fend for themselves during the next firestorm. The combination of California's Mediterranean climate with extended periods of drought, strong Santa Ana winds, and large amounts of combustible fuels have made the region one of the most fire-prone environments on earth. There will never be enough fire engines, fire fighters, or helicopters to guarantee the personal safety of each and every citizen during a wildfire. The only reasonable defense is one based on individual, personal responsibility. Every citizen needs to become fire literate and help create and maintain low fire risk communities. To do otherwise fosters an attitude of dependency on a safety net that does not exist. The only legitimate policy is to be honest with citizens by informing them another fire is coming and that they need to be ready to defend themselves without government help.

The most crucial component of developing an effective fire safety program is education. FireSafe Councils have been set up throughout the state to help communities prepare for fire, but many more are needed. Although fire officials had long considered the Scripps Ranch community in San Diego County high risk, few within the area fully understood that danger; eucalyptus trees hanging over homes, wood shake roofing, and long streets ending in cul-de-sacs created the ultimate fire trap. The whole place was waiting to explode, and did the first morning of the Cedar fire.

A coordinated, long-term educational commitment will help keep both long time residents and new arrivals informed about what fire means in southern California and how best to survive one. This must go beyond real estate documents warning of various hazards primarily designed to release property sellers and their agents of liability. Fire education needs to be part of the public school curriculum as well as one of the primary objectives of countywide fire departments. Without the broad based coordination county fire departments can provide, too many embers can fall through the cracks. This applies not only to homeowner, but firefighter safety as well. Many times an engine company is sent up a narrow road to fight a fire without the confidence of knowing the structure they are being asked to protect is in compliance with standard fire safety regulations.

Learning about fire and how to properly establish defensible space around your home is the first half of the "survival in southern California" equation. The second half relates to the natural space in which we have chosen to live. As the fires of 2003 have taught us, we cannot simply construct our own environment and plop it down wherever we please without considering the natural surroundings.

This perspective is not about hugging trees. It's a matter of survival. Without understanding the natural areas around us, not only do we lose the enjoyment these areas can provide, but also the awareness we need to stay safe in a fire-prone environment. Since chaparral is the most extensive plant community in California it becomes the most important part of the survival equation to understand. But our understanding needs to occur in a timely manner because much of the chaparral is literally burning up. Our connection and appreciation for the system is crucial if we hope to protect and properly manage it for the future.

Although chaparral has been shaped by fire, it is highly sensitive to when and how frequently fires occur. The natural interval between chaparral fires is unclear but was probably anywhere between 30 to 150 years. Whatever it was, a completely new fire regime exists today. The natural interval, based on ignition from random lightning strikes in the wilderness, vanished thousands of years ago when human beings became a significant influence in California. As the population has grown, so have the brush fires. Under adequate rainfall, chaparral can build up a sufficient seed bank and recover after a fire within 10 to 20 years, depending on the location and species mix. But when fires occur more frequently, the chaparral is threatened with type conversion, the process whereby one plant community replaces another through some kind of disturbance. Over vast areas of southern California, intervals between fires have compressed so much that chaparral has been completely eliminated. In its place are acres of non-native, weedy grassland. Examples can be seen west of Highway 52 near the Miramar Air Station, along Interstate 5 between Castaic and the Tejon Pass, and through the Cajon Pass on Interstate 15. Current drought conditions have magnified the problem.

Some resource managers are finally recognizing the need to protect chaparral from increased fire frequency, but the task is a difficult one. Very few stands of beautiful, old growth chaparral remain, where massive trunks of manzanita help support canopies reaching as high as 18 feet. Once the preferred habitat of the California grizzly bear (Storer and Tevis 1955), these remarkable elfin forests are some of the state's most prized possessions.

But why protect chaparral? What is it good for? It's so thick it can only be explored by using established trails. Over time it can create enough fuel to drive 100-foot flames into the sky. And it doesn't have trees. A closer look is important.

Chaparral provides critical watershed necessary to maintain our quality of life. Without the shrubs, rain would slam into the ground with greater energy causing increased levels of erosion and flooding negatively impacting water quality, drainage infrastructure, and waterways. Grass covered slopes do not provide the same benefits as deep-rooted shrubbery and have their own sets of problems such as being easier to ignite, lengthening the fire season, and reducing biodiversity. Huge numbers of people enjoy chaparral as a wildlife habitat for a wide variety of activities including hunting, bird watching, hiking, and solitude. The capital required to deal with the loss of chaparral would be enormous. On a philosophical level, chaparral is our own native landscape. It has an aesthetic value and its presence creates a sense of place for us. It has natural wonders found nowhere else on earth.

Fire, Chaparral, and Survival in Southern California has been written to help all of us who live here strengthen our connection to the native environment in a way that will not only improve our quality of life, but will also help save our lives when the next wildfire arrives on our doorstep. Traditionally, details about the plants and animals of a particular region are restricted to nature guidebooks, separate from all other aspects of the human existence. Although this is a reasonable approach, it reinforces the disconnection between our daily lives and that of our surrounding natural environment. A thorough understanding of natural history is crucial in order to preserve the quality of life southern Californians enjoy today. Such knowledge will help us balance our immediate short-term desires with long term planning and determine what level of natural heritage, wilderness and native open space we want to protect. With the rapid pace of growth, leaving the decision up to future generations is no longer an option.

There are many voices in this book, each with a wealth of experience living within and studying the chaparral of southern California. But the message delivered is a consistent, coherent one that will offer you an honest description of what we know today about the chaparral and its intimate relationship to fire.

As you continue investigating the subject it will become quite clear there are a significant number of opinions relating to fire management that are opposed to one another. It is difficult for the average individual to wade through it all and decide who is right. Try it. But be sure you look at the data and analyze it for yourself. Do not allow a well drawn map or a persuasive argument hijack your objectivity. Analyze the data and ask questions, even if it makes you or those you ask uncomfortable or defensive. I have found in my own work there is a tendency to accept observations that confirm my own conclusions and beliefs without subjecting them to a more rigorous examination. It's a tendency I struggle with all the time.

Sometimes it just takes listening with a new perspective and examining data with a more critical eye to help see the truth.

R.W.H.
September 2004
Metaphor Café
Escondido, California

List of Figures

1-1 Chaparral Coverage in Southern California xii
1-2 Percentage of Shrubland in Southern California National Forests 2
1-3 Wrentit 3
1-4 Creation of a Rain Shadow 5
1-5 Mediterranean Rainfall Patterns in Southern California 6
1-6 Southern California Chaparral Communities 9
1-7 Grizzly Bear 11
1-8 Differences Between Coastal Sage Scrub and Chaparral 13
1-9 The Mountain Lion 14
1-10 Mountain Lion Attacks on Humans in California 15
1-11 Chaparral Plant Drought Strategies 16
1-12 Reproductive Response to Fire 18
1-13 Fire Cues, Fire Response, and Reproductive Cycles of
     Selected California Chaparral Plants 24
3-1 Estimated Insurance Losses for Catastrophic Wildland Fires
     in the United States 48
3-2a Most Devastating California Wildfires 49
3-2b Selected Major Fires Outside California 50
3-3 Fire Triangle 51
3-4 Fire Square 51
3-5 Path of the Cedar Fire Through Wildcat Canyon, San Diego County 53
3-6 Strategic Fire Suppression 57
4-1 Natural Chimneys 76
4-2 Ridgelines 76
4-3 Reducing Fire Risk When Designing a New Home 78
4-4 Retrofitting an Existing Structure to Reduce Fire Risks 79
5-1 Establishing Check Dams 95
5-2 Evaluating the Use of Chain Link Fences 95
5-3 Placing Boards 96
6-1 Area Burned Per Decade and 10-Year Running Annual Average
     During the 20th Century for Nine Counties in
     Central and Southern California 100
6-2 Decadal Variation of Area Burned and Human Population for
     Riverside County 101
6-3 The Twelve Largest Fires in the Santa Monica Mountains 1928-2001 106
6-4 Map of Santa Monica Mountain Area 108
6-5 Fire Hazard vs. Ecological Risk 110
6-6 Fire Perimeters for October 2003 Fires in Southern California 113
6-7 The 2003 Southern California Firestorm 113
6-8 Size of Fires in Two Southern California Counties 115
6-9 Decadal Changes in Human Populations and Fire Frequency 115
6-10 Seasonal Distribution of Fire Occurrence and Area Burned in
     Los Angeles County 116
6-11 Fuelbreak East of Scripps Ranch, San Diego County 118
6-12 Historical Fire Perimeter Map of San Diego County 119
The Essential 64 Plants and Animals of Southern California Chaparral 134

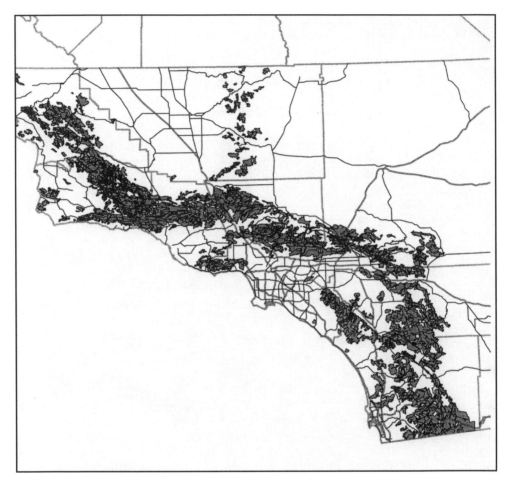

Fig. 1-1 Chaparral Coverage in Southern California. *Dark patches represent all chaparral types.*
Map generated from data collected by the GAP Analysis of Mainland California Project
(http://www.gap.uidaho.edu/gap/).

1

Chaparral,
California's Unknown Wilderness

Chaparral is California's most extensive plant community. It is also the state's most characteristic wilderness, dominating foothills and mountain slopes from the Rouge River Valley in southern Oregon to the San Pedro Martir in Baja California. Chaparral provides the deep green backdrop for Santa Barbara, the soft hues surrounding the gold country along the western slopes of the Sierra, and a valuable wilderness retreat for a rapidly growing San Diego. Take a drive into the hills surrounding nearly every southern California metropolitan area and you are immediately immersed in chaparral (fig. 1-1).

The first publication exclusively focusing on California chaparral was a 48-page U.S. Forest Service bulletin written by Fred Plummer in 1911 entitled appropriately, *Chaparral, Studies in the Dwarf Forests, or Elfin-Wood, of Southern California*. William Cooper's 1922 publication, *The Broad-Sclerophyll Vegetation of California*, was the first to approach chaparral from an ecological perspective. He disregarded Plummer's paper as "totally inadequate" in its claim to cover "both the purely scientific and economic standpoints" of the system.

It wasn't until 1923 when Francis Fultz wrote *The Elfin Forest* that the plant community was popularized as a place of natural wonder and beauty. In describing its role as a watershed Fultz wrote, " . . . Nature knew her business when she developed the chaparral . . . How defenseless the mountains are without their coat of chaparral against the elements."

Until this book the only readily available publication on California's dominant wilderness has been Winfield Head's 1972 personal narrative, *The California Chaparral, an Elfin Forest*. Affectionately called Uncle Buddy by friends and family, Bud and his wife Grace (a.k.a. Aunt Billy) drove their big, yellow station wagon "roughing it" throughout the wilds of San Diego County. His book is a heartfelt description of what he found there.

Because of the chaparral's unique pervasiveness, the community should be as well known as the redwoods or the desert sands of the Mojave. Unfortunately, chaparral not only suffers from a severe case of incognito but identity theft as well.

Upon entering one of the four National Forests in southern California visitors are greeted with "Welcome to the Forest" signs. They look around and wonder, "What forest?" Wander the isles of health food markets and you'll find chaparral in a jar, between chamomile flower and chickweed seed. "High Chaparral" was one of the most successful television westerns in the late 1960's. Unfortunately, none of these examples have anything to do with the entity they pretend to describe. All of the "forests" in southern California are primarily chaparral shrublands, not stands of timber (fig. 1-2). The "chaparral" sold in stores is actually the dried, crushed leaves of a common desert shrub, the spindly creosote bush *(Larrea tridentate)*. "High Chaparral" was filmed outside Tucson, Arizona, far from the green hillsides of the show's namesake. (The actors did, however, wear chaps.) It's no wonder folks have quizzical looks on their faces when I ask, "Have you been to the chaparral lately?"

NATIONAL FOREST	TOTAL ACRES	ACRES IN CHAPARRAL AND OTHER SHRUBLAND	PERCENT SHRUBLAND
Los Padres	1,774,520	1,149,277	64%
Angeles	662,409	474,506	71%
San Bernardino	664,830	346,940	52%
Cleveland	420,245	370,654	88%

Fig. 1-2 Percentage of Shrubland in Southern California National Forests. Despite overwhelming dominance of chaparral in southern California open space, few residents are familiar with its presence. Data source USFS.

The word "chaparral" is derived from *chaparro*, the Spanish term for "place of the scrub oak." When Spaniards first explored California, they were struck by the landscape's similarity to what they knew back home so they used the same name to describe it. *Chaparro* was later Anglicized to chaparral, with one of its first recorded references found in a letter written by William H. Brewer in 1860. Describing a trip into the mountains behind Los Angeles, Brewer wrote, "It was very steep, many precipices obstructed us, and when there were no rocks, there was an almost impenetrable thicket, or chaparral, as it is here called."

Chaparral – The name elicits visions of romantic nights at the rancho when California life was much less hectic. Once called elfinwood, a term that inspires visions of tiny fairies flitting between boughs of manzanita, chaparral can also be considered a place of tightly held secrets (photo 1). When experienced only through car windows, this "impenetrable thicket" appears as an amorphous green carpet, a stunted forest of dense, bushes, refusing entry to any curious onlooker; not an easy place to have a picnic. Upon closer inspection, however, accessible edges reveal themselves, made possible by old roads, pathways, and previous burn scars. Once entry has been achieved the visitor is engulfed by a remarkable array of fire-adapted plant life, delicate colors, and a comforting quiet. Soon the ears become acclimated, and sounds begin to emerge. Off in the distance, hidden deep in the shrubbery, a secretive little bird with a long tail introduces itself. Its call, recognized by those who consider wild southern California their home, is known as "the voice of the chaparral." Of all the interesting life forms found there, it is the sparrow-sized wrentit that best characterizes this shrubby habitat; ubiquitous, yet hidden, its secrets revealed only to those with patience and a willingness to listen (fig. 1-3).

Fig. 1-3 Wrentit. *Artist: Zackery Zidinak*

Properly defined, chaparral is a semi-arid, shrub dominated association of *sclerophyllous* woody plants shaped by summer drought, mild, wet winters, and naturally recurring fires every 30 to 150 years plus. *Sclerophyllous* is a term coined by German botanist, Andreas F. W. Schimper in 1898. Referring to Mediterranean climatic regions in his classic 844 page *Plant Geography Upon a Physiological Basis* he said, "The mild temperate districts with winter-rain and prolonged summer-drought are the home of evergreen xerophilous (dry-loving) woody plants, which, owing to the stiffness of their thick, leathery leaves, may be termed *sclerophyllous* woody plants."

Meaning "hard-leaved" in Greek, *sclerophyllous* leaves are advantageous in a semi-arid climate because they reduce evaporation through a variety of traits including waxy coatings, thicker cell layers, and recessed "stomata," the pores in leaves permitting evaporation and the exchange of oxygen and carbon dioxide. Chaparral is primarily a California phenomenon, although a type of "mock chaparral" exists in parts of Arizona, the central Rocky Mountains, and Northeastern Mexico.

As direct connections to the land have slowly disappeared for most Californians, so too has familiarity with chaparral. We pay a heavy toll for this alienation; homes burn, lives are lost, and we forget the value of retaining informed contact with wild space. Reconnecting with our natural surroundings is no longer just a casual pastime for bird-watchers or wilderness enthusiasts; it is a matter of survival for all of us. This chapter is designed to assist you to reconnect, providing a quick familiarity with the chaparral ecosystem. Although the species described are primarily from California's southwestern most counties (San Diego, Riverside, and Orange), most can be found throughout the southern California region wherever chaparral exists. The fundamental details concerning chaparral ecology apply statewide.

The Seasons

Do the amber colored leaves that traditionally decorate the walls inside elementary school classrooms accurately reflect what is happening outside during the months of autumn? Is fall really a time of red maple leaves and hibernation? Not in southern California. Since drought, not freezing snow, determines our seasons, the transition from one to the other is more subtle. And with help from the garden hose and sprinklers, suburban dwellers can live in a green, springtime setting all year. But out in the chaparral, seasonal changes continue to pace the rhythm of life; a Mediterranean melody with three notes instead of four; fall, spring, and six or more long months of drought.

Fall is subtle, lasting only a few short weeks in June, punctuating spring and drought. Marked by a brief yellowing of the hillsides as some of the leaves on shrubs like ceanothus and manzanita are discarded, fall prepares the chaparral for long months of desiccation ahead; scarcity of water demands conservation and springtime foliage becomes a liability by releasing too much moisture. Although autumn in the chaparral is more of a short interlude than a full season, it remains a critical component of the system's life cycle. By mid-July, drought has settled in; growth slows to a crawl, cicadas buzz in the heat, and ceanothus seed capsules snap open in the dry air.

Usually in November, just when it seems as if life is about to shrivel up and disappear from lack of water, a hint of moisture arrives. The ground stays damp longer in the morning from lingering nighttime dew. Serious clouds begin to form. Finally, the first concentrated delivery of rain arrives and quenches the shrubland's thirst. "Spring" has arrived. The traditional winter months become part of the chaparral's season of growth.

So while much of the country is preparing for cold, the chaparral is emerging from its defensive posture. Bright green fingers of wild cucumber vines *(Marah macrocarpus)* (#22) crawl upon the ground, searching for something to grasp. Creamy bushrue flowers *(Cneoridium dumosum)* (#53), California's own native citrus, create clumps of contrast to olivaceous hillsides. Ceanothus buds begin to swell, and will soon powder the chaparral with white or azure blossoms (#47). Perhaps, instead of snowflakes and holly leaves, southern California classrooms in December should be decorated with boughs of red-berried toyon *(Heteromeles arbutifolia)* (#52), scrub oak acorns, and sprigs of fragrant white sage *(Salvia apiana)* (#33). Such native decorations would be an excellent way to strengthen the connection children already have with nature and may help reawaken the same in the adults around them. One wonders how different the American view of the natural world would be if the Pilgrims had landed in San Pedro Bay instead of Plymouth.

The Climate

The distribution of chaparral in southern California is shaped by five different factors: 1) **latitude**, 2) **coastal mountains**, 3) **the ocean**, 4) **air mass movement**, and 5) **Santa Ana winds**.

At the equator, warm, moist air rises. As it cools, rain is squeezed out and dry air cells drop back to earth approximately 30 degrees **latitude** north and south of the equator. These areas are where the world's great deserts appear. However, in six special places a combination of local conditions holds back the desert and creates unique, semi-arid shrubland ecosystems: central Chile, the Cape of South Africa, southwestern and southern Australia, the Mediterranean Basin, and California.

In California, **coastal mountains** block moist, **ocean** air blowing further inland. Pushing upslope, the air cools. Cold air holds less moisture than warm air, so condensation occurs and rain falls. By the time the air gets over the mountaintops it's parched, leading to the creation of the Mojave and Anza-Borrego deserts (Fig. 1-4). There is just enough rain on the western side to support a wide variety of plant communities. The higher the elevation, the richer the vegetation becomes. This applies to latitude as well. Santa Barbara has more rainfall than San Diego, and consequently more lush growth. Regions with 8 to 39 inches average annual rainfall can support chaparral as the dominant vegetation type (Keeley 2000). In areas with less than 8 inches or higher evaporation rates, chaparral is replaced by coastal sage scrub. Conifer and mixed evergreen forests begin dominating above 30 inches of rainfall. (Barbour and Minnich 2000).

Contrary to popular opinion, coastal southern California is not a desert. The average annual rainfall for San Diego is just over 10 inches, gradually increasing inland with elevation to over 33 inches for Cuyamaca State Park. The Anza-Borrego Desert has less than 6 inches per year.

One remarkable feature of southern California vegetation is the variation seen as related to slope orientation, especially in drier San Diego County. Because of

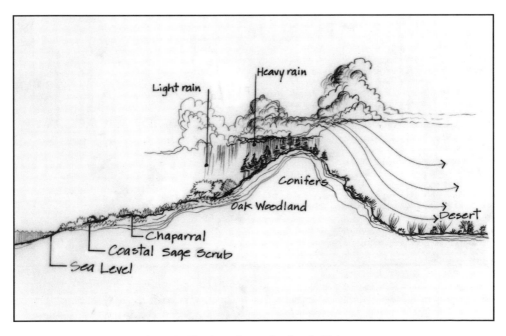

Fig. 1-4 Creation of a Rain Shadow. *Artist: Stephen L. Halsey*

decreased solar radiation and thus reduced rates of evaporation, north-facing slopes have more verdant growth than south facing slopes. This is different from what is observed in other regions of the country. In eastern forests you see miles of dense vegetation no matter what direction you look. Across the Mojave, you see desert all around. But in southern California, plants live on a knife-edge. There is just barely enough moisture to maintain their existence. Any slight, localized environmental change will tip the balance and rob enough water to drastically alter vegetation type. Consequently, one can stand between hillsides and see two completely different plant communities: thick chaparral on a north-facing slope, and sparse coastal sage scrub on the south. This is one reason why California is one of the most ecologically diverse regions on earth; there are multiple types of habitat within a few feet of each other (photo 2).

For most of the country, summer is a time for rainstorms. Not California. A huge, subtropical high-pressure cell over the Pacific Ocean dictates the region's overall climate. As this **air mass** moves northward in the summer, it blocks cold, polar storm fronts from reaching California. In the winter, the air mass backs off and moves toward the equator, allowing storms to break the drought. Hot, dry summers and mild, wet winters (our spring) characterize California's weather pattern and define a Mediterranean-like climate, creating one of the most pleasant environments on earth (fig. 1-5).

Average Monthly Rainfall for Southern California Chaparral Regions 1961-1990

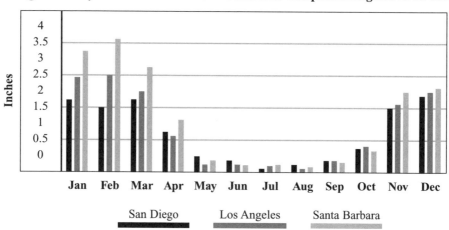

Fig. 1-5 Mediterranean Rainfall Patterns in Southern California. Shows average monthly rainfall distribution patterns for three different southern California locations, and demonstrates the characteristic Mediterranean climatic cycle of dry summers and wet winters. Data source: University of Utah, Department of Meteorology.

The last, and perhaps most notorious factor shaping southern California chaparral, is **Santa Ana winds**. Created when heavy, cool air masses from the interior deserts rush onto the coastal plain between September and May, these dry winds quickly heat up as they drop to lower elevations and can exceed sixty miles an hour. Dropping humidity below measurable levels, Santa Ana winds create extremely dangerous fire conditions and are responsible for causing the most catastrophic wildfires in California.

Origin: Past and Future

Things have not always been the way we see them today. This appears obvious, but when trying to imagine past and future landscape configurations we are constrained by visions of the present. Along with trying to visualize that most of southwest California was attached to the western side of northern Mexico 20 million years ago, we also must understand the flux of complex climatic changes that have occurred. It is extremely difficult to imagine what a particular location looked like when it has moved so much.

Approximately 14 million years ago, summer rains began decreasing on the land that was to become modern southern California. Forests thinned, exposing under-story plants to more light. Beginning about 10 million years ago, based on charcoal deposits, fires appeared to dramatically increase (Axelrod 1989). Adaptations to with-stand drought and survive fire were selected for, and plants requiring more moisture were pushed into canyons and higher elevations. Two million years ago coastal uplift occurred, creating some of the modern elevational variation we see today. Interglacial periods during the Pleistocene (1.6 million to 10,000 years ago) saw the chaparral expand and contract depending on moisture levels. As recently as 15,000 years ago, chaparral covered the Vizcaino Desert in Baja California, about 200 miles further south than it does today in the Sierra San Pedro Martir, Baja California (Rhode 2002).

Whenever the first humans arrived on the North American continent (there is strong evidence that a large contingent entered at least 11,000 years ago), their numbers were probably not significant enough to have a meaningful impact on the landscape until 5,000 years ago (Keeley 2002). However, once established, early Native Americans regularly burned chaparral in an effort to increase favored natural resources (herbaceous seed crops and deer), reduce grizzly bear contact (chaparral was their favored habitat), and as a weapon against tribal enemies. To a limited degree, Spaniards continued the practice in order to expand grazing land (Kinney 1887). Once Americans arrived on the scene, fires caused by ranchers, miners, and hunters became so frequent the United States government recognized something needed to be done to protect valuable water-sheds. U.S. Forest Reserves were first established in 1891 in part to address this concern. On December 20, 1892, the boundaries of the first reserve in California were drawn in the San Gabriel Mountains above Los Angeles, becoming part of the Angeles National Forest in 1908.

It is impossible to determine how much chaparral has been lost since humans began altering the landscape. Currently there are an estimated 8.6 million acres of chaparral in California (Jones and Stokes 1987). This represents nearly 9% of the state's total acreage of 99.82 million acres. Between 1946 and 1987 it has been estimated chaparral decreased as much as 1.5 million acres by urban expansion, road, reservoir, and power line construction, range "improvement" and wildfire (Bolsinger 1989). Range improvement is a utilitarian description for eliminating native vegetation for the purpose of increasing livestock grazing pasture.

At first it may seem confusing that chaparral can be eliminated by fire since conventional wisdom portrays the system as fire adapted. Conventional wisdom is frequently overly simplistic. Not all fires are alike. Different types of chaparral have adapted to specific fire regimes. A fire regime includes several important variables including frequency (intervals between fires), intensity (the amount of heat released), and seasonality (when fires burn). If the interval between fires is too short, chaparral is unable to restock its seed bank in the soil to properly recover. Time required between burns to insure chaparral recovery can be as long as 20 years for south facing stands suffering long term drought conditions or a minimum of 10 years for chaparral growing under less stressful parameters. Fires occurring more than once a decade will wipe out all non-sprouting chaparral shrubs (Keeley and Fotheringham 2003). Chaparral eliminated by high fire frequency is replaced by smothering tracts of non-native, weedy annuals, most of which produce the irritating stickers found jabbing through your socks after a causal walk outdoors (photo 3). This process whereby one type of plant community replaces another is called "type conversion."

Although there are still large tracks of chaparral throughout California, the combination of increased fire frequency and development will seriously compromise the ecosystem's health and integrity over the next century. Preservation through wilderness or park designations is only marginally successful because fire knows no boundary. For example, one of the last remaining stands of old growth chaparral in San Diego County, the Agua Tibia Wilderness, was mostly destroyed by a series of fires over a 12 year period between 1987 to 2000. The area had not burned for well over a century, not since at least 1877 (Chester 2004). With the growing development pressure in nearby Temecula, chances are that fire frequency will increase and threaten the wilderness with type conversion to non-native, weedy grassland.

As California's population continues to grow, available flatland is quickly diminishing and developers are spying the backcountry for additional building opportunities. Considering development, increased fire frequency, and the possibility of continued drought conditions, the future looks extremely difficult for southern California's remaining stands of native chaparral.

Chaparral Types

Chaparral is filled with groups of unique individuals. As one becomes familiar with the system, a surprisingly wide variety of distinct communities appear. One hillside may be covered with a pure stand of chamise *(Adenostoma fasciculatum)* (#50), while directly across the canyon, clumps of red-barked manzanita *(Arctostaphylos* species) (#23) will be mixed with white flowering ceanothus. All are chaparral plant communities, yet each has its own distinct appearance and species mix. Being able to identify the differences creates a new level of recognition of patterns you never knew existed before. This is the basis for becoming an accomplished citizen naturalist. Once you are able to notice subtle distinctions, because you know what belongs and what doesn't, the natural environment becomes an integral part of your existence. Small changes and new observations turn into exciting, new discoveries as you add them to your quiver of connections with the natural world around you.

There have been several efforts to classify chaparral plant communities, with one of the most recent identifying over 50 different variations or series (Sawyer and Keeler-Wolf 1995). Although these categories are helpful when doing detailed work, they are overwhelming to the average citizen trying to grasp the overall picture. Therefore, I have consolidated them into seven basic types found in southern California, based on the most dominant plant species present (fig. 1-6). Where no particular species dominates the scene, meaning at least 60% of the cover is composed of a single species, the default classification "mixed chaparral" applies. As with any attempt to categorize natural patterns, it is important to understand they are regionally specific and apply to the most frequent distributions. One type of chaparral will blend into another without easily defined interface zones. Boundaries have been dramatically influenced by past human activity as well. Animal grazing, farming, and repeated burning have drastically changed the distribution of natural communities. What is a weedy hillside today may have been an old-growth chaparral stand 100 years ago.

TYPE	DEFINING SPECIES	SPECIAL SITE CHARACTERISTICS
Red Shanks	*Adenostoma sparsifolium*	Above 2000 ft. 6-9 ft. tall. Minimal leaf litter (>1/2"). Light green, airy appearance.
Ceanothus	Various *Ceanothus* species	Generally below 3600 ft. 3-9 ft. tall. Minimal leaf litter (>1/2").
Chamise	*Adenostoma fasciculatum*	Common on lower elevation south-facing, xeric slopes, and mesas. 3-6 ft. tall. Minimal leaf litter (>1/2"). Most common single species chaparral type.
Mixed	No overwhelmingly dominant species	
a. xeric form	*Adenostoma, ceanothus,* and *Arctostaphylos* species	Typically on south-facing slopes. Minimal leaf litter (>1/2").
b. mesic form	*Heteromeles arbutifolia* *Rhamnus crocea* *Prunus ilicifolia* *Malosma laurina* *Rhus integrifolia* *Quercus berberidifolia* *Cerococarpus betuloides*	Typically on north-facing slopes. Can be 10-18 ft. tall. Deep leaf litter (up to 8"+). Many broad-leafed species. Most diverse chaparral type.
c. maritime	*Ceanothus verrucosus* *Quercus dumosa* and endemics including *Arctostaphylos glandulosa crassifolia* *Baccharis vanessae* *Pinus torreyana*	Coastal areas. Usually > 6 ft. tall. Under the influence of coastal fog belt. One of the rarest chaparral associations due to development.
Manzanita	*Arctostaphylos* species	Generally higher elevations. 3-6 ft. tall.
Scrub Oak	*Quercus berberidifolia* *Q. wislizenii* *Q. cornelius-mulleri*	North facing slopes below 3000 ft. and all slopes above 3000 ft. 4-12 ft. tall. Moderate leaf litter (> 7").
Montane	*Arctostaphylos* and *Ceanothus* species	Above 4500 ft. Usually > 4 ft. tall. Compact shape, extremely dense and dominated by resprouters.

Fig. 1-6 Southern California Chaparral Communities. *Listed by increasing relative density with red shanks chaparral the least dense, montane the most. Adapted from Hanes (1977) , Marion (1943), and Halsey (unpublished data).*

Although the largest and most pristine stands of chaparral occur in southern California between 500 to 4,500 feet in elevation, smaller patches exist along the coast such as those on Carmel Mountain in San Diego County. Stands of red shanks chaparral can found at 7,000 feet in the San Jacinto Mountains in Riverside County. However, if there is one defining characteristic of nearly all chaparral, it is the presence of chamise *(Adenostoma fasciculatum)*, the ecosystem's most pervasive shrub.

Red shanks chaparral (photo 4) is composed of yellowish green, finely leaved *Adenostoma sparsifolium*. As its Latin name implies, this shrub has an airy, light appearance, easily distinguishing it from denser, surrounding species. Frequently growing in nearly pure stands, red shanks chaparral is found in four widely separated populations; southeastern San Diego County into Baja California, the lower slopes of the San Jacinto Mountains southward to Volcan Mountain, small patches in the Santa Monica Mountains, and several large stands in north-central Santa Barbara and southern San Luis Obispo Counties. After fire, *Adenostoma sparsifolium* is a vigorous resprouter.

Ceanothus chaparral (photo 6) can also form nearly pure stands, but is often mixed as a dominant with other shrubs such as chamise *(Adenostoma fasciculatum)* and scrub oak *(Quercus berberidifolia)* (#28). More the 40 species of ceanothus, commonly called California wild lilac, exist in California. The group is split into two groups. Approximately half of the species (mostly subgenus *Ceanothus*) resprout after fire, while the rest (subgenus *Cerastes* with rare exceptions) depend on fire-stimulated seed germination to repopulate after flames have moved through.

Chamise chaparral (photo 5) is the most common chaparral type dominated by one species. In fact, chamise *(Adenostoma fasciculatum)* is also the most common California native shrub west of the Sierra Nevada mountain range. Occasionally found in nearly pure stands, chamise has tiny, needle-like leaves, which help the plant conserve water as well as making it extremely flammable during dry weather.

Mixed chaparral (photo 1) includes all the miscellaneous stands without a single species dominating the scene. Mixed chaparral can be further divided into three distinct forms: xeric, mesic, and maritime. **Xeric** relates to increased rates of surface evaporation and a relative lack of moisture as opposed to **mesic** which describes environments with reduced rates of surface evaporation and higher moisture availability. **Xeric mixed** chaparral is found on south facing slopes where direct sunshine increases evaporation and produces conditions where plants suffer severe water stress during time of drought. Chamise *(Adenostoma fasciculatum)* and various *Ceanothus* species are common components.

California native shrublands reach their most diverse and tallest development under **mesic mixed** conditions. Most of the magnificent old growth stands of 100 year old plus chaparral are of this type, where deep red manzanita trunks are more than waist thick, canopies reach eighteen feet into the sky, and narrow animal pathways weave themselves through shaded galleries. California grizzly bears thrived here (fig. 1-7), using the same trails for generations, placing their paws in the same depressions over and over until the trails became a series of potholes. Despite the grizzly's extinction, some of these trails may still exist in remaining old growth chaparral stands. The last grizzly in southern California was shot in the southeastern corner of Orange County up Trabuco Canyon in the Santa Ana Mountains in January, 1908. The final recorded sighting in the entire state occurred in 1924 around the vicinity of Sequoia National Park, the bear's last refuge from a rapidly changing world (Storer and Tevis 1955).

*Fig. 1-7 California Grizzly Bear (*Ursus arctos californicus *Merriam). Now extinct in Southern California, the grizzly bear was once the dominant predator in the chaparral. The southern California grizzly was the largest of them all and was considered a subspecies* (magister) *by C. Hart Merriam. Artist: Zackery Zdinak.*

Maritime mixed chaparral is a specialized form distinguished by its coastal location and an assemblage of rare, endemic (restricted to a particular locality) plant species. Warty-stemmed ceanothus *(Ceanothus verrucosus)* and Nuttall's scrub oak *(Quercus dumosa)* are two characteristic species. Due to coastal development, very few examples remain. One stand preserved by the Torrey Pines State Park in San Diego County is unusual in that it also contains trees, the Torrey pine *(Pinus torreyana)*. This is the rarest pine in the United States and exists in only one other location, on Santa Rosa Island off of the Santa Barbara coastline. Both populations combined, there are probably fewer than 10,000 individuals remaining.

Manzanita chaparral (photo 7) is the type most people visualize when they think of chaparral because of the rich, blood red bark of its characteristic species. Combined with beautiful urn shaped flowers, manzanita shrubs *(Arctostaphylos* species) are undisputedly one of the most beautiful plants in California. There are nearly 60 different species in the state, the most common in the southern portion being Eastwood manzanita *(Arctostaphylos glandulosa)* and Bigberry manzanita *(Arctostaphylos glauca)* (#23). Five species have underground burls allowing them to resprout after a fire. The rest are usually killed by the flames and depend on chemicals in charred wood to stimulate the germination of their seeds. Due to the extreme hardness of manzanita wood, this type of chaparral is virtually impossible to penetrate, with or without chaps.

Scrub oak chaparral (photo 8), the *chaparro's* original namesake, is primarily found on northern facing slopes. Scrub oaks are not the traditional, large, sheltering oaks found dotting the landscape, but rather shrubs with beautifully gnarled boughs, small leaves, and impoverished acorns; all reflective of their semi-arid environment. Some of the oldest chaparral stands in San Diego County consist of this type with the dominant scrub oak species being *Quercus berberidifolia* (#28). Along the coast, Nuttall's scrub oak *(Quercus dumosa)* replaces *Quercus berberidifolia* as the predominant species but with lower density.

Demonstrating the evolutionary selection pressures that limited water can exert on an organism, an interesting variation occurs in the southern distribution of the interior live oak *(Quercus wislizenii)*. This species, normally a very large tree growing up to 70 feet tall, becomes a smaller shrub when found in chaparral, *Quercus wislizenii frutescens*.

Montane chaparral is determined by elevation and structure rather than species mix. Found above 4,500 feet, this type is subjected to colder temperatures and is frequently covered by snow for months at a time. These selective pressures have produced an extremely dense, low growing cluster of species frequently found as understory plants in coniferous forests. The canopy, 2 to 4 feet tall, is so rigid and intertwined it seems as if one could walk over the top of it. Various manzanita, *Ceanothus* species, and scrub oak are some of the most common plants found in montane chaparral.

Coastal Sage Scrub

If conditions become too dry for chamise or xeric mixed chaparral, another shrubland type appears, coastal sage scrub (fig. 1-8). The two plant communities frequently intergrade, especially where slope angles alternate between north and south facing exposures. More limited in distribution than chaparral, coastal sage scrub can be found just north of San Francisco and southward into Baja California. Typically found below 3,000 feet, the simplest way to distinguish this more open shrubland from its dominant relative is by its density (photo 9). Due to the brittle nature of its characteristic species, lower stature, and lack of intertwining, woody branches, coastal sage scrub can be easily walked through, hence the nickname, soft chaparral. On a warm day, the aromatic vapors filling the air from leaves of plants like black sage *(Salvia mellifera)* (#33), white sage *(Salvia apiana)*, and California sagebrush *(Artemisia californica)* (#10) are unforgettable. A few larger shrubs common to chaparral like laurel sumac *(Malosma laurina)* (#5) and lemonadeberry *(Rhus integrifolia)* (#6) are frequently found in the mix. During the drought season, they appear like islands of greenery floating in a sea of grays and tans. The umber tones of spent flower clusters on California buckwheat *(Eriogonum fasciculatum)* (#44) in late summer turn hillsides deep red at sunset, reflecting the day's last rays of light.

Distinct from chaparral, most coastal sage scrub plant species are semi-summer deciduous. During the dry season they lose the majority of their leaves. Those remaining are small and often curled up to reduce water loss. Once the rains return, coastal sage scrub is the first community to respond since the leaves of resident plants require less energy to produce than the thick, sclerophyllous foliage typically found in chaparral species. After fires, most of the plants recover by resprouting rather than germinating from seed. As time after fire increases, the 2 to 5 foot tall canopy remains open allowing for continual recruitment of seedlings and permitting herbaceous plant growth.

Unfortunately, since coastal sage scrub is primarily distributed at lower elevations and along flat, coastal mesas, it has been heavily impacted by development. The U.S. Fish and Wildlife Service has estimated less than 10% of the habitat remains. It has more than 100 rare, sensitive, or endangered species including the California gnatcatcher *(Polioptila californica)*, horned lizard *(Phrynosoma coronatum)*, and San Diego barrel cactus *(Ferocactus viridescens)*. Even less appreciated than chaparral, coastal sage scrub is one of California's most threatened natural environments.

CHARACTERISTIC	COASTAL SAGE SCRUB	CHAPARRAL
Dominant plant species	California sagebrush, white sage, black sage, California buckwheat, laurel sumac, lemonadeberry, broom baccharis	chamise, scrub oak, ceanothus, manzanita
Moisture	Fine-textured soils and/or angle of exposure to sun reduce available moisture. Rainfall varies.	Average annual rainfall range between 8-39 inches
Elevation	Lower elevations, south facing slopes and flat lands below 3,000 ft. Common along the coast.	Typically 500-4,500 ft. Most common at lower elevations on north facing slopes.
Vegetation height	2 to 5 ft.	4 to 18 ft.
Density	Generally open appearance	Extreme density with up to 450% greater biomass than coastal sage scrub.
Plant type	Brittle stemmed and herbaceous species	Woody shrubs in mature chaparral. Some geophytes. Herbaceous growth limited to periods after fire and in openings.
Reaction to drought	Mostly evade by being semi-summer deciduous. Some can tolerate like laurel sumac and lemonadeberry.	Some loss of leaves, but most species tolerate with thick, ever green foliage.
Post-fire response	Mostly resprouters.	Resprouters. Many species require a fire cue for germination and resprouters.
Primary threats	Development, grazing. Nearly 100 sensitive species.	Type conversion by repeated fires over short periods of time (less than 10 years). Development.

Fig. 1-8 Differences Between Coastal Sage Scrub and Chaparral. Data based on DeSimone (1995), Keeley (2000), Mooney (1977), Halsey (unpublished data).

Animals

Because of its density, uniform cover, and nonexistent understory of herbaceous plants, the diversity of chaparral animal life is low when compared to a forest ecosystem. However, the animals that do call the chaparral their home are an interesting assortment of highly territorial survivors. There are two in particular that a shrubland visitor will invariably notice the sparrow-sized wrentit and the big-eared woodrat.

The wrentit *(Chamaea fasciata)* (#2) is one of the most homebound bird species in North America, restricting its movement to less than 2 acres. Despite being visually secretive, both male and females sing all year-round allowing their location to be pin-pointed by sound, a descending whistle having the beat of a bouncing ping-pong ball. Rarely is a mated pair found apart unless finding food for their young. At night the female sits in the nest and the male sleeps alone on a nearby perch. His call is often the last bird sound heard across the chaparral at dusk. When the offspring finally leave their nest, the parents once again share the evening roost. They snuggle up so tightly that it is difficult to distinguish two birds amongst the bundle of feathers.

The big-eared woodrat *(Neotoma macrotis)* (#1) is conspicuous not by actual sighting, but by the home in which it lives. Built of a pile of sticks, woodrat nests can be over five feet tall and eight feet across. With furry tails and large Mickey Mouse ears, woodrats look like arboreal gremlins as they scurry along limbs and branches at night searching for favored foods including seeds, acorns, leaves, and fungi. Unlike the wrentit, these nocturnal creatures are quite promiscuous, with the male mating with multiple females each breeding season. The nest is the domain of mother and daughters since males disperse from their birth den rather quickly, roaming the shrubland with generally bad attitudes and territorial imperatives (Kelly 1990). Due to the male's aggressive nature in defending these territories, a significant number of potential fathers are unable to find a mate and fail to become successful breeders.

One animal you are not likely to see, but has certainly seen you without your knowledge, is the mountain lion *(Felis concolor)*. With the grizzly bear gone, mountain lions are now the top chaparral predator (fig. 1-9). Their primary food source is deer, but smaller animals including rabbits, raccoons and rodents comprise the other half of their diet.

Fig. 1-9 The Mountain Lion. *Artist: Zackery Zdinak.*

Like fire, mountain lions are an inevitable part of the southern California experience and there is little you can do to prevent coming near one if you spend a significant amount of time in or near chaparral. Occasionally they let you see them, rarely will they choose to attack. However, the risk of attack is real and it is important to take the threat seriously (fig. 1-10). Do not venture out alone in areas with recorded sightings. Maintain constant, close contact with children who are with you whenever exploring southern California backcountry. Being aware and respectful of these animals is as much a part of reconnecting with our surroundings as knowing how to prepare for wildfire.

DATE	LOCALE	COUNTY	VICTIM	INJURY
1890, June 19	Quartz Valley	Siskiyou	Boy, 7	Death
1909, July 5	Morgan Hill	Santa Clara	1 woman/ 1 child	Death (rabies)
1986, March 23	Caspers Regional Park	Orange	Girl, 5	Serious
1986, October 19	Caspers Regional Park	Orange	Boy,6	Minor
1992, March 12	Gaviota State Park	Santa Barbara	Boy, 9	Minor
1993, August	Los Padres National Forest	Santa Barbara	Boy, 6	Minor
1993, September	Paso Picacho Campground	San Diego	Girl, 10	Minor
1994, April 23	Auburn State Rec. Area	Placer	Woman, 40	Death
1994, August 16	Dos Rios	Mendocino	Woman, 48	Minor
1994, Dec. 10	Cuyamaca Rancho State Park	San Diego	Woman, 56	Death
1995, March 20	Angeles National Forest	Los Angeles	Man, 27	Minor
2004, January 8	Whiting Ranch Wilderness Park	Orange	Man, 35	Death
2004, January 8	Whiting Ranch Wilderness Park	Orange	Woman, 30	Serious

Fig. 1-10 Mountain Lion Attacks on Humans in California. Contacts and attacks from mountain lions have increased dramatically since 1986 probably due to reduction of mountain lion habitat. Adapted from Tom Chester (2004b).

Relationship to Drought

An organism has two basic ways to coexist with stressful conditions: tolerate or evade. Chaparral plants use both methods by employing four different strategies in response to drought. They can be classified as **avoiders, persisters, retreaters,** or **chameleons** (fig. 1-11).

Depending on soil conditions, drought **avoiders** can develop roots 30 feet long to access water deep underground (Keeley 1998b). Their leaves are designed to conserve water with protective, waxy surfaces. These coatings, plus additional supportive cells inside, create the characteristic sclerophyllous foliage characteristic of many chaparral shrubs. To further reduce water loss, stomata are concentrated on leaf undersides. Some, like those of many *Ceanothus* species, hide stomata in deeply sunken pits. These hefty leaves are expensive to make in terms of energy utilization so they have to last a very long time. For example, leaves on toyon *(Heteromeles arbutifolia)* (#52) last an average of two years in the sun and nearly seven years in the shade (Castellanos 1986).

Heavy foliage and focus on water conservation has a price: slower growth. Restricted stomata reduce the intake of carbon dioxide, seriously compromising the process of photosynthesis. This represents a classic irony for chaparral plants. When summer delivers necessary sunshine and warmth, lack of water limits photosynthetic activity. Consequently, the community as a whole has shifted its growing season into

DROUGHT STRATEGY	CHARACTERISTICS	EXAMPLE SPECIES
Avoiders	Avoid drought by long roots and hard/thick (sclerophyllous) leaves.	*Malosma laurina, Rhus integrifolia, Quercus berberidifolia.*
Persisters	Tolerate drought by physiological adaptations and movements (leaf angle, stomata closure). Do not have long roots. Some with sclerophyllous leaves.	Non-sprouting/shallow rooted ceanothus and manzanita *(Artostaphylos)* species.
Retreaters	Annuals evade by using an annual life cycle. Plants with underground storage (geophytes) evade by dying back above ground during dry months.	Annuals: popcorn flowers (*Cryptantha* and *Plagiobothrys* species). Geophytes, like lilies.
Chameleons	Evade by being semi-summer deciduous.	*Mimulus aurantiacus,* many coastal sage scrub species like *Salvia mellifera* and *Artemisia californica.*

Fig. 1-11 Chaparral Plant Drought Strategies. *Being able to survive water stress is critical in a Mediterranean climate. Chaparral plants do so by using one of four different strategies.*

earlier months. Cooler temperatures in winter and spring do not permit optimal photosynthetic rates, but at least there is enough water to keep the process going.

Drought **persisters** are the battle-hardened Green Berets of the chaparral. Due to their tough physiology, they can withstand extreme levels of internal water stress; enough to kill a drought avoider. *Ceanothus* species, characteristic drought persisters, can survive more than seven times the internal water stress than laurel sumac, a typical avoider (Keeley 1998b). Water stressed plants are damaged by embolisms within their xylem tubes, the internal water pipes of a plant. Once the tight chain of water molecules breaks, moisture can no longer reach plant tissues and they die.

Persisters thrive in the open, doing poorly in shade. In contrast to avoiders, these plants soak up the sun and reach their maximum photosynthetic abilities with 66% maximal sunlight levels (Oechel 1982). During the driest days, these plants can completely shut down their stomata.

Persisters partially overcome the lack of deep roots by an intricate network of lateral ones near the surface. Chamise extend roots up to 7 times the area of its canopy (Kummerow 1981), with most being concentrated in the top 8 inches of soil and going no deeper than 2 feet (Kummerow et. al. 1977). To avoid direct sunlight, many persisters like the manzanitas (*Arctostaphylos* species) have leaves permanently pointing straight up. *Ceanothus* species use a similar strategy, but are a bit more flexible. They can change individual leaf orientation as the sun moves across the sky.

Drought **retreaters** hide in order to fight another day. There are two basic groups of plants practicing this survival technique: annuals, and plants that retire underground during the dry season, the geophytes ("earth plants" in Greek).

Although annuals make up about thirty percent of the native species found in California's Mediterranean climate zone they are relatively absent under the chaparral canopy (Keeley 2004b). Only after a fire do they appear in large numbers when cover has been eliminated and sunlight is available. Quickly growing after the first rains, these plants produce a large seed crop before ending their short lives, baking as dry stalks in the summer sun. Geophytes are perennials that emerge from an underground storage organ, like a bulb or enlarged tuber, then die back to ground level during the dry season. Members of the lily family are included in this group, producing some of the most beautiful wildflowers found in the chaparral, especially after a burn.

To conserve water, drought **chameleons** are semi-summer deciduous, shedding most of their springtime foliage during the dry season, retaining only smaller, curled versions. The fragrant sages in the mint family use this strategy. They possess dimorphic leaves, meaning "two forms." A pair of buds is subtended by a larger, though slightly shriveled leaf below (photo 10). This allows the plant to quickly respond to momentary supplies of moisture by expanding the larger leaves in order to increase photosynthetic activity. The buds are ready to grow the following winter-spring to produce either full-sized leaves or new branches. In the case of white sage, leaves are covered with minute, whitish hairs, further reducing water loss through evaporation by reflecting light and diminishing air movement over the leaf's surface.

Although mostly components of the coastal sage scrub community, drought chameleons are frequently interspersed within chaparral, especially where the two vegetation types meet. Many chameleons, like black sage, are responsible for the minty scent hanging in the air during a warm summer day. These aromas come from volatile oils produced by leaves that may serve to reduce evaporation rates.

Fragrances, such as those of sage, being one of the strongest cues for memory, can stimulate vivid recall of past experiences associated with a certain scent. Lester Rowntree (1939), one of California's most famous botanists, described one such incident in her book, *Flowering Shrubs of California:*

> *Fragrance is a marked characteristic of the chaparral. Especially after rain its scent is as typical of California as is the scent of orange blossoms. All the stands of it everywhere have the same basic aroma – something like that of Chrysanthemums – overlaid here by one perfume, there by another, as the various shrubs come into flower.*
>
> *Early one spring, after several days of scouting, I stopped at a hotel in a small California town to clean up. The little maid, coming in with an armful of towels, stopped short in the middle of the room, threw back her head, and began sniffing the air like a warhorse, while I watched her in some perplexity.*
>
> *"Chaparral!" she said wistfully. "Oh! You've been in the chaparral."*

Subtle color shifts and changing scents distinguish California's chaparral seasons in a much more subdued, sensual way than traditional seasonal markers. Chaparral plants live within a thin band of existence, like insects skating on the surface of a quiet stream inhabiting a space between two different worlds. Living in neither forest nor desert, chaparral organisms do not have the luxury of abundant water nor the ability to store it (with the exception of geophytes). They must be able to quickly exploit moisture when available and survive in between. It is a remarkable evolutionary achievement.

Fire Adaptations

Fire is viewed as separate from life, a destroyer of things. When studying biology in school, the subject is conspicuously absent from the curriculum, even at the university level. The omission is regretful because in many ecosystems, fire is as important as rainfall in shaping community structure and the organisms that live there. In especially fire-prone environments like California chaparral, a lack of specialized fire adaptations prevents a species from existing there. This does not mean the chaparral "needs to burn" to remain healthy or that it is immune from fire as a destructive force. It merely illustrates the system's ability to continue existing in the face of a powerfully disruptive force under natural conditions.

In their response to fire, chaparral shrubs and herbaceous perennials can be classified into five different groups, each with its own survival strategy: obligate resprouters, obligate seeders, endemic fire followers, facultative seeders, and frequent fire followers (fig. 1-12).

STRATEGY	STUMP SPROUT	SEEDS	PLANT TYPE	EXAMPLE
Obligate resprouter	Yes	Transient seed bank. No fire response. Seed life: less than one year.	Shrub, Herbaceous perennials	*Quercus berberififolia, Heteromeles arbutifolia, Prunus ilicifolia.* Geophytes
Obligate seeder	No, plant dies	Large seed bank. Germinate after fire. Seed life: decades.	Shrub, Herbaceous perennials	Most *Arctostaphylos* species. 50% of *Ceanothus* species. *Dicentra chrysantha* Serotinous pines
Endemic fire followers	No, annual life span	Large seed bank. Germinate only after fire. Seed life: decades.	Annuals	*Emmenanthe penduliflora Phacelia grandiflora Phacelia brachyloba*
Facultative seeder	Yes	Large seed bank. Germination can be fire dependant or not. Seed life: decades.	Shrub, Herbaceous perennials	*Adenostoma fasciculatum Malosma laurina* 50% of *Ceanothus* species. 5 *Arctostaphylos* species.
Frequent fire followers	No, annual life span	Polymorphic seed banks. Germination enhanced by fire cues. Seed life: dormant-type for decades.	Annuals	*Antirrhinum coulterianum Lupinus bicolor Cryptantha micromeres*

Fig. 1-12 Reproductive Response to Fire. *Chaparral plants are able to recover from fire by using one of five strategies. Obligate refers to an organism with only one lifestyle. Obligate resprouters survive a fire only by resprouting. Facultative refers to a double lifestyle. Facultative seeders survive fire by resprouting and by post-fire seed germination.*

Obligate resprouters are possibly relic species from a time when the climate of southern California was sub-tropical and fires played a smaller evolutionary role than they do today. Consequently, these plants are found in more mesic environments such as north-facing hillsides and canyon bottoms. They survive burns because of their ability to stump sprout. Their seeds, frequently surrounded by some fruity covering, are short-lived and likely do not survive into the fire season, either succumbing to decay or by being eaten. A thick layer of leaf litter is typically required for their successful germination, which is one reason seedlings of obligate resprouters are seldom observed in mature chaparral stands less than fifty years old (Keeley 1992). Toyon *(Heteromeles arbutifolia)* (#52) and holly-leafed cherry *(Prunus ilicifolia)* are obligate resprouters.

Obligate seeders die in fires, but their populations recover because their seeds survive to germinate. Most are fire-dependant, producing seeds requiring some kind of fire cue such as heat, charred wood, or smoke to stimulate their germination. Obligate seeder shrubs are typically found in concentrated, even-aged stands. These homogenous populations exist for two reasons. First, their seeds are small and do not have structures encouraging animal or wind distribution. Most go no further than the canopy directly below the mother plant (Keeley 1991a). Secondly, since the seeds respond to the same fire cue at the same time, all the adult plants have the same birthday. Cupleaf ceanothus *(Ceanothus greggii)* (#47) and bigberry manzanita *(Arctostaphylos glauca)* (#23) are classic obligate seeders. In contrast to obligate resprouters, obligate seeders are frequently found in xeric areas like ridge tops, flat mesas, and south-facing hillsides.

Serotiny, used exclusively by conifers, represents an interesting twist to the obligate seeding strategy. Serotiny refers to conifers that produce serotinous cones, meaning they remain closed and on the tree for a year or more after maturity, opening to release their seeds only after being fire-stimulated. The seeds then scatter over the burned ground, setting the stage for the next generation. The seeds do not depend on a fire cue per se, rather the heat of the fire to let them free. Although trees are not a component of chaparral, there are localized populations where conifers punctuate the shrubbery, especially as remnants of larger stands in the past and at higher elevations. The Tecate cypress *(Cupressus forbesii)*, restricted to Orange and San Diego Counties and northern Baja California, is one example. These are truly remarkable trees with crimson bark and tiny cones about the size of a quarter. One old growth population, nestled within the canyons of the northern Santa Ana Mountains, contains an individual with a trunk eight feet in diameter.

There are various levels of serotiny. The Coulter pine *(Pinus coulteri)* has a varied serotinous nature depending on the community in which it lives. In some stands, serotiny is uncommon, but for trees within chaparral the cones can remain attached and closed for as long as 25 years (Lanner 2002). Interestingly, the Torrey pine, found in maritime mixed chaparral is only partially serotinous. Although it will release its seeds over several seasons without a heat stimulus, it can retain cones for up to 15 years (Lanner 2002). A noteworthy population of Knobcone pine *(Pinus attenuata)*, whose cones are tightly sealed with resin, exists on Pleasants Peak in the Santa Ana Mountains. Since these trees are unable to compete with the surrounding chaparral, they are found successfully inhabiting islands of nutrient poor serpentine soil where shrubs are stunted and sparse.

In addition to obligate seeding woody species and perennials there are a number of annuals that have overwhelming dependence on fire for proper germination. These are the **endemic fire followers**, partially responsible for the explosive post-fire wildflower bloom observed after winter rains (frequent fire followers make up the rest). Once they have grown, set seed and died, most of these species will not reappear until after the next fire. As with obligate seeding shrubs, these fire following annuals, like *Phacelia brachyloba* (#15), can blanket entire hillsides to the exclusion of almost any other species.

Facultative seeders play both sides of the fire survival game; seed germination as well as being able to resprout from a root burl. These include dominant shrubs such as chamise *(Adenostoma fasciculatum)* (#50), laurel sumac *(Malosma laurina)* (#5), and whitebark ceanothus *(Ceanothus leucodermis)* (#48).

Ceanothus and manzanita, the definitive chaparral shrubs, have a number of facultative members. Of the five manzanitas that resprout, only one, *Arctostaphylos glandulosa,* is common in southern California. About half of the ceanothus, mostly in the subgenus *Ceanothus*, resprout. An interesting variation exists with the common blue flowering Ramona lilac, *Ceanothus tomentosus* (#47). The northern California populations in the Sierra Nevada are resprouters, but disjunct (widely separated) populations in southern California are non-sprouters. There is speculation the loss of the resprouting trait may have something to do with the evolutionary selection pressures created by climatic change, but the answer remains elusive (Schwilk 2002).

Some facultative seeders, like *Arctostaphylos glandulosa* and chamise, are fire dependant. Their seeds require a fire cue to germinate despite their resprouting ability. This duplicitous response to fire has led at least one fire ecologist to humorously suggest the species are in serious need of genetic counseling (J.E. Keeley 2004, personal communication).

Frequent fire followers are annuals with polymorphic seeds, a percentage of which remain dormant in the soil and are cued to germinate after a fire. The common bicolor lupine *(Lupinus bicolor)* (#27) and the little popcorn flower *Cryptantha micromeres* (#16) are in this group.

Earth Plants

Geophytes deserve special mention regarding response to fire. These are strictly herbaceous (having only soft, fleshy plant parts) and emerge from an underground storage organ such as a bulb, corm, or enlarged root. Monocot geophytes are the plants that produce some of the most magnificent wildflowers after a fire. Species such as wild hyacinth *(Dichelostemma capitatum)* (#60), mariposa lily *(Calochortus species)* (#57), and soap plant *(Chlorogalum parviflorum)* (#55) color the scene with delightful blossoms perched on tall, thin stalks waving in the breeze. Paradoxically, these plants emerge from deep underground structures that are unaffected by the flames above. Their prolific response to fire raises an intriguing question. Why would fire have any influence on their flowering patterns? Claudia Tyler and Mark Borchert (2003) did a nine-year investigation of one geophyte, Fremont's camus *(Zigadenus fremontii)* (#58), and provided some answers.

In their study area within the Santa Ynez Mountains, northwest of Santa Barbara, they found camus produced an abundant number of flowers and seeds the spring following a burn. In an unburned section nearby, not only were camus flowers scarce, but the few blossoms produced rarely made any seeds. However, the bulbs grew the largest and greatest number of leaves when compared to those in the burned area. As the research progressed it was discovered in nearly all subsequent years after the fire, the same plants that flowered so profusely showed dramatically reduced leaf production. The plants rarely flowered again.

Tyler and Borchert have suggested that in mature chaparral, camus gradually collects energy obtained through photosynthesis and stores the surplus in its underground bulb. Once fire eliminates the canopy, high light levels stimulate the plant to tap into those energy reserves to produce flowers. The results can be dramatic. Acres of land that have not seen camus flowers in years are suddenly covered by them. The following year, the plant's energy stores exhausted, only puny leaves are produced. Another impressive round of flower production is virtually impossible.

What of the seeds? Tyler and Borchert discovered that within 4 years all viable seeds germinated. Fremont's camus does not form a persistent seed bank. This means the survival of the species depends on long-lived adults that can span the time between fires. Further research is needed on other species, but from the camus investigation it appears that increased sunshine is the primary cue for the explosive, post-fire flowering response of the geophytes. However, it is important to remember just because one study reveals data supporting a particular hypothesis, it does not necessarily eliminate all others.

In an experiment on a South African fire-lily *(Cyrtanthus ventricosus),* it was demonstrated that it would flower only after being treated with smoke (Keeley 1993). Plants exposed to sunlight alone do not germinate. It turns out that the flower buds are preformed within the bulb. No matter what time of year the fire occurs, the fire-lily will blossom 5 days later. Although this is unlike any species found in North America, it does demonstrate the wide variety of responses plants can have to periodic flames.

Developing Fire Survival Strategies

Evolution has shaped the chaparral and continues to do so. However, it is important to understand what exactly is evolving. To say individual chaparral plants have "adapted" to fire over time in order to survive is incorrect. Species evolve and adapt, individual living things do not. Plants cannot slowly change in order to survive an explosive inferno. They either have what it takes before hand or die. This is one of the basic principles of evolution.

The sprouting behavior of laurel sumac (#5) is an example. Upon casual observation it appears this plant has adapted to survive fire because the entire above ground portion can be incinerated yet the root stock remains alive. Within weeks, little green shoots emerge from the blackened base and after a few years the plant returns to its original size. Has laurel sumac adapted to fire in the chaparral? Not exactly. Long before the chaparral fire regime began developing approximately 10 million years ago, laurel sumac was a re-sprouting, forest understory plant. The resprouting behavior is nothing new, but a perfect example of pre-adaptation; a characteristic that provides an organism some future advantage in a changing environment (Wells 1969). Laurel sumac did not obtain re-sprouting because of fire, it already had it. As the environment changed by becoming drier and more susceptible to fires, laurel sumac was able to survive because of a fortuitous characteristic it possessed beforehand. Other species not as fortunate were extirpated.

As time went on, a finer evolutionary process took over. Every individual is slightly different. There is always variation within a population. Some laurel sumac plants were better at resisting fire than others. Those "better resisters" produced more offspring than individuals more seriously damaged, creating a population of even better fire survivors. This is where the adapt over time idea comes from. Once a trait is selected by nature, in this case resprouting, evolution selects those individuals with better versions of the trait than others and the species as a whole becomes better adapted to fire in the chaparral. After the trait was selected, the species as a whole evolved through time improving the fire resisting characteristic. The same process goes on with all living things. The better individual survives and passes on those better characteristics to the next generation.

Obligate seeding shrubs, such as the majority of ceanothus and manzanita species, could be considered the true "chaparralians" because their life cycle requires a fire regime specific to the chaparral ecosystem. They are the new kids on the block. Their specialized fire adaptations have been fined tuned as California became dominated by a Mediterranean climate over the past 14 million years.

Fire Cues

If the complete yearly seed crop from chaparral plants were to germinate after the first winter rains, every species would be betting its entire inheritance on a single event. This is not the best survival strategy, especially in a semi-arid environment. So the question arises, when is the optimal time for germination and how is this time signaled to the seed?

Plants compete with each other for space, light, water, and nutrients. Post burn sites are like pirate's plunder. Huge amounts of acreage are cleared, the competition has been scorched, sunlight is everywhere and nutrients once locked away in the stems and leaves are lying about like gold coins. Seedlings also get a reprieve from plant nibblers since fire dramatically reduces herbivore populations. Those remaining must contend with bare ground without cover, not the best place for rodents and rabbits to scurry about unprotected from predators. This is the kind of situation designed for an evolutionary drama. Plants with seeds resistant to germinating until conditions are right, like after a fire, have an advantage over those without such innate dormancy mechanisms. Over the past 10 million years, a significant number of species have evolved under such conditions, becoming dependent on specific fire regimes for their continued reproductive success. The three primary fire cues utilized for signaling the proper germination time are **heat, charred wood,** and **smoke.** Fire cues work by either physically altering the seed coat or chemically influencing the tissues beneath.

Without water, seeds cannot germinate. Since an impermeable seed coat encloses embryos within many chaparral seeds, germination will not occur until those barriers are broken by heat. Some species produce polymorphic seeds, meaning some require heat while others do not. For example, yellow rock rose *(Helianthemum scoparium)* (#19) splits its seed production by producing some that germinate easily with just moisture while others require temperatures approximately 250 degrees Fahrenheit for a minimum of 5 minutes. There are limits of course. Temperatures nearing 300 degrees Fahrenheit prove fatal to the little embryos (Keeley 1991b).

The other two fire cues capable of inducing seed germination are chemicals from **charred wood** or **smoke**. Chemicals leached from these substances alter internal membranes within the seed, stimulating growth. The shrub chamise *(Adenostoma fasciculatum)* (#50), and caterpillar phacelia *(Phalecia cicutaria)* (#15), a common fire-following annual, are examples of species responding to such chemicals. Interestingly, nearly all the species responding to charred wood show even higher germination rates when exposed to smoke, so apparently similar processes and chemicals are involved but are delivered more effectively with smoke. In fact, dormant seeds that show only 40% to 60% germination success from charred wood achieve 100% germination rates when exposed to smoke. Matilija poppy *(Romneya coulteri)* (#42) and whispering bells *(Emmenanthe penduliflora)* (#13) fall into this smoke-loving group. All show 0% germination with moisture alone and none of them are known to respond to heat (Keeley and Fotheringham 1998). Before drawing too many conclusions from this data, however, it's important to understand that it is more difficult to control the amount of chemical leaching off charred wood than it is when applying smoke. The lower percentage germination with charred wood data may be more reflective of experimental procedures than an accurate measurement of what happens in nature (Keeley, personal communication).

In experimental tests, smoke treated soil or smoke treated water elicit the same basic response as charred wood and direct smoke. The exact identity of the chemicals involved or the mechanism explaining how germination is induced has yet to be identified. G.R. Flematti et al. (2004) claimed to have isolated the active ingredient in smoke, but they failed to provide evidence demonstrating fire cues were required for stimulating or enhancing the germination of the seeds they tested. The search goes on.

One intriguing story relating to seed dormancy has to do with the exquisite golden eardrops *(Dicentra chrysantha)* (#40). This member of the poppy family can grow six feet tall and has delicate, yellow flowers with four delicate petals that look like curled earrings. This perennial exists only during the first few years after a burn, so it is clear some fire cue is required for germination. However, in multiple laboratory studies conducted by J. E. Keeley and colleagues on more than 50,000 seeds over a period of 15 years, the plant's seeds failed to germinate in response to any known fire cue. After a few insightful discussions around the lab table, they decided to bury the seeds for a while to see if some in-soil ripening was required. It was. Seeds of golden eardrops require at least a year of soil contact before they will germinate, and only then after exposure to smoke. Bush poppy *(Dendromecon rigida)* (#39) and woolly bluecurls *(Trichostema lanatum)* exhibit similar hard-to-germinate characteristics (Keeley and Fotheringham 1998).

When studying how plants respond to fire, it is important to differentiate between the actual response to fire and how the plant survives in the absence of fire. For example, deerweed *(Lotus scoparius)* (#26), an obligate seeder, responds after fire by seed germination. The adult plant dies. However, when examining the species entire reproductive cycle, its seeds will sometimes germinate in the absence of fire. Being an obligate seeder does not necessarily mean it is completely fire dependent, it just means the species responds to fire only by germination (fig. 1-13).

Another potentially confusing point relates to facultative seeders when comparing plants like chamise and laurel sumac. Both resprout and both germinate after fires, yet they have radically different reproductive cycles. Chamise is fire dependent (seeds require heat for germination), and laurel sumac is not, although some of its seeds survive after the burn to germinate. Keeping fire response and the whole reproductive perspective separate is important to avoid becoming confused.

Seeds Responding to Heat

COMMON NAME	SPECIES	FIRE RESPONSE	REPRODUCTIVE CYCLE
Cupleaf ceanothus	*Ceanothus greggii*	Obligate seeder	Fire dependant
Whitebark ceanothus	*Ceanothus leucodermis*	Facultative seeder	Fire dependant
California fremontia	*Fremontodendron californicum*	Facultative seeder	Fire dependant
Deerweed	*Lotus scoparius*	Obligate seeder	Mostly fire dependant, but has polymorphic seeds
Yellow rock rose	*Helianthemum scoparium*	Obligate seeder	Mostly fire dependent, but has polymorphic seeds
Laurel sumac	*Malosma laurina*	Facultative seeder	Fire independent, enhanced germination
White sage	*Salvia apiana*	Facultative seeder	Fire independent

Seeds Responding to Charred Wood and Smoke

COMMON NAME	SPECIES	FIRE RESPONSE	REPRODUCTIVE CYCLE
Whispering bells	*Emmenanthe penduliflora*	Endemic fire follower	Fire dependant
Golden eardrops	*Dicentra chrysantha*	Obligate seeder	Fire dependant
Matilija poppy	*Romneya coulteri*	Facultative seeder	Fire dependant
Eastwood manzanita	*Arctostaphylos glandulosa*	Facultative seeder	Fire dependant
Chamise	*Adenstoma fasciculatum*	Facultative seeder	Fire dependant
White snapdragon	*Antirrhinum coulterianum*	Frequent fire follower	Fire independent, enhanced germination
Caterpillar phacelia	*Phalecia cicutaria*	Frequent fire follower	Fire independent, enhanced germination
White sage	*Salvia apiana*	Facultative seeder	Fire independent

Fig. 1-13 Fire Cues, Fire Response, and Reproductive Cycles of Selected Southern California Chaparral Plants. Data based on results from most recent laboratory research. Adapted from Keeley (1991b) and Keeley and Fotheringham (1998).

The search to discover the dynamics of post-fire germination is an amazing story involving both scientific discipline and imagination. The first species to be shown to respond to charred wood was whispering bells *(Emmenanthe penduliflora)* in 1977 by D.T. Wicklow. There are other plants that retain their secrets. For example, mission manzanita *(Xylococcus bicolor)* (#24) may or may not require some fire cue for germination. The species commonly resprouts, but seedlings of the species appear to be non-existent or extremely rare in both mature chaparral stands and post-fire environments. We do not know whether something in the environment has changed enough to prevent germination or there are other mechanisms involved.

Type Conversion

Ever since humans have been in California in significant numbers, the chaparral has been vulnerable to both purposeful and accidental elimination. It probably all started approximately 5,000 years ago when there was a dramatic shift in the diet of Native Americans. The huge Clovis spear points used to take down mastodons and other large mammals disappeared from the North American archeological record about 5,000 years ago and were replaced by mortars and other stone grinding tools. One source of energy, large mammals, was replaced by another: plants, seeds, and roots. However, deer remained important and Native Americans practiced land management to increase their numbers.

As chaparral re-dominates an area several years after a burn, deer populations slowly decrease as the amount of herbaceous browse declines. One of the ways to bring the deer back is to burn again (Biswell, et al. 1952). There are large numbers of documented accounts from early explorers that described Native Americans continually burning the landscape. For example, in 1792 Jose Martinez wrote, "In all of New California from Fronteras northward the gentiles (Indians) have the custom of burning the brush," (Simpson 1938). The mosaic pattern of various types of plant communities seen today in California may very well be an artifact of Native American land management practices, especially where more open habitats intrude into pure stands of chaparral (Keeley 2002). No doubt Native Americans knew that complex mosaics of habitat supported larger deer populations than chaparral alone (Tabor 1956). Unfortunately, this artificial disturbance also set the stage for the successful invasion of Eurasian weedy annuals with the arrival of Spanish missionaries in the early 1800's.

Then, beginning in 1862, California experienced a devastating dry spell. 40% of the entire state's livestock perished. In ranch lands surrounding the little pueblo of Los Angeles, 70% of the animals died searching for food and water. Sheep outlasted the cattle and nibbled down whatever was left, roots and all (Cleland 1951). Drought was nothing new to California and its native flora of course, but the combined pressure of overgrazing and competition from exotic weeds created an ecological disaster. Native forage was devastated and much of the ground lay bare. A huge niche opened up and weeds from another Mediterranean climate across the Atlantic Ocean took advantage of the situation with a vengeance.

Because they grow faster and have more aggressive seed dispersal mechanisms, exotic weedy annuals quickly fill in areas scraped clean of vegetation, burned too frequently, or disturbed by other types of activity. Instead of ceanothus and manzntia, disturbed chaparral is typically type-converted to non-native, weedy grassland with exotic grasses like wild oats *(Avena fatua)* (#63), foxtail chess *(Bromus madritensis)*, and ripgut *(Bromus diandrus)* (#64) along with non-grass immigrants such as filaree *(Erodium* species) (#62), mustard *(Brassica species)* (#61), and various thistles.

Under natural fire regimes, chaparral replaces chaparral (photos 14-18). But as fire frequencies increase, exotic grasses and weeds can easily establish themselves and begin the process of type conversion (photo 11). One possible reason for this is because the amount of fuel available to burn in recovering shrublands is less than in mature stands, thus creating a cooler fire. Cooler fires allow weed seeds to survive, whereas hotter chaparral fires do not. As the amount and type of fuels continues to change in favor of lighter ones, the invasive species alter the fire regime and then flourish under the new environment they create (Brooks, et al. 2004). These plants dry out earlier in the spring and thus increase the length of the fire season in the chaparral (Keeley 2000). In addition, they create fine, high surface to volume ratio fuels making them highly combustible (Rundel 1981), increasing the probability of ignition.

The change in fire return intervals and number of fires has been dramatic in some southern California counties over the past century (Keeley et al. 1999).

- In Los Angeles County from 1910 to 1950 there were 357 brush fires. From 1951 to 1997 they increased to 1,392.
- In Riverside County the fire return interval before 1951 was 225 years. After 1950, it decreased to 38 years.

Interestingly, while the number of fires increased during the period studied, the mean fire size decreased. For example, before 1951 the mean fire size in San Diego County was 2,319 acres. After 1950, it was 1,344 acres. This is important in terms of invasive weeds because smaller burns with large perimeter-to-area ratios are more readily invaded than larger ones (Turner et al. 1997). The presence of fuel breaks and roads adjacent to and within chaparral stands make for ready sources of non-native weed seeds (Keeley 2004b).

The first chaparral plants to vanish when fires increase are the obligate seeders, as demonstrated after two fires on Otay Mountain in southern San Diego County. The first fire occurred in 1979. In 1980, a second fire reburned a portion of the 1979 scar due to the presence of dry annual ryegrass *(Lolium multiflorum)*, which had been seeded on the mountain as an erosion control measure. The impacts were dramatic. Except for a few individuals, the obligate seeder *Ceanothus oliganthus* was completely eliminated from the site. Chamise *(Adenostoma fasciculatum)*, the most common species before the fires, was reduced in density in various study plots by up to 97%. This is interesting because chamise is a facultative seeder, able to resprout as well as germinate after a fire. Apparently the second blaze caught the exposed young sprouts when they were the most vulnerable and the supporting burl did not have enough stored energy to develop new ones (Zedler et al. 1983). All the seedlings that had germinated after the 1979 fire were killed in the 1980 fire.

This type of ecological damage has occurred time and time again throughout southern California as increased fires, aided by inappropriate and largely useless post-fire erosion control measures, have transformed large tracks of native chaparral into non-native, weedy grassland. In fact, until recently, type-conversion of shrublands in favor of grass was an official government land management policy (CDF 1978). Based on the average of many investigations, the threshold below which chaparral will be type-converted is anywhere between 10 to 20 years depending on summer drought and individual site conditions (Haidinger and Keeley 1993, Keeley 1995, Zedler 1995, Jacobson et al. 2004). Anything less threatens the chaparral's continued existence.

Chaparral Mythology

Due to stories passed along by well meaning enthusiasts and a number of flawed conclusions published in scientific journals, several misconceptions concerning chaparral have cemented themselves into the public consciousness. Three of the most prominent concern, chemical interactions between plants (**allelopathy**); relative health of older chaparral stands (**senescence**); and so-called **"unnatural" accumulation** of plant material in California brushlands.

Chemical inhibition, or **allelopathy**, suggests plants are capable of suppressing the growth or germination of neighboring competitors. Although an intriguing idea, actual chemical inhibition in nature has been notoriously difficult to prove. In 1990 plant ecologist J. H. Connell wrote, "To my knowledge, no published field study has demonstrated direct interference by allelopathy in soil . . . while excluding the possibility of other indirect interactions with resources, natural enemies, or other competitors."

This lack of scientific verification, however, has not prevented the concept from being presented as a well-understood phenomenon in science texts as well as along chaparral nature trails. Dramatic explanations are seductive, especially if they provide interesting answers to intriguing problems. If repeated often enough, they become dogma and influence thinking for decades.

C.H. Muller, an accomplished botanist from the University of California, Santa Barbara, suggested chemical inhibition explained the lack of plant growth under the canopy of mature chaparral stands in southern California (Muller, et. al. 1968). According to his hypothesis, chemicals washed off the leaves of chamise and manzanita shrubs and suppressed the germination of seeds in the ground below. When the chaparral burned, flames denatured the toxic substances in the soil and released the seeds from inhibition.

The problem with this explanation is that the soil chemicals suspected of suppressing growth actually increase after a fire. In addition, the dormancy found in chaparral plant seeds is innate, not caused by some outside environmental factor. The seeds are dormant before they hit the ground. Post-fire seedling response in chaparral can be easily explained without considering chemical inhibition (Halsey 2004).

Muller also suggested allelopathy was the cause for bare zones often found around purple sage *(Salvia leucophylla)* and California sagebrush *(Artemisia californica)* in the coastal sage scrub community (Muller, et. al. 1964). Later investigations revealed these bare zones are primarily the work of herbivores, not volatile substances from the plants themselves (Bartholomew 1971) (photo 12).

To little furry rodents like the California mouse *(Peromyscus californicus)* and the pacific kangaroo rat *(Dipodomys agilis)* the world is a dangerous place. Cover is critical to their survival since they are on the dietary preference list of local carnivores like coyotes, snakes, and hawks. Consequently, they have a tendency to remain under shrubbery with only occasional, quick forays into surrounding grassland to nibble on available seeds or new growth. They will stray only as far as they can quickly leap back to safety. Bare zones, therefore, can be viewed as "calculated-risk terrain" where rodents have a fair chance of grabbing food without getting caught. Bare zones are bare because herbivores exploit the space in order to grab available snacks.

Do volatile compounds in certain coastal sage scrub plants ever play a role significant enough to make a difference in naturally occurring vegetation patterns?

"As far as I know, the question of why grasses grow within bare zones during wet years, despite animal activity, has never been adequately addressed," Bob Muller said when reflecting upon his father's work. "Why don't animals always eliminate seedlings, regardless of the level of moisture?"

The allelopathic explanation favored by C.H. Muller provides a reasonable hypothesis for this phenomenon; heavy rains leach toxins from the soil, removing inhibitory chemicals and permitting seedling success. However, without further investigation the question remains unresolved (Halsey 2004).

John Harper (1975), a prominent plant population biologist from England explained that, "the critical issue is to determine whether such toxicity plays a role in the interactions between plants in the field. Demonstrating this has proved extraordinarily difficult – it is logically impossible to prove that it doesn't happen and perhaps nearly impossible to prove absolutely that it does."

The second misconception deals with chaparral health, or rather, the idea chaparral becomes **senescent**, decadent, or trashy as it becomes older and unburned for more than 50 years (Hanes 1971). This has unfortunately led credence to the assumption chaparral "needs" to burn every 20 to 30 years to in order to renew itself, suggesting the necessity of using prescribed burns as a resource management tool. Field research has failed to support this notion. Specifically: the continued ability of chaparral stands nearly a century old to maintain productive growth has been confirmed by multiple investigations (Hubbard 1986, Larigauderie et al. 1990); the accumulation of living material (biomass) steadily increases for at least 45 years in chamise chaparral (Specht 1969) and probably more than 100 years in other types, especially north facing stands; and shrubs in older chaparral communities are not constrained by limited soil nutrient levels (Fenn et. al. 1993).

While it is true some individual specimens of certain *Ceanothus* species will die as a stand reaches 20-40 years of age (Keeley 1975), others such as *Ceanothus greggii* var. *perplexans*, remain an important part of chaparral stands over 90 years old (Keeley 1973). Rather than being a function of age, individual ceanothus shrubs apparently expire due to water stress during prolonged droughts lasting several years in a row (Schlesinger and Gill 1978). When spaces do appear in the chaparral, living plants quickly fill the void. For example, chamise shrubs that have not experienced fire for at least 80 years continually send up new stems from their base (Zedler and Zammit 1989).

Not only do mature shrubs continue growing over time, but seeds from the majority of species common to north facing, mesic chaparral stands require long fire-free environments before being able to germinate. Moisture protecting shrub cover and leaf litter are needed to nurse the seedlings along. Plants such as scrub oak *(Quercus berberidifolia)* and holly-leafed cherry *(Prunus ilicifolia)* fall into this category. In the San Gabriel Mountain area of Los Angeles County, a 60-year-old chaparral stand contained large numbers of these seedlings (Patric and Hanes 1964). Two other common chaparral plants requiring mature growth for seed germination are toyon *(Heteromeles arbutifolia)* and mountain mahogany *(Cercocarpus betuloides)*. So rather than being a "senile" habitat of dying shrubbery, many mature chaparral stands are just beginning a new stage of growth after fifty years of age.

Although chaparral is a fire-adapted ecosystem and some types do accumulate significant amounts of dead wood, the system certainly does not need prescribed ignitions to remain healthy, especially in light of the increased number of fires occurring in southern California shrublands today. The idea chaparral needs to burn is related more to human perceptions than any ecological process.

The last misconception is probably repeated more than any other: past fire suppression efforts have allowed an **"unnatural" accumulation** of brush to develop within the chaparral, leading to huge, catastrophic wildfires. This belief appears to be based on the misapplication of studies relating to dry ponderosa pine *(Pinus ponderosa)* forests showing that undergrowth has increased over the past century due to successful fire fighting activities. In the past, surface fires burned through these forests at intervals anywhere between 4 to 36 years, clearing out the understory and creating a more ecologically balanced system (Swetnam and Baisan 1996). However, this conclusion has nothing to do with California shrublands.

Detailed analysis of historical fire data has shown that not only have fire suppression activities failed to exclude fire from southern California chaparral as they have in ponderosa pine forests (Keeley et. al. 1999), but the number of fires is actually increasing in step with population growth. Research showing differences in fire size and frequency between southern California and Baja California (Minnich and Chou 1997) has been used to imply larger fires north of the border are the result of fire suppression, but this opinion has been seriously challenged by numerous investigators (Zedler and Seiger 2000, Keeley and Fotheringham 2001, Mortiz 2003).

Chaparral is composed of shrubbery, not trees. Whenever it burns, everything goes, no matter the age. This is characteristic of a crown fire regime as opposed to the surface fire type found in ponderosa forests. A young, 5-year-old stand of chaparral has already produced more than enough material to fuel and carry a catastrophic wildfire across the landscape (Halsey, unpublished data). Overall, how old a recovered chaparral stand happens to be has very little to do with its chances of burning (Moritz et al. 2004).

There is no question chaparral is extremely flammable, especially during dry weather conditions. As stands grow older, they continue to build up fuel in the form of both dead and living plant material. This is a natural process and part of the normal chaparral life cycle. Indeed, proper vegetation management, including strategically placed prescribed burns near communities, is an important fire management tool. However, past fire suppression practices or environmental regulations limiting vegetation treatments in wild spaces cannot be blamed for the wildfires we see today.

What does understanding historical fire regimes have to do with modern chaparral wildfires? The debate over what is natural or unnatural when compared to the past is largely irrelevant to Californians trying to survive within a fire-prone ecosystem. Wildfires are going to happen and they are happening with increased frequency. The important question now is how do we protect life and property, allow for future growth, and continue to preserve a valuable natural resource? Although our control over the environment has increased dramatically, humans remain an integral part of nature. We must assess our impact objectively and decide as a society what value native landscapes possess and how important it is to retain some connection to them. We must also recognize fire will always be a part of the Californian experience, with or without chaparral. In a fire-prone environment like ours, poorly designed structures can promote and spread devastating firestorms as well as uncut brush. Considering the inevitably of fire in southern California, it's best to learn how to let fire burn around us instead of through us.

Becoming Familiar

For the naturalist, southern California is paradise. Within a day's drive one can observe more habitat types than anywhere else in the world. This environmental diversity has produced a unique array of singularities unmatched by any other region on earth. It has also created the most pristine Mediterranean shrubland remaining in the world today: the chaparral.

As the fires of 2003 have shown, being detached and unfamiliar with our surrounding natural environment can have serious consequences. It leads us to build our homes in unsustainable places and become aliens in our own land. By becoming familiar with the plants, the animals, and the natural cycles found within the chaparral, our awareness will broaden and we will be less likely to be surprised by the next natural event, be it fire, flood, or drought. Our lives will be enhanced because we will be able to see and hear more. We will also come to recognize the call of the energetic, little wrentit not only as the voice of the chaparral but that of our home as well.

2

When the Fire Comes

On July 19, 1973, Steve Arrollado became a seasonal firefighter for the California Department of Forestry and Fire Protection (CDF). He was 18 years old and had just graduated from Santana High School in San Diego County. He was excited about his future and thought working for the CDF would be a good way to find a career and a clearer vision of what might lie ahead.

A quiet, handsome young man, Steve was known to his friends and family as a hard working individual who had a penchant for making others feel at ease in otherwise uncomfortable situations. For example, the tension between younger and older kids in school is often the cause of conflict, especially in the P.E. locker room. As one of Santana High's varsity football players, Steve used his influence and spirit of cama-raderie to help make incoming freshmen feel comfortable and unafraid. "I was in eighth grade and just starting cross-country," friend Clayton Howe remembered. "He took me aside one day and boosted my confidence by telling me that my sport was so much harder than his. Here was this big football hero trying to make me feel important. I'll never forget it. Steve had a personal character way beyond his years."

On August 11th, Steve was called to help fight a wildfire in Bell Valley, just south of the little town of Potrero, in southern San Diego County. The fire's behavior suddenly turned ugly and Steve was quickly overcome by smoke. As he attempted to escape, his clothing caught fire and he was critically burned. After being dragged out of the flames by his companions, he was flown by helicopter to Grossmont Hospital, and later transferred to University Hospital's burn unit. After a very difficult two weeks, his lungs finally failed. He died on August 28th.

Steve's death was a tremendous blow to both his families; the one at home and the CDF. To have lost a hero at such a young age made it especially devastating. His colleagues, however, made sure the lessons learned would not be forgotten. It wasn't long before fire-resistant clothing was developed and issued to all CDF firefighters. As time went on, Steve's story spread throughout the firefighting community and continues to be used today in training schools across the world to help prevent similar tragedies.

On August 21, 2004, 31 years after Steve's death, a ceremony was held at CDF Headquarters in San Diego County to honor the fallen firefighter and to unveil a bronze plaque in his honor. It is set in a monument constructed of granite rock collected at the site of the Bell Valley fire. After his family pulled off the memorial's shroud, the traditional three rounds of three rings on a fireman's bell were struck. James Arrollando, Steve's brother, reminded everyone how important it was to appreciate one's family and friends everyday. Because of how quickly changes were made after the 1973 incident, the chances of firefighters returning home safely to enjoy such connections have improved significantly.

The risks Steve Arrollando took continue to challenge those who seek to help protect life and property from California wildfires, a job requiring not only valor, but also patience; patience for those who fail to understand the importance of individual responsibility in maintaining homes and communities able to withstand the embers and the flames. Although California maintains a vigorous firefighting force, it is not capable of defending every home and saving every life when wildfires overwhelm available fire fighting resources.

Ninety-seven percent of the fires starting in California wildlands are extinguished by the initial attack phase, an impressive track record by any measurement. But what happens with the other 3%? Once fire escapes initial control, extended attack efforts begin with the commitment of more personnel and equipment. If this fails, the fire is considered major and all available resources are employed to fight the flames. Although suppression efforts take place from beginning to end no matter the size or severity of a fire, there is a limit to what can be done during severe fire weather. Pushed by strong Santa Ana winds, the flames will only stop when conditions improve on their own. Once containment has failed and a fire turns into a major incident, the primary task of emergency personnel is to try to evacuate citizens in harm's way while protecting as many structures as possible. The number of aircraft, fire engines, and firefighters available do not determine the life span of a wildfire. It is the fuel, the slope, and most importantly, the weather that dictate when and how the fire will die (photo 13).

The 2003 Cedar fire in San Diego County, as large as it was, could have wrought twice the devastation without the fortuitous weather change late Sunday, October 26. If the Santa Ana wind conditions had persisted another day, not an unusual event in southern California (Fosberg 1965), the flames could have easily made a run to the Pacific Ocean by continuing down the Highway 52 corridor, reaching Mt. Soledad and burning into La Jolla and other beach communities.

On the Cedar fire's southern flank, embers jumped Interstate 8 at two locations, Harbison Canyon and Viejas, igniting spot fires that could have burned all the way to Mexico. Fortunately, with the wind shift, fire management personnel were given sufficient time to halt the fire's southern progression. However, it was not soon enough to save the community of Crest, an area that was devastated 30 years before during the 1970 Laguna fire. At the Viejas crossing, blowing embers ignited 3 year old growth in the 2001 Viejas fire burn scar. The flames were on their way to ignite 30 year old chaparral across the Sweetwater River canyon when reduced winds and lower fuel levels permitted hand crews with aerial support to cut a successful fireline. Unfortunately, favorable weather conditions did not exist for long. After a brief lull, the westward blowing Santa Ana winds were replaced by an onshore flow and the fire rapidly moved eastward into the Laguna Mountains and Cuyamaca State Park. One of the region's few coniferous forests was devastated. A series of strategically placed prescribed burns performed over the previous three years just north of Pine Valley reduced fire intensity enough to allow firefighters to set up a defensive zone nearby. Although the town survived unscathed, many other mountain communities were not as fortunate. The fire's eastern march was finally stopped as weather conditions improved dramatically and the flame front entered the 2002 Pines fire scar.

Blame

It is difficult for many to accept the uncontrollable. With support mechanisms in place smoothing the bumps in life, the urban dweller may forget the intimate connection that still exists between civilization and nature. The multitude of safety nets designed to remove risk are taken for granted. When an event occurs that exposes the fragility of human society's protective barrier against the randomness of the natural world, the community lashes out. Be it cougar attacks, floods, or fires, someone must be found to blame. The public reaction during the Cedar fire illustrated this phenomenon well as described in the CDF report detailing the California fire siege of 2003:

> *Even during the height of the firefight, elected officials and the news media criticized the fire agencies of not fighting the fire aggressively enough. The Incident Commanders and Agency Administrators now had the fire to fight as well as a need to respond to the rapidly growing political and public demand for information and answers. Dividing responsibilities, Agency Administrators tried to handle the large number of interviews, press conferences and the negative media coverage, while the Incident Commanders focused on the efforts of their people on the firefight. The negative reaction from outside the fire was widespread and loud.*
>
> *The fight continued as the wind had shifted to a westerly and the fire headed east towards Cuyamaca and Julian. Firefighters were working long hours, not leaving their posts until relief arrived. The critical public reaction had a negative affect on the morale of the firefighters who were working in extreme conditions and risking their lives to save people and property.*

On September 29, 2004, 11 months after the southern California firestorm, the San Diego Board of Supervisors held a meeting to assess the progress fire fighting agencies had made to better prepare for future wildfires. The tendency to hold someone responsible for the devastation was reflected in the meeting's description in the Board's agenda. "As we learned first hand during the disaster and in the reports that followed, there was a litany of inadequacies in our emergency response system at the time of the fires."

The uncontrollable nature of the wildfires was barely addressed during the 3 hour meeting. The outstanding service performed by federal, state and local firefighters in saving countless lives and structures was never acknowledged. The only significant testimony given regarding the responsibility of individual homeowners was offered by Richard D. Hawkins, the fire and aviation officer for the Cleveland National Forest. He indicated how 41 out of 50 homeowners in Sherilton Valley participated in a FireSafe Council sponsored brush removal program. "When the Cedar fire arrived in Sherilton Valley," Hawkins testified, "we only had enough firefighters to try and save the nearby community of Descanso. Without much support from the firefighters, the 41 fire-safe homes survived the Cedar Fire. The other 9 homes were lost."

In the summary statements, only Supervisor Bill Horn stressed the need for citizens to take more initiative for personal fire safety.

If there had been more helicopters or another set of fire trucks, the reasoning went, the Cedar fire would never have gotten out of control. A resident from Mussey Grade, a rural area south of Ramona, shouted out during a post-fire community meeting that there should have been more firefighter fatalities if they had been doing their job right. During another gathering, residents from the semi-rural neighborhood of Crest claimed the fire department stood around and let their homes burn.

The Cedar fire started approximately five miles southwest of where eleven fire-fighters were killed while battling the Inaja on November 25, 1956, in the same type of vegetation and rugged terrain. Cedar fire commanders knew the risks involved when they arrived on scene with approximately 350 fire control personnel within an hour of the fire being reported on October 25; impenetrable, twelve-foot high chaparral, steep canyon walls, and approaching Santa Ana wind conditions. Not a lot could have been done without risking the lives of hundreds of firefighters. When the winds picked up an explosive inferno blasted over 18 miles by the following morning. It was an unstoppable force. At the height of the Cedar fire, 9 acres of landscape were being consumed every second. "When a fire does that," Larry Hood, a US Forest Service fire specialist said, "your efforts are turned from the firefight to firefighter and public safety. You just hope you can get all the people out of the way in time."

Emotions run high during disasters. People hurt deeply. With time, the ability to rationally examine what really happened improves. What has become clear after the 2003 firestorm is that people had become so unfamiliar with the environment in which they lived and so dependent on outside assistance that they had lost control of their own lives. They had neglected to prepare for the inevitable because they had forgotten, or more likely, they had never fully understood the awesome power nature can deliver. Additionally, fire literacy is not a priority in a highly mobile society where newcomers arrive daily from places where the threat of suburban conflagration does not exist.

Neighborhoods

"Nobody ever told us this could happen. The neighborhood seemed so safe. There were always half a dozen kids running up and down the cul-de-sac. We all looked out for each other, you know." Ellie stopped talking for a moment as she stared across her front yard at the charred remnants of her neighbor's homes. "The houses were so nice. They all had big bay windows in front."

Ellie and her husband bought their home in Scripps Ranch, a community on the northern border of San Diego, in September 2002 after moving from the east coast. Out of a group of several dozen homes in her neighborhood, Ellie's, the house next door, and one on the corner were the only structures left standing after the Cedar fire.

"You know, you buy a home and assume it's a safe place to raise your family," Ellie continued. "You figure that if anything horrible like this was coming, the fire department would take care of it and things would be okay. But after it was all over, several of my neighbors told me that someone had come around a few years ago and warned everybody that the neighborhood was a firetrap. He said if there was a fire, the chances were officials wouldn't risk firefighters' lives by sending them down here. No one ever told us that when we bought our home. Not the realtor, not the city, no one. We wouldn't have bought the place if we had known that."

In the large stack of papers homebuyers are required to sign in southern California are Natural Hazard Summary disclosure documents detailing a dwelling's vulnerability to earthquake, flood, and fire. On maps issued by the CDF, most of the Scripps Ranch community is classified as within a "Very High Fire Hazard Severity Zone".

Ellie's neighborhood was situated in a shallow basin surrounded by small hills, all covered with dense vegetation. During quiet evenings, little animals would venture out of the chaparral and visit the backyards of the island suburbia. With neatly cared-for homes, it was slice of civilization within the heart of wild California. Traffic was minimal as the roads all ended in cul-de-sacs There was only one way out.

Ellie walked around the outside of her house and pointed out burn scars on the building and property. "The reason our home was saved was because a few neighbors broke through the barriers posing as members of the press and joined a couple of retired firefighters who had been sent down to put out hot spots. They told me later they had no idea houses were still standing."

Once one home ignited, the flames would run along the property's wooden fence, burn the adjoining side yard gate connected to the next house, and begin engulfing that structure. "You can see what happened here", Ellie said while pointing at a charred fence post. "The men kicked over my side gate to keep the flames from catching the eaves on fire. They used the hose while it lasted to stop things from flaring back up again."

The green hose lay on the ground in a wandering spiral of melted plastic.

Ellie and her son evacuated after a neighbor pounded on her door and said a fire was just over the hill. They pulled out of their driveway around 8:45 AM. "I told my son, 'whatever you do, don't look back.' Well, of course he did and he told me later that flames were already burning fences at the end of the street."

Based on various eyewitness accounts, the eastern part of the neighborhood was in flames all morning. Later, after a lull, the western part of the neighborhood caught fire in the early afternoon. The last home burned to the ground around 5:30 PM, 8 hours after the fire first hit the area. Nine homes were destroyed in the second wave of flame (photo 28).

Harbison Canyon

Just south of Interstate Highway 8, about 10 miles east of El Cajon, rests the community of Harbison Canyon. Before the Cedar fire many of the homes existed on pads carved out of hillsides overlooking the canyon bottom. Most were older structures surrounded by the usual collection of yard stuff, woodpiles, and shrubbery frequently associated with living in the backcountry. A newer development near the highway represents a reverse image: tiled roofs, stucco facades, and neatly manicured lawns. It was designed with fire in mind.

"Around 3:00 PM Sunday I saw the fire on the other side of the Interstate and felt pretty safe," Bob Krause said, a resident of the new, fire-safe community. "But just in case, I sat out in the yard with hose in hand. I had just seen a guy up in Ramona on television defending his house by putting out spot fires, so I figured I could do the same if the situation demanded it."

Bob's house was built according to the most recent fire codes. The structure was covered in stucco without exposed wood surfaces. Eaves were barely six inches wide and the roof was covered with curved tile. Landscaping around the house consisted of a backyard pool, ice plant, lawn and several species of drought tolerant shrubbery. Adjacent to the property was dedicated open space with weedy grasses and shrubland. Although most of the building was set back the required distance, one corner was less than 30 feet away from potentially explosive woody fuels.

"To my surprise the fire jumped the Interstate. I couldn't believe it. The wind was blowing so hard thousands of embers were flying ahead making all these spot fires. I sat there with my mouth open, stunned (photos 19-20). I finally got up to turn the hose on. Within a few minutes the flames had moved a couple miles and were beginning to burn the small canyon right by my house. By the time I realized what was happening, little fires were igniting all around my place, in front of me, beside me, behind me. It was like I was in a war zone. I dropped my hose and ran down the driveway to my car as fast as I could. I'm lucky to have gotten out of there alive."

When he was allowed to return to his home, there was little left other than the façade around the front doorway; the rosea ice plant *(Drosanthemum floribundum)* in the back yard was vaporized, portions of the wrought iron fence had melted, and plastic yard furniture left only dark stains on the concrete (photo 21).

"The neighbor across the way, who lost his home, had asked the homeowner's association to clear brush further away from his property line a couple weeks before the fire, but they refused. They sited laws regulating disturbance of dedicated open space and their desire to maintain the area's natural appearance."

Although additional distance from the shrubbery would have eliminated the risk of ignition by direct heat radiation, it may not have prevented the homes in Bob's neighborhood from burning down. One of the primary causes for structural loss during wildfires is flying embers slipping through openings and igniting the building from the inside. Winds created by severe weather conditions or the fire itself can propel embers a mile or more from the fire front (Countryman, C.M. 1974, and CDF 2004). There are no guarantees during wind-driven fires.

Prepared
Susan Conniry

"What are your plans for the weekend?" asked the principal of the high school where my husband and I work.

Without hesitation I replied, "We'll be at home on fire watch." It was Friday the 24th of October, 2003, the day before the Cedar Fire started. We didn't know of course how events would unfold that Friday afternoon, but we knew that the scene was set. It was dry, really dry. And hot. Powerful Santa Ana winds were predicted with wind gusts as high as 60 miles per hour. San Diego County was experiencing severe drought, its landscape tortured from the long dry spell. With the humidity less than 3%, coupled with the preceding facts, my husband and I were intensely aware of the need to be on "fire watch."

We make a point of being alert and aware. Our home sits in the midst of chaparral country, on acreage with a 25% grade. The only way out is either up or down the canyon on a windy two-lane street designated as a rural collector road. In the wilderness and urban survival courses we teach, we have a simple motto, "create awareness without precipitating panic." We encourage people to be prepared, to act responsibly by taking precautions, and to learn to take care of themselves in an emergency situation. This type of proactive behavior takes the pressure off our emergency personnel, particularly in an urban setting. As is the case in many large cities, San Diego County emergency personnel departments are strained on a regular basis to take care of the population, let alone in a crisis situation.

Every year we spend many months weed whacking and clearing brush, creating a "defensible space," a space even wider than the fire department recommends. And as we thinned the brush, we planted succulents to cover the ground creating a "green zone" around our house. We installed the required 5000-gallon water storage tank that gravity feeds to the house and a fire hydrant. I remember the day the tank and hydrant were approved. Instead of feeling safe in case of fire, it was quite the contrary. As the Fire Marshal checked his approval list, he said, "You are on your own, way out here." He added, "By the time the trucks arrive, it might be too late. You may want to consider taking personal precautions as well in order to be better prepared." We told him we understood.

"We teach kids preparedness," we told him.

He smiled. We had a sense that he was thinking, *at least these folks get it.*

For over 15 years we continued to be alert to the possibility of fire, the need to evacuate if circumstances dictated, and the necessity of making our home as fire-safe as possible. Every summer we went through fire drills. Our best time to gather, load, and be out the gate was seven minutes. One year we had just completed our drill and returned home, congratulating ourselves on a job well done, when a fire broke out north of the property about 300 yards away. We were back in the vehicle in a matter of moments, faster than usual, still in escape mode from the drill. That fire was put out in a matter of hours and we returned home before nightfall, but with all the experiences and effort we still felt vulnerable. We felt that we needed to do more to protect our home. We were great at running away, but we needed to know that we'd have a home to come back to.

In 2002, my husband Tom and I reassessed the potential of fire engulfing our home. We knew that even with appropriate defensible space established, a composite shingle roof, and exterior stucco walls, the wooden deck surrounding our home preserved our vulnerability to flying embers.

Tom makes things when he can't find what he wants in the stores. He designs it, builds it, tests it, and re-designs until it is just right. He decided the deck needed some sort of sprinkling system, but nothing was available that met his specifications. So he purchased copper pipe and some landscape misters and created a misting system that attaches to the metal roof of the deck. In operation, the water covers the entire span of the deck and seeps through cracks, soaking the ground up to 4 to 6 feet away from the house. We felt we were finally prepared for the firestorm, whenever it would come.

On the night of October 25th we went to sleep on our deck about 9:00 PM, a normal pattern for us in the summer. Around 1:00 AM, I woke up coughing and choking. Ash was covering our faces, our blankets, and the deck. I turned on the radio to the local emergency news channel. Nothing. Then on the hour, during the regular 2 minute news program, the announcer said there was a small fire located in the four corners area of Ramona. That was it. Nothing more.

With wind gusts already up to 50-60 miles an hour blowing toward us from that location, and the amount of ash already at our house, I knew we had a problem and woke my husband. "Tom, I have a bad feeling about this."

We got up and got ready. We didn't wait for someone to tell us to go, we never have. But because we have evacuated several times before and the fire went the other way, we delayed so Tom could drive the quad up our dirt road to the top of the property and take a look. At first he didn't see anything. But then, like an apocalyptic nightmare, it began. He heard it, a strong rumbling sound like a runaway freight train. He saw what looked like the sun rising. It wasn't the sun; it was the entire landscape on fire for as far as he could see. He turned to view Wildcat Canyon Road, our only exit, and was dismayed to see that it was bumper-to-bumper traffic. Our chances of getting out were abysmal. But by the time he got back to the house the traffic had suddenly vanished. The road was clear. Tom yelled, "Susan, it's time to go. Now!"

The last thing we did before we left was turn on the misting system. It was connected to the 5000-gallon water storage tank that gravity feeds to the house. Misters would continue to pump out water until the storage tank was empty. This independence of the city's system was important because we knew that during a fire electrical lines would burn down and power would be cut off.

The next 36 hours were a blur. We watched from the shore of Lindo Lake as the fire raged across our canyon, heard propane tanks blow, and knew in our heart that our home was gone.

After the firestorm passed and the smoke had cleared a little, a friend, who also happens to be a Los Angeles Fire Marshal, took my husband back up the canyon to see what was left. As they slowly drove passed burned power lines and destroyed vehicles, they could see some structures had survived the fire. Not many, but some. They entered our property, much of it still on fire, oak trees smoldering, the ground smoking. Some of the oaks continued to burn for weeks before they fell to the ground. They passed two burned vehicles, a melted recreational vehicle, and the smoking remains of our neighbor's house. Our outdoor classroom was reduced to twisted metal and several outbuildings were gone, with nothing to show that they ever existed. It didn't bode well. But around the corner, standing in an oasis of greenery, stood our geodesic dome. As they walked closer, they could see the fire had surrounded the place, burned the landscape logs, and was still smoldering right up to the back door. But the deck was untouched. 5000 gallons of water from the misting system had soaked an area nearly 6 feet wide all around the house. "My God," our friend said, "the fire couldn't work against the humidity of the wet earth. The misters saved your house (photo 22)."

I called several radio and TV stations and pestered the newspapers to do a story, sharing with others how a simple misting system played an important part in saving our home. None appeared interested. Perhaps they just wanted horror stories, the tragedies, not stories of survival. I don't know.

We returned and camped out in our home after the fires were finally extinguished. It took 11 days for running water and power to return and 7 weeks for telephone service, but we got on with our lives and were back to work within a few days. We consider our selves extremely fortunate. Several of our canyon neighbors were killed while fleeing the flames.

A week after the devastating fire, the principal at our school reminded me of our conversation before I left work on that Friday, the day before it all happened. "How did you know?"

Reflections on a Firestorm
Michael Wangler

When I met my class Sunday morning at 7:00 AM on October 26th, the wind had already been blowing hard since midnight and the air was heavy with thick, black, acrid smoke. The first major Santa Ana wind event of the fall season had arrived and was fanning a fire several miles to the north and east of our suburban San Diego campus. We were scheduled for an all day field trip to the local mountains to study, among other things, the ecology and biogeography of fire in Mediterranean ecosystems. We were all a little nervous about the fire, but I tried to reassure the group that there was little to worry about; after all, Santa Ana winds and backcountry fires are regular and predictable events for this time of year in southern California. So predictable in fact, that one anticipates their arrival in much the same way that a New Englander might look to the changing fall colors as a sign that autumn has indeed arrived. I also figured I could use the fire as a teaching tool to illustrate materials recently discussed in class. Little did I know how powerful a lesson this fire would become.

Three hours later, we were near the headwaters of the Sweetwater River in the Cuyamaca Mountains dodging fallen branches and fighting to maintain balance as a fierce gale roared through the forest canopy above us. To the west were several giant plumes of black smoke boiling and churning like a squall line of severe thunderstorms set against a perfectly blue autumn sky. The scene was surreal: spectacularly beautiful yet troubling and dangerous as tree limbs snapped like match sticks all around us and sheets of black smoke began filling in the sky directly above. By noon, the state park was under evacuation order – it was time to go home.

The news of what was happening back home was not good. Neighborhoods were being evacuated, houses were burning, and the choking black smoke paralyzed the city. The main fire had already burned over 70,000 acres, traveling over 30 miles in only a few hours, and had just jumped a 14-lane freeway near the Miramar Air Station. To the west, the San Diego neighborhoods of Scripps Ranch and Tierrasanta were burning and the southern flank of the fire was rapidly approaching the east county communities of Alpine, Blossom Valley, Harbison Canyon, and Crest. My neighborhood, just across the river from Alpine was not immediately threatened, but when I arrived home everyone was packing their valuables and preparing to evacuate.

A few neighbors and I gathered on the ridgeline just above and to the east of our sparsely populated valley and watched through binoculars in disbelief as 50-100 foot flames raced through Alpine, jumped the interstate and burned through the communities of Harbison Canyon and Crest. The fire was moving so fast that some houses appeared to spontaneously combust well in advance of the main fire line, yet others were left virtually untouched as the flames leaped over and around one structure while completely engulfing another. As nightfall approached, I joined the steady line of cars and loaded pick-ups heading down into the city along the only remaining east-west evacuation route that had not yet been closed by the fire.

On the 27th I awoke to a blood red sky; the smoke illuminated from below by the rising sun as it peeked over the burned-out silhouette of Shadow Mountain. The winds had died down overnight, allowing for the heavier smoke to settle into the finger canyons adjacent to my parent's house, creating the optical illusion of dense fog on this bone-dry morning. The smell in the air, however, was no illusion. I lingered outside and stumbled across what appeared to be a charred manzanita branch that had blown in from the north and had been delicately deposited on the fine layer of ash that covered the driveway. Its characteristic gnarled and twisted growth pattern was still well preserved. If washed to the sea and buried by sand and mud, it might one day serve as a window to the past, hinting at the magnitude of this conflagration that was all too real in the present. I pick up the branch and crumbled it in my hands.

On the 28th I was trapped. The city was still shut down, completely immobilized by the smoke. Fires remained out of control. More houses lost, more lives turned upside down. Unable to go home or to work due to road closures and power outages, I was unwilling to go outside for fear of poisoned air. For all of the human tragedy and loss I had witnessed, nothing had quite prepared me for what was about to happen. For me, this was to be the saddest day of all.

The wind shift that had been forecast arrived with a vengeance and drove the main fire up into the mountains where it burned more than 90% of the Rancho Cuyamaca State Park, including the southern-most stand of ponderosa pine on the west coast. These old yellow trees had seen dozens of fires over the centuries, but this firestorm was unlike anything they had ever experienced and the stand was charred to a crisp. Along with it, several neighborhoods surrounding the historic gold mining town of Julian suffered almost unimaginable losses. Ninety percent of the homes in the town of Cuyamaca were destroyed and only 4 of over 200 homes in Harrison Park were standing after the firestorm had blown through.

I was devastated by the news and openly cried for the first time in years. This was, after all, my true home. The wild oak and pine-covered hills of eastern San Diego County had always been my refuge – a place where I could go to re-center myself and reconnect with the earth. It is a place where old growth conifers mingled with ancient oaks, where mountain lions were free to roam across vast stretches of undeveloped land, and where the rich and penetrating smells of the forest served as a primeval reminder of our ancestral roots. This was indeed a sad day and a further loss of wildness for us all.

On the 29th clouds and rain replaced the smoke and desiccating winds. The early morning air was crisp and refreshing with a hint of salty ocean air wafting on the breeze. It was as though the fires had never happened and it was just another beautiful autumn morning, but the piles of charcoal gray ash that had accumulated under the eaves brought me quickly back to the reality of what had just happened. I know the land will recover and forests will someday return, but I worry that these fires will fuel the emotional rhetoric that surrounds the current debate over how best to manage our forests. I can only hope that nature's resiliency is stronger than the human desires for manipulation and control; that this wild garden be left to its own devices for renewal and regeneration; and that we finally see that our attempts to control nature are not only futile, but are ultimately counterproductive to our efforts at achieving the ends we desire.

Fire is as much a part of the western landscape as are the snow-capped mountains and brilliant sunsets that capture our imagination, and connect us so deeply to this unforgiving place. Wallace Stegner once said, "Those of us who live in the arid west need to get over the color green if we are to ever truly live as natives to this place." I would further expand on that and suggest that we also need to get over our fear and loathing of fire. Fires have helped to shape the West for millennia, and will continue to do so for many thousands of years to come. It's time that we reexamine our current assumptions on how best to manage our fire-prone ecosystems. We need a shift in our collective consciousness that transforms our perception of fire as merely a destructive scourge to the land to a more holistic view that recognizes fire as a natural and inherent part of the western landscape that not only has the capacity to destroy, but also serves as a catalyst for regeneration and renewal.

Insects and Chaparral Fires
Michael Klein

Insects and other invertebrates have lived on the earth for a very long time. There are fossils dating back to the Devonian Period, some 350 million years ago. By the Paleozoic and Mesozoic Eras, some 300 million years ago, they were abundant in numbers and species. Over these millions of years they have not only survived, but thrived.

How the insect world reacts to fire and habitat conversion after a fire can be as diverse as there are species. Many insects living in a fire stricken area are destroyed in the blaze. Many survive because they live below the surface. As plants regenerate, insects return and help in reestablishing the chaparral plant community by pollination and also by aiding in the decomposition of dead wood. Like many plants, some insects are fire adapted.

Fire beetles (*Melanophila* species) are attracted to heat and smoke and can even be observed in areas where flames are still present. They are also called "jewel" beetles because of their iridescent colors. The beetles find still smoldering areas with infrared receptors on their thorax and fly straight toward them. The female will bore into the charred wood and lay her eggs. When the eggs hatch, the larvae eat the wood, aiding in the process of decomposition. Smoke flies (*Microsania* species) can be observed in the smoke of campfires and are usually some of the first insects to arrive after a burn. Little is known about this group and why they are so attracted to smoke. The larvae are known to feed on fungi.

Harvester ants (*Pogonomyrex* species) can be seen in large numbers within recently burned areas as well, dispersing seed. Tachinid flies (family Tachinidae) and blow flies (family Calliphoridae) can also be seen patrolling recently burned areas looking for charred mammals, birds, or reptiles, to lay their eggs on.

Insects or other invertebrates have the same requirements as certain plants and animals that may require varying ages of habitats to establish and stabilize. An example of this is pollination. A recent initial study of the pollination of Lakeside ceanothus (*Ceanothus cyaneus*) seems to indicate the potential candidate pollinators are one or two species of blister beetles (family Meloidae) (Klein, unpublished data). Chaparral fires, although important for ceanothus propagation, may be catastrophic to blister beetle populations depending on the time of the year the fire happens.

A little butterfly found almost exclusively in San Diego County and northern Baja is the Hermes copper (*Lycaena [Hermelycaena] hermes*). Its caterpillar will only eat one species of plant, the spiny redberry (*Rhamnus crocea*). Observations in San Diego County suggest it takes 18 years before they will recolonize a burned area. The October 2003 Firestorm destroyed approximately 90% of the known territory of this butterfly. If the previously occupied areas do not recover to their natural environment due to type conversion, recolonization may never occur. If they only recolonize in disconnected, isolated groups, they may not be able to maintain successful breeding populations. A subsequent loss of genetic variation could lead to extinction. It will take 20 years before we know for sure.

Up to 1,000 Hermes copper individuals were documented in 2001 in my study area at the Crestridge Ecological Reserve in eastern San Diego County. In June 2004, which is the primary flight time of the adults, no specimens were observed. Out of 18 documented Hermes copper locations, a total of only 98 butterflies were observed for the entire 2004 season. Remove a caterpillar's host plant and it is more than likely the butterfly will not be found in the area except for those species that are known to disperse long distances. Unfortunately, many of the southern California butterflies are not known to be long distance fliers, so large fires can effectively remove these species from an area for years.

Since there are a number of butterflies found specifically in certain types of chaparral, they can be important indicators of the habitat's health during the post fire recovery period. The gold-hunter's, hedge-row, and mountain mahogany hairstreaks (#4) have larger ranges than the Hermes copper so they may not have been as seriously impacted by the 2003 fires. Although the plants will recover, it is unknown what age they need to be before the caterpillars will utilize them again.

Rebirth
Bill Howell

I have walked the paths of Mission Trails Regional Park for more than a decade, appreciating the wildness right near my home. I also help train trail guides there who lead the public on interpretive hikes. So when flames of the Cedar fire (2003) engulfed my park, I took it personally. Mission Trails, nearly 6,000 acres, flanks the eastern edge of San Diego and remains undeveloped and relatively untamed. The fires burned half the park and destroyed or damaged many homes nearby.

A few days after the firestorm had subsided, I took a walk in the park. With my camera and a ranger, we surveyed an area along Oak Canyon that had been surrounded by healthy stands of 20 year old mixed chaparral. To chronicle the rebirth, I returned each week to this special place of formerly green slopes, with its flowers and fruits of many shades and the scents of sumac and sage. The colors were no more. Black painted the panorama and the air smelled of smoke. The vibrant landscape had been replaced with burnt twigs, carpets of ash, and broken boulders.

The scene before the fire included the lavender-blue blossoms of Ramona lilac, tiny rose-like clusters on chamise, and feathery white curlicues on the fruits of mountain mahogany (#51). They were all gone as were the bruise-red fruits of mission manzanita, the holly berries on toyon, and the fuzzy, scarlet fruits and pendulous petals of the fuchsia-flowered gooseberry. The calls of birds, the squeaks of squirrels, and the rustle of leaves had vanished in the scorch and smoke.

As we walked, I noticed subtle wisps of pale ash on darker char; they were mini-cremations of little critters that couldn't flee. Other remains were clearly braised bones of rodents or rabbits, a snake, and even a deer. Many animals escaped, but not all. Boulders were cracked; slabs had splintered. There was enough moisture in the natural crevices when the flames blasted by to cause instantaneous steam. This hot vapor advanced the natural exfoliation of granitic rock from decades to seconds.

Shrubs destroyed in the wildfire were already resprouting from the tops of their burnt skeletons. Little red, taco-shaped leaves emerged from on a burl and revealed the identity of the charred stump; laurel sumac. It will come back fast, if autumn rains are adequate they will be full-grown in a few years.

Honeysuckle, bush mallow, and spiny redberry were next to show leaves from stumps. Toyon, mission manzanita, and mountain mahogany followed with scrub oak close behind. Early on, chamise emerged from gnarls, but on close observation revealed little seedlings surrounding the mother plant. Post-fire, this chaparral member sprouts from the base but its seeds survive and germinate too. Chamise does it all.

I returned many times over the ensuing months and continued to observe the changes. Months after the fire, the cooked remains of pure stands of Ramona lilac remained lifeless. No sprouts. They appeared to be ebony snags with no hope, until one day little green seedlings popped up around them. There was a future after all.

After a light rainfall showered the area, many more seedlings emerged from the dark soil. I wondered what species they were. Some I could identify right away; for others

I would have to wait for larger leaves or flowers. Other than nonnative grasses, some of the earliest arrivals were various lily relatives, like wild hyacinth, early onion, and the undulate leaved soap plant. All over there were tiny filaree leaflets, sprouts of popcorn flower, and the arrow-shaped leaves of morning glory.

One of the most noticeable plants to appear early, with unmistakable coiling shoots and unruly tendrils, was wild cucumber, even before the rains (#22). This is no surprise because it possesses a huge tuber beneath the soil and can survive years of drought with minimal effect. The untamed stems and leaves of this wild vine spilled over rocks, tumbled down slopes, and greened entire hillsides within weeks after the burn. Black became green.

One day I noticed that gentle showers had encouraged a moldy carrot-colored goo, an inch high and over a foot wide in some places, emerging from charred creases on hillsides and between scarred rocks (photo 23). The magic mold grew so quickly I wondered if this handsome, but weird fungus was going to turn all the darkened slopes orange. In another week, except for a few hidden crevices, it was gone. For nearly two decades since the last fire the single-celled spores had remained viable in the soil, waiting for the proper fire cue and a little sprinkle to stimulate growth. It was a fire-following slime mold about which not much is known.

I anticipated the arrival of some flowers because of previous experiences with burns. They did not disappoint. The deep indigo corolla of Parry's phacelia stood tall on fuzzy stems. Whispering bells followed with dangling little pale yellow blossoms that rustle in the wind when dry. They grew next to Indian pinks with blood red petals perched precariously on floppy stems with sticky leaves. With new green foliage enhancing the darkened landscape, carpets of blue, yellow, and red are a welcome aftermath of a chaparral wildfire.

On another day I focused on white, quarter-sized disks scattered about. They were the disarticulated doors of trapdoor spiders. This inch-long arachnid digs a narrow hole, nearly a foot deep, in the clay soil, lines it with silk, and weaves a hinged flap for protection. The door is camouflaged on the top and covered with white silk on the under-side. When the fires come, the spiders hide in the bottom of their tunnels and wait for their fate. Hot chaparral fires pass by quickly and some spiders live and some do not. I don't know how they tolerate the smoke, but soil is a good insulator and many burrowing mammals like gophers and certain mice endure chaparral fires in their hideaways. Arthropod burrowers survive the same way. I poked around the territory and noted that some doors had popped off at the hinge and lay nearby, while others remained covered with an occupant inside. Some nooks were empty with partially rebuilt coverings as if the spider had started to repair and died of wounds. Who knows? Before the flames cleared the land, I was unaware that trapdoor spider populations in the chaparral were so significant.

One plant I had looked for, but had never seen at Mission Trails, was the giant of the *Phacelia* clan. A "fire follower," the books had stated. So when I first observed the downy leaves breaking through the dust, I was not aware I was about to be surprised. Soon, fuzzy leaves were on stalks 3 feet tall, with yellow buds. I waited for the flowers to erupt. The blossoms were blue, and then I knew: *Phacelia grandifora*. With a corolla 2 inches across, deep purple veins, and 5 dangling stamens surrounding a two-parted style, it was unmistakable. Two months after the overwhelming heat removed botanical life from the area, it was, indeed, "a fire follower."

I watched painted lady butterflies flit through the burned area when there was absolutely nothing botanical to visit. They would land on a rock, bask in the sun and fly on. They seemed to just be passing through, in no hurry. As vegetation returns from the wildfires of the fall, butterflies and other flying insects locate the fresh greens. Additional bugs arrive gradually and birds, too, are unhurried in their comeback. House finches were some of the earliest to flock to the cindered habitat. They liked to play in the dust. Early one morning, high on a singed sycamore limb, a black-headed grosbeak serenaded his world as if there had never been a fire. He sang all by himself to a silent spring.

Exactly a year ago, on this very trail, I noted a lonely plant with 3 flowers. I took lots of pictures, because I had never seen it here before. Why should I? After all, it was the fire poppy and the last wild fire in the area was nearly 20 years ago. It must have come from one of those rare seeds that differed from the rest. But after the recent inferno, thousands of fire poppies emerged from the ashes. Their orange-red petals dominated the dark wasteland in a spectacular celebration of recovery. Each petal lasts a day, but the image lasts a lifetime (#1).

More of the unmistakable feathery leaves of the poppy family emerged from the char. Its large gray leaves slowly progressed into plants with blossoms quite un-poppy-like. As the ocher buds erupted they resembled characters in a miniature toy land. Two of the golden petals curved back and the middle two fused to form a fantasy figurine. Golden eardrops they are called and may grow above your head, though several years later they're gone. I had learned that this yellow-flowered fire lover will return only after the seeds have cured in the soil and then exposed to charred wood or smoke. In early classifications, this plant had been placed in an old family called Fumeriaceae, which in Latin means, "smoke-family." Some things are best left alone (#40).

It was an adventure to return to the same places in the park each week and watch the cindered real estate evolve into a botanical display more colorful and more diverse than before. Fire is devastating; rebirth exhilarating.

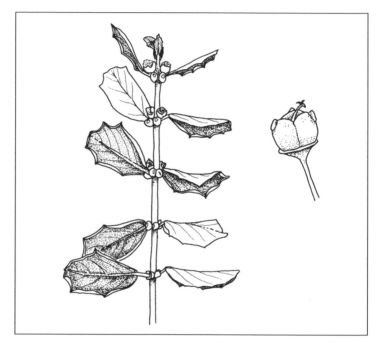

Ceanothus crassifolius

Fire, Chaparral, and Survival in Southern California

3

Fires and Firefighters

Wildfire is capricious. Behavior of the flames can change so quickly that it is impossible to know exactly what will burn next, how hot it will be, or whether or not firefighters will find themselves in mortal danger. Despite this, there are patterns that are repeated again and again. Fire personnel are trained to anticipate these patterns to make sure they do not find themselves in predictably dangerous situations. Being upslope a potential fire chimney area, such as a canyon, is one of the more obvious risks. But even relatively safe areas can quickly become hazardous because fire creates its own weather, changing conditions in a split second. This was one of the main factors leading to the entrapment of firefighter Steve Rucker's engine company. His crew was engulfed in flames during the Cedar fire in Wynola, a small community west of Julian. Rucker was killed, Captain Doug McDonald was seriously burned, and engineer Shawn Kreps and firefighter/paramedic Barrett Smith suffered minor injuries. The home they were trying to protect was surrounded by more than 100 feet of clearance.

In the infamous 1949 Mann Gulch fire, 13 firefighters were killed as flames were pushed up a canyon by 20 to 30 mph winds with 40 mph gusts. As the fire emerged from the forest into an open, grassy area the wind was free to blow without interference. Moving between 170 to 280 feet per minute, the tall grass fire flame lengths probably reached 16 to 20 feet (Rothermel 1993). Considering the difficult terrain, high altitude, and forward spot fires created by flying embers, the men didn't have a chance of outrunning the inferno. One of the 3 firefighters who survived the experience did so by lighting an escape fire with a book of matches. He lay down in the burned off area and the fire passed right over him. This strategy is now taught internationally in firefighter training schools.

Fires also have a tendency to follow the same paths. One of the fears during the Simi fire in the October 2003 fire siege was that it would repeat the same run previous burns had taken, through the canyons of Malibu and all the way to the Pacific Ocean.

These included the Hume fire of 1956, the Wright fire of 1970, the Piuma fire of 1985, and the Old Topanga fire in 1993. All were wind driven and all became some of the most horrific, damaging fires in the United States. In fact, since 1970, 12 of the nation's top 15 most destructive wildfires have occurred in California, all during extremely high winds, and low humidity (fig. 3-1).

DATE	LOCATION	IN 2002 $ (000,000)
Oct. 20-21, 1991	Oakland and Alameda Counties, California	2,245.4
Oct. 25-30, 2003	San Bernardino and San Diego Counties, California	2,040
Nov. 2-3, 1993	Los Angeles County, California	466.9
Oct. 27-28, 1993	Orange County, California	435.7
Jun. 27 -Jul. 2, 1990	Santa Barbara County, California	364.8
May 10-16, 2000	Cerro Grande, New Mexico	146.3
Jun. 23-28, 2002	Rodeo-Chediski Complex, Arizona	120
Sep. 22-30, 1970	Oakland-Berkeley Hills, California	115
Nov. 24-30, 1980	Los Angeles, San Bernardino, Orange, Riverside, and San Diego Counties, California	90.5
Jul. 26-27, 1977	Santa Barbara, Montecito, California	59.4
May 17-20, 1985	Florida	55.2
Oct. 23-25, 1978	Los Angeles and Ventura Counties, California	41.4
Nov. 16-17, 1980	Bradbury, Pacific Palisades, Malibu, Sunland, Carbon Canyon, and Lake Elsinore, California	34.9
Oct. 9-10, 1982	Los Angeles, Ventura, and Orange Counties, California	29.8

Fig. 3-1 Estimated Insurance Losses for Catastrophic Wildland Fires in the United States, 1970-2003. Despite the size of the 2003 fires, the Oakland Hills fire, at only 1,600 acres burned, remains the most costly in terms of insurance dollars due to number of lives and expensive homes lost. Adjusted 2002 $ by the Insurance Information Institute. Oct. 25-30 firestorm losses are preliminary estimates. Source: Property Claim Services/Insurance Services Office, Inc. (ISO); Insurance Information Institute.

Extreme Fire Weather

There are two basic types of wildfires in California. The first is **fuel-driven**. This is typically the type that burns in the first half of the fire season, from the middle of May through September. Although they can still be ferocious, control typically can be accomplished by using traditional fire management strategies such as exploiting previously constructed firebreaks, using ground crews and employing aerial support (photo 24). The second basic type of wildfire is **wind-driven**. These are the monsters that turn catastrophic and occur during the worst of the Santa Ana wind season from mid-September through January.

Santa Ana winds are created when fall and winter storms over the desert plains of Utah and Nevada create a high pressure, cold air mass. As this heavy volume of air pushes outward it blows southwest into southern California, blasting its way through mountain passes at over 75 miles per hour, toppling trucks on Interstate 15 traveling through Cajon Pass. These hot, dry winds can raise temperatures from the mid-70's to nearly 100 degrees within a day.

Santa Ana winds are more than just a meteorological curiosity. They impact both man and beast in peculiar ways. San Diego County farmers have reported that when the devil winds blow, stressed poultry produce 15% fewer eggs, cows give three to four pints less milk per day, and avocados twist off trees by the thousands. Psychiatrists say the winds increase depression and inflame emotions. Raymond Chandler, the author who brought us the exploits of detective Philip Marlowe, described Santa Ana nights as times when, "every booze party ends in a fight. Meek little wives feel the edge of the carving knife and study their husband's necks." Skin flakes, hair flies out of control, and jolts of static electricity turn a simple touch into a shocking event. For writer Joan Didion it's, "the wind that shows us how close to the edge we are."

Santa Ana winds also dry the brush and create conditions conducive to explosive wildfires. Such was the case on October 21, 1996. Due to either a tossed cigarette or a deliberate act of arson, roadside weeds were ignited along Harmony Grove Road outside Escondido. Within seconds, the fire raced up the hillside into the community of Elfin Forest. Within 4 hours, the fire consumed 8,600 acres and more than 130 homes along its westward, 7 mile path. The one constant variable for this and all other catastrophic fires is wind (fig. 3-2a and 3-2b).

Catastrophic California Wildland and Interface Fire Events

DATE	NAME	COUNTY	ACRES	DEATHS	STRUCTURES	WIND CONDITIONS
Sept 1889		Orange	800,000 est.	?	?	Santa Ana
Sept 1889		San Diego	200,000 est.	?	?	Santa Ana
Sept 1923	Berkeley	Alameda	50 city blocks	0	624	60 mph gusts
Sept 1932	Matilija	Ventura	220,000	0	0	Santa Ana
Oct 1943	Hauser Creek	San Diego	10,000	10	0	Santa Ana
Nov 1956	Inaja	San Diego	43,904	11	5	Santa Ana w/40 mph gusts
Nov 1961	Bel Air	Los Angeles	6,090	0	505	Santa Ana w/50 mph gusts
Sept 1970	Laguna	San Diego	175,425	5	382	Santa Ana
June 1990	Painted Cave	Santa Barbara	4,900	1	641	Sundowner winds
Oct 1991	Oakland Hills	Alameda	1,600	25	2,886	50 mph gusts
Oct 1996	Harmony Grove	San Diego	8,600	1	110	Santa Ana
Oct 2003	Cedar	San Diego	281,666	14	2,232	Santa Ana
Oct 2003	2003 Firestorm	14 fires	748,017	24	4,443	Santa Ana

Fig. 3-2a Most Devastating California Wildfires.

Selected Catastrophic Western Wildfires (Outside California)

DATE	NAME	COUNTY	ACRES	DEATHS	STRUCTURES	WIND CONDITIONS
Aug 1949	Mann Gulch	Montana	4,339	13	0	20-30 mph 40 mph gusts
Sept. 1988	YellowStone *248 total fires*	Montana and Idaho	1,585,000	2	67	High winds
July 1994	South Canyon	Colorado	1,856	14	0	50 mph gusts
May 2000	Cerro Grande	New Mexico	47,650	0	235	50 mph gusts

Fig. 3-2b Selected Major Fires Outside California.

The speed and ferociousness of wind-driven fires are hard to imagine for anyone who has never experienced them. The novice might think he or she would have time to gather family members and personal treasures under such conditions before danger became imminent. This may have been one of the contributing factors in the number of lives lost in the Cedar fire. Unknown to most, wind-driven flames can move fast enough to catch birds in flight. Upon first observing the 1996 fire cresting over a nearby ridge, many Harmony Grove families had only seconds to leap into a vehicle and escape. During the Cedar fire, flames overwhelmed a number of individuals as their cars were engulfed by fire and smoke and fire from all sides. As horrible as this loss of life was, it could have been much worse, particularly considering what could have occurred near two San Diego County Indian gaming casinos during the 2003 firestorm.

As flames blasted over the mountains toward the Barona Indian Reservation, CDF Battalion Chief Ray Chaney arrived on the scene with a sheriff deputy and immediately ordered the doors locked, preventing anyone from leaving. Shortly thereafter, huge flames cascaded into the canyon, filling the exit route through Wildcat Canyon with intense heat. CDF Division Chief Bill Clayton brought a similar situation under control at the Valley View Casino in Valley Center. Smoke from the Paradise fire was already entering the building when Clayton arrived and the scene was chaotic. The mostly elderly gamblers were all frightened, a horse suffering from burns somehow found his way into the casino, kicking one of the patrons by a slot machine off his stool, and another man collapsed from a heart attack. Remarkably, panic was held in check and more than 50 people were saved from running outside into the flames.

Based on the catastrophic nature of these kinds of wind-driven fires, the traditional fire triangle model (fig. 3-3) used as a teaching tool in fire safety programs needs some modification. Its shape does not take into account the dominating role of extreme weather in wildfires. Instead, a fire square is more appropriate (fig. 3-4). The top horizontal portion represents extreme weather producing catastrophic fire within. Knock out this top section and the triangle is reformed, describing fires under normal conditions. Without winds to push the flames and low humidity to dry the fuels, fires do not become the beasts they did in the 2003 firestorm.

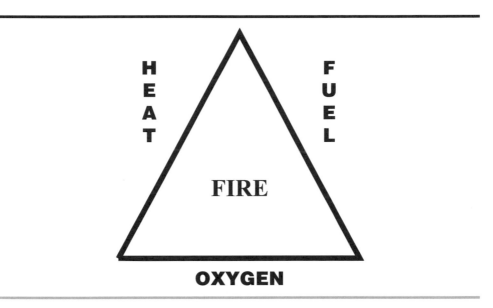

Fig. 3-3 Fire Triangle. This is the basic model describing the necessary components for fire to occur.

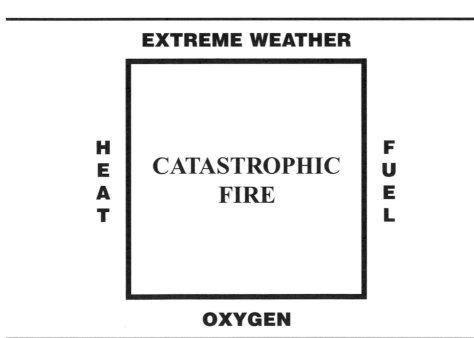

Fig. 3-4 Fire Square. A modification of the fire triangle to take into account the important role weather plays in wildfires.

A Conversation with Ray Chaney

The headquarters of The California Department of Forestry and Fire Protection in southern San Diego County lacks the grandiose façade of some government buildings. The front entrance is through a glass door barely distinguishable from the other openings along the plain walls of the single-storied structure. When entering the reception office there's a sense of modesty to the place. On the walls are a few large photographs of CDF planes dropping red fire-retardant, ground crews fighting orange flames; lots of orange flames. Otherwise, the environment is unassuming. A long central hallway accesses various offices and conference rooms with chalkboards and a few tables and chairs; a perfect place to find unsung heroes.

Battalion Chief Ray Chaney came out to meet me and we walked into one of the conference rooms to talk. A CDF veteran of twenty years, Chaney was destined to fight fires. "My dad was a firefighter."

As one of the first to witness the fledgling Cedar fire spread its terrible wings, Chaney was in a unique position to see the fire develop. He was also instrumental in saving hundreds of lives.

"I'd run a few scenarios estimating how a fire would move if it started in Cedar Creek, so I had a good idea about which way it would go. I drove down to Barona Mesa, just south of San Diego County Estates when the wind hit. The hills started exploding. I projected the fire's path and realized it would be heading straight toward the Barona Casino. I grabbed a sheriff's deputy and we raced over to Wildcat Canyon."

"What time was that?"

"There was no time that night," he answered. "It was probably around 12:30, but I can't be sure. Everything happened so fast."

Chaney blocked traffic from entering the canyon and then drove down to a car racetrack just north of the casino. "There were about 75 to 100 people on site getting ready for Sunday races. I found the track manager and told him to get everyone out of there immediately, making sure they headed north, not south into the canyon. We circled the track and announced the same thing on the truck's PA system."

After making sure the racetrack evacuation was going smoothly, Chaney blasted down Wildcat Canyon Road toward the casino. He glanced into his rearview mirror and saw the fire cross the road behind him. He was ahead of it by only a few minutes. "As I drove, I thought about what would happen if people panicked at the casino and tried to outrun the flames. The image of that 'highway of death' scene from the Gulf War, where hundreds of vehicles and bodies were strewn for miles, entered my mind. All it would have taken would have been one car crash or just traffic backing up trying to get down the road. When the flame front hit, there would have been no escape. The only hope I could see was to have everyone shelter in place at the casino and wait it out."

Chaney stopped in at the nearby fire station, briefed them of the situation, then ran into the casino and told the manager they needed to talk quickly, privately. "You've got about 10 minutes before a 100 foot wall of flame hits this place. If anyone leaves here, they're going to die. Secure the exits. Do not let anyone out."

The large golf course would provide an excellent buffer for the buildings, but the parking lot posed a problem. It was Saturday night and the lot was filled with cars.

All it would have taken to ignite one of the vehicles would have been a few embers entering through an opened car window. One would ignite another. "I told the officers to patrol the lot. If any vehicles caught fire, they had to put them out, fast!

"Despite the speed of the fire, the driving Santa Ana winds were relatively moderate. With faster winds, you can more accurately predict where the fire front will go. The topography plays a more important role with moderate winds. Instead of the fire going straight over hills, it moves around them. (fig. 3-5)

"The front split in two after hitting San Vicente Mountain with one section moving toward the racetrack and the other through Featherstone Ranch. The casino area got hit with the Featherstone branch first. It was a pretty deadly one, two punch. When the first wave came it was like an orange tornado with millions of swirling embers. Plastic fences around the casino were melting and burning trees were falling onto the roadways. It was impossible to see."

Further down the canyon, deputies were trying to evacuate residents, but the fire was moving so fast and the homes were so dangerously dispersed it proved impossible to reach everyone. California Highway Patrolman Joe Jones, a decorated veteran of the Gulf War, was one of those who tried to save as many as he could despite the overwhelming risks. He later told Chaney over a cup of coffee that the Gulf War was lightweight compared to what happened in Wildcat Canyon that night.

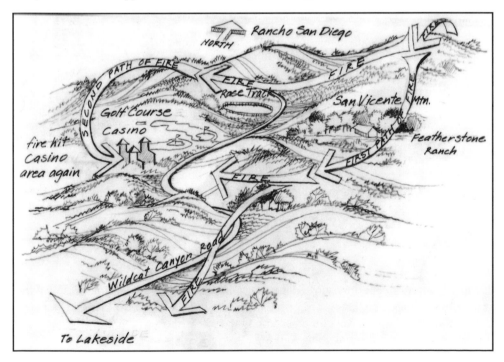

Fig 3-5 Path of the Cedar Fire Through Wildcat Canyon, San Diego County.
Artist: Stephen L. Halsey

"Somewhere between 2:00 to 3:00 AM, 33,000 acres burned," Chaney said. "You do the math. The real heroes of this fire are the deputies and other emergency personnel who drove down those narrow roads trying to reach people. A lot of them were not familiar with the area and only had maps to go by. Taking the wrong turn in Muth Valley toward San Vicente Reservoir would have meant certain death. When you can't see because of the smoke, getting lost and disorientated is an easy thing to do."

Chaney organized additional search, rescue, and suppression efforts with other emergency personnel in the area as he drove down Wildcat Canyon himself. "Visibility was almost zero so I had to drive by watching the white line down the center of the road. At one point a wire from an electrical pole slapped across the hood of my truck. I immediately lifted my hands off the steering wheel so I wouldn't get fried. As the wire slid off the back, it became pretty clear that since I was still alive, the thing wasn't hot. I checked to make sure everyone with me was okay, and then kept going. Hand crews ahead of me were cutting the burning trees that had fallen across the road. In all my years fighting fires, I had never experienced anything like this. The speed, the violence, the intensity; it was unprecedented."

Chaney showed me a moving computer graphic demonstrating how fast the fire moved. It rolled forward like spilled red paint. The speed at which it traveled between 6:00 to 8:00 AM toward the Scripps Ranch community was phenomenal. Ray pointed at the western edge of the fire front. "The fire here was pretty much done by 10:00 AM. Good thing the winds stopped when they did. Clairemont and Pacific Beach would have been next."

"Do you think anything more could have been done to save those people in the canyon who died," I asked him.

Ray shook his head. "It was moving so fast and those homes were so deeply embedded in wild areas with only one way out. There just wasn't enough time."

One of the suggestions Ray offered to help prevent fire casualties in the future is the construction of community protection zones. "Bulldoze a 10 to 20 acre patch within at-risk communities and create a park with lots of parking space. Everyone understands and knows the pre-evacuation plan and everyone goes to the park when a wildfire threatens. There could be a wireless phone there and families could call and tell us their status. 'I'm here with my three kids and ten of my neighbors.'"

Ray turned off his computer and told me he had to go. "We're building a pool and my wife and I are meeting with the contractor."

"You got kids?"

"Yeah, little ones."

Maybe future firefighters, I thought to myself.

On the way out, Ray showed me some fire education pamphlets he was working one. "People just need to know. They need to understand fire is part of living in southern California. They should have a little poster on their refrigerator with a list, 'A fire is coming at you – what are you going to do?'"

As I drove out, I passed by the recently dedicated memorial to Steve Arrollando, the young CDF firefighter who was killed in 1973. He graduated from high school the same year I did and died 2 months later. We would be the same age now. I slowed my car down for a moment and offered him a salute.

How We Fight Brush Fires
A perspective offered by two veteran firefighters[1]

"The Viejas fire in '01, the Gavilan fire in '02 and then again during the Cedar fire in '03. It's always the same damn thing."

Jim Hart, a veteran firefighter in San Diego County, leaned against a his truck and shook his head. Soot was buried deeply into his skin and a cigarette hung from his hand like an old bandaged finger. He was taking a break after spending all night trying to keep his firefighters alive. He was one of the incident commanders coordinating suppression efforts on a fire raging in the local foothills. "The media, the politicians, they blame the fire service and lack of aircraft for the loss of homes. Every time. People don't have a clue how fires are fought. They think if they've tended a campfire or watched brushfires from a lawn chair, they're instant experts. Right."

He looked at me with blood-shot, squinted eyes and took a long drag off his cigarette. I'd have liked to think he was just trying to imitate some Clint Eastwood character, but I could tell he really didn't like me very much. I'm one of those reporters, one of those media people. I was there to interview him for a story I was writing, and it wasn't starting out very well.

Hart's radio crackled some indecipherable emergency personnel speak the same time his cell phone started ringing. I stood there pretending to be occupied with my notepad.

"How old are you?" he barked after snapping his phone shut.

"Ah, 31," I answered.

"Look, lets go sit down."

We went over to an area with picnic tables, or rather a table. The others had burned the night before. Hart held his two hands up, joining them together by touching his thumbs and first fingers at their tips to form a triangle shape. "See this? It's a triangle." He stared at me waiting for some sheepish grin on my behalf. I didn't grin. "First of all, you need to understand the basics about why fires behave the way they do. The Fire Triangle is one of the first things a young firefighter is exposed to when learning about fighting chaparral fires. Most of my early training was related to understanding this kind of stuff, like depriving a fire of fuel by building a fireline, or depriving it of oxygen by throwing dirt on it."

"Yeah, I remember that in grade school. The fire department came over and taught us all that: fuel, oxygen, and heat. Deprive the fire any one of these and it can't burn." I felt excited about the memory, but Hart ignored my enthusiasm.

"Each great wildland firefighter is a master of fire behavior. He has to be otherwise it will kill him. And there's another triangle, the one based on behavior." Hart thrust his fist up and delineated each of the three components by popping up a finger, pausing each time. "Type of vegetation, weather elements like wind and humidity, and topography

---

[1] As told to Richard W. Halsey by two anonymous firefighting veterans. Although the names of the characters are fictional, the details presented are completely factual.

of where the burn is. The essence of a successful fire suppression operation is understanding how these three things interact."

I scribbled the fire triangle in my notes and suggested maybe I should take a firefighter class.

"Yeah," Hart deadpanned.

The chaparral vegetation of southern California presents an immense challenge to firefighters. While separating the fire from the fuel by constructing firelines is the same method used elsewhere in the United States, it is certainly a more daunting task when working in the thick brush compared to grasslands or open forests. Laying fire hose or cutting fireline through chaparral is full of hazards and frustrations. Manzanita dulls the saws, whitethorn ceanothus penetrates the firefighters clothes with 2 inch long thorns, and moist areas usually contain a large amount of poison oak. And typically, the fire is on steep slopes with gravity taking a tremendous toll on firefighter stamina and balance. Not only does gravity affect the firefighter's ability to stand upright on a steep slope, it also promotes a significant amount of rolling material as the fire removes vegetation upslope. Some rocks rolling downslope towards fire personnel are life threatening. Other hazards faced by the firefighter include swarms of angry yellow jackets disturbed by fireline construction, the presence of yucca plants that can pierce the toughest of clothing, and the hazards of being hit by fire retardant or a water drop from support aircraft. Chaparral fires have resulted in the counties of southern California holding the dubious distinction of having the most wildland firefighter fatalities of any region in the United States. "Chaparral fires spread faster than we can cut our firelines," Hart said before stopping for a moment. "What's your name again?" he asked me.

"O'Malley, Tom O'Malley."

"Yeah. Well, because of how fast these things can move, we place a lot of emphasis on having predetermined locations to contain them. Fuelbreaks, fire breaks, and fire roads are all examples of this."

"Fuelbreak, fire break?"

"A fuelbreak is an area along a road or on a ridge where the chaparral has been converted to lower fuel volume plants like grass to help with fire control. A fire break is the same kind of area where all the fuel has been completely removed, like a preexisting fireline."

"Fuel?"

Hart gave me one of those looks again. "Bushes. Leaves. Sticks. Vegetation is fuel."

"So how *do you* start to fight a fire, I mean from the beginning?"

"Fires usually start on the edge of a road. Some jerk throws out a cigarette, sparks fly off some chain dragging on the ground, a number of things. Once we get there, fire engine crews lay fire hose from the base or heel of the fire and up both flanks. If it's not contained right then, hand crews, bulldozers, and aircraft join the fight. Hand crews and bulldozers build fireline to physically separate the fire from the fuel."

"The fire triangle," I interjected. Hart ignored my effort to become involved in the conversation.

"Then engine companies apply water and foam along the fireline to cool the fire edge or extinguish it. It's like a war, O'Malley. We use a combination of ground and air resources to defeat the enemy."

"You lose guys."

"No. There's no tolerable loss philosophy in firefighting that justifies the death of firefighters or civilians during fire suppression operations. It's not part of the attack."

"It happens sometimes though," I said with an uncertain tone in my voice.

Hart stopped talking for a moment and finished his cigarette. He dropped the butt on the ground and smothered it with his boot. Then he picked it up and put it into a little zip-lock baggie he pulled out of his back pocket. I learned later one of his best friends was killed fighting a fire when both of them were first starting their firefighting careers. He had persuaded his friend to join up.

Firefighting requires that everyone operate within established rules and guidelines related to safety. For example, throughout a fire suppression operation, each firefighter is briefed on the location of their escape routes and safety zones, should the behavior of the fire suddenly change, threatening their safety. Typically, the safety zone is inside the fire perimeter in a well-burned area that has cooled enough to provide refuge. Other examples of safety zones include non-flammable environments such as irrigated pastures, golf courses, and rocky areas.

Hart opened up a water bottle and drank the whole thing, throwing the empty into a nearby, charred trashcan. It bounced off the rim and rolled onto the ground. "NBA I'm not." He picked it off the blackened earth and dropped it in the can. "You've got to establish an anchor point for suppression operations," he said. "Anchoring the fireline to a road or some natural feature like rock faces or cliffs prevents any fire spread behind your crew and provides the initial firefighter safety zone" (fig. 3-6).

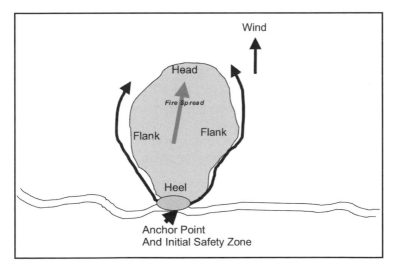

Fig. 3-6 Strategic Fire Suppression.

"So what about the helicopters and the planes. When do they come into play?"

Hart rubbed his nostrils with the back of his dirty hand and snorted out some air. "The key role of air tankers is to lay fire retardant along the flanks and across the top of the fire to slow down the spread (photo 26). They don't put the fire out. They just help us limit its spread."

"Not according to the television," I said with a laugh. Hart snorted again, then grinned. I was getting somewhere.

"In windy conditions, air tankers aren't worth a lot because the retardant drifts with the wind, or the flames just jump over the retardant line they make. Helicopters support firefighters on the ground as well, but are a lot more flexible. We use them for not just dropping retardant, but also water and foam. They go up for reconnaissance, logistical support like airlifting food, water, and equipment to firefighters, and can transport crews to remote portions of the fire. But like other aircraft, and this is the part the media doesn't get, the effectiveness of helicopters drops a lot once wind speeds increase to 35 miles per hour or more."

Most of helicopters used in southern California are either the medium sized ones that carry 350 gallons per drop or the larger helitanker, which averages 1850 gallons per drop. Like air tankers, helicopters do not actually put fires out, but are an essential tool in allowing firefighters on the ground to get a fireline and hose line around the blaze, which is referred to as containment. Air tankers drop their retardant loads just outside the fire perimeter, covering the unburned vegetation with retardant to temporarily abate the spread of the fire. Helicopters use retardant in the same way but are more likely utilized to drop water or foam directly on the edge of the fire, resulting in a significant reduction in heat and fire spread and allowing firefighters on the ground to be successful.

In general, aircraft are not effective firefighting tools during high winds. During windy conditions, embers can be blown in front of the main fire producing spot fires as far as one and one half miles ahead of the main fire. Therefore, even if aircraft were effective in hitting their targets in the wind, the fire is likely to jump over the location where retardant, foam, or water has been applied. As the winds die down, aircraft become more effective, helping firefighters get an upper hand over a wind driven fire.

"I've heard there was a pilot who had to dodge a piece of wood or something like that while flying over one of the fires. Was that in San Diego, or . . . ?"

"No, near Hemet. Chris Kniebes and Cameron Douglas were flying a four-engine DC-4 at around 1,500-2,000 feet. They were preparing for a fire retardant drop when they spotted this 4 x 5 sheet of plywood spinning around about 100 yards to their left. It was just hovering there, rotating end over end in the same place. Chris told me later that his plane, along with several others, experienced windshield pitting from the gravel up there. Gravel at 2,000 feet. Those are extreme firestorm conditions, my friend. People think any rookie with a flying license can go up there and make a drop. What they don't understand is that the weather has to change before we can get a handle on these large fires and contain them. No clue (photo 27)."

"Hart," a voice came out of the cab window of a fire truck, "I'm taking part of your crew to do some mop-up on the south ridge."

"Okay." Hart turned back to me. "Fires aren't controlled until every burning ember has been extinguished within 100 to 300 feet of the fireline. Hand crews and engine companies have to take care of that. If a single ember on either side of the fire-line remains it can result in fire escaping containment days after it's been officially declared over. The firefighting isn't done when the public stops seeing the smoke. It can last several more days."

"How many fires do you guys deal with every fire season?" I asked.

Hart shook his head, not at me, but at the naïve public audience within his own head. "You know, most of the wildfires that occur is San Diego County are controlled by the first engine company to arrive on the scene. You don't usually hear about those. It's the more difficult fires that require all of the tools like hand crews, bulldozers, and aircraft." Hart pulled out another cigarette and lit it. "Come over here for a minute." He stood up from the picnic table and nodded to the right.

We walked over the crest of a hill and could see the suburban edge of the city tempting the wilderness with little dispersed networks of streets and homes in shallow canyons and along ridge tops.

"The biggest change I've seen over the years in fighting chaparral fires has been this; the increased development, the thousands of structures built in the middle of flammable chaparral vegetation. These places represent a huge threat to the safety of firefighters because of the homeowner's failure to maintain defensible space. The presence of these homes is a major headache to us when trying to run an efficient fire suppression effort. It's hard to contain the spread of a fire when most of your workforce is tied up saving threatened residences rather than working to contain the perimeter of the fire. The loss of this focus on perimeter control can lead to bigger fires, fires that are even more threatening to communities."

"Doesn't someone like the Fire Marshal have authority to keep people from building in dangerous places," I asked.

"You've got to be kidding me O'Malley. You think they'd give us the power to tell people they can't put a house where they want because they might die or one of our firefighters might burn to death trying to protect it? Not a chance."

"So what do we do? There's got to be something we can do to keep all these homes from burning down all the time."

"Look, there've been fires that we haven't been able to stop for a hundred years and there will be lots more in the future. Ever heard of The Great Idaho Fire of 1910? It burned over 2 million acres in just 36 hours. Then there's the recent drought. As it has dragged on, we are seeing more problems controlling fires under hot, dry weather or fall Santa Ana wind conditions. And by all indications, that global warming thing is a reality and fires are becoming more severe because of it. It is not about aircraft. People need to have some basic understanding of how fires are fought and when fires can't be stopped."

"We spend too much time in our cars," I said. "When I taught school for a few years most of the kids had never been into the mountains, much less understand what chaparral was. Fire was something they only saw on television."

"It's not about mountains O'Malley. The winds can take the next fire into La Jolla. When you look at the environment and truly understand that some fires just can't be stopped, only then will people see the real value of fire prevention or creating defensible space around their homes. The best firefighters can hope for during a wind driven fire episode is a safe assignment created by enough defensible space around the structures they're protecting. When communities are threatened by fire, there's lack of defensible space, and buildings are not fire resistant – it's called heavy losses."

"Maybe they won't forget this time."

"We get two things every decade O'Malley; a big fire and another fire conference where everyone sits around and talks about what they forgot since the last one. Yeah, a few building codes change, but in a county like San Diego that routinely votes down proposals for enhanced levels of fire service, and continues to approve development in chaparral areas, the problem of protecting communities from wildfire is increasing every year. All this noise about getting a few more firefighting aircraft will not solve anything."

"So what do you need?"

Hart smiled, "If I were king . . . Tell them this; tell them new developments have to be as fire resistant as we can make them. And all those older homes; the owners need to walk around and figure out how to retrofit the place to be more fire resistant. This includes intelligent management of vegetation. And if the county wants to buy things, more aircraft would help, but additional ground resources like fire engines would have far more impact during these wind-driven events."

Hart's cell phone rang again. He talked for a few minutes and then turned to walk back to his truck. "Got a new fire in Riverside County. Gotta go."

"Thanks for the time."

Hart stopped for a moment and rubbed the back of his neck. "Teacher. You were a teacher. That's where I've heard your name before. Where'd you teach?"

"Mark Twain Elementary."

"My nephew went there. Rudy Shaffer."

"Yeah! I had him as a student. Sharp kid."

"Heard you were really good. The kids liked you."

"Thanks."

"That story you're writing. Do the same good job. Get the message out. We'll have another fire. It's just a matter of time."

From the Ozarks to Marin
Chris Blaylock

In August of 2000, the National Fire Plan set forth a new policy on wildland fire in America. One aspect of the plan called for increased focus on the wildland-urban interface, the area where homes and vegetated wildlands meet. Soon after, a non-profit group known as the Student Conservation Association (SCA) developed a program to address the education requirements of the new plan. Trained in the finer points of defensible space, SCA interns set out to engage homeowners and help them protect their own homes. It was through this grass-roots program that I first entered the complex world of fire.

Heroes and Heroines Abound

The firefighter holds a special place in America's heart. When disastrous circumstances conspire against us, the firefighter rushes to our aid. When infernos threaten to rob us of life and property, firefighters take a stand. The firefighter will march fearlessly into the heart of Hades to protect total strangers. The firefighter will forgo sleep till the battle is finished.

Indeed, the firefighter is a modern day hero. We stop what we are doing to watch their engines pass by, knowing they speed somewhere surely exciting. We don t-shirts and hats emblazoned with their insignia. Ask a young child what he wants to be when he grows up and he'll probably say, "Spiderman!" Ask him what he wants to do and he may say, "Be a firefighter."

However, in all the romanticism and well-deserved mythos attributed to firefighters, the true depth of firefighting has been obscured. Many people don't realize that most of firefighting occurs before the fire ever starts. Whether it be keeping tools in peak condition so they don't fail at the worst moment, running drills and rehearsing potential situations, or identifying and mitigating hazardous conditions, firefighting is – in large part – preparation. It is therefore not only the men and women wielding hoses and axes who have the opportunity to be heroes, but land-managers, city planners, and homeowners as well.

Salt of the Earth

I certainly didn't realize the full depth and complexity of firefighting until I entered the fire world professionally. Though raised in San Diego, my introduction to fire prevention and safety began in southern Missouri. In the Ozark hills I led a community outreach effort to raise defensible space awareness in the wildland-urban interface. Our team was part of the Student Conservation Association's Fire Education Corps program. Fire Education Corps teams accomplish their goals by going straight to the homeowner, door to door, and providing a channel of communication between communities and the neighboring agencies that host the teams.

Communication in the Ozarks was, flat out, behind the times. The area lacked a functioning 9-1-1 emergency system and some departments didn't have maps to identify the homes in their jurisdiction. This may have been just as well; many streets didn't even have names. If a homeowner happened to know the phone number to their local firehouse they'd be left to explain where they lived in relative terms.

Dispatch: "Van Buren Fire. What's the emergency?"
Homeowner: "Help! Some kids set fire to the field behind my house!"
Dispatch: "Okay. Where do you live sir?"
Homeowner: "Well…you go out to the old mill and head left at the fork, there's an old double-wide there, just keep going past that"

One homeowner told me it once took over 20 minutes for the emergency crews to find his house. He lived less than 2 miles from the firehouse.

That season our team of interns managed to map several hundred homes for local emergency response crews. We gathered defensible space data for each home and entered it into a Geographic Information System (GIS) database. During the project we never got to see fire on the ground, but we could be sure that the work we were doing would eventually make the difference in saving someone's home, perhaps even life.

Possibly a more powerful accomplishment, we were able to organize a defensible space demonstration project that brought together the efforts of community members, a local church group, the local volunteer fire department, as well as state and federal agencies. Though the local volunteer firefighters still had insufficient equipment, their job would be that much safer in the event of a wildland fire.

The project not only demonstrated defensible space but the importance of cooperation in fire prevention. All it took was a few concerned citizens to serve as catalysts. Though I would soon leave that post, the organizational structure we set up continues. As of this writing, 3 more towns have been mapped and GIS risk hazard assessment is being used to help local fire officials plan projects. My next assignment would bring me back home to California with its huge population and relative wealth, but similar need for greater coordination.

From Ashes it Bloomed

Traveling north across the Golden Gate Bridge, one leaves the concrete confines of San Francisco into the open wilds of Marin County. Small communities branch off the trunk of Highway 101, stretching into the grassy valleys and eucalyptus forests that make up vast state and federal lands. Marin residents cherish their natural surroundings where suburban streets fade seamlessly into the brush and trees. In fact, much of Marin is a textbook example of the wildland-urban interface.

From these homes that dot Marin's steep slopes, one can view the San Francisco Bay with Alcatraz in the foreground and the Bay Bridge, Berkeley, and Oakland behind. In fall of 1991, that view included a new feature; thick smoke billowing up from the Oakland hills.

Like a mirror image reflecting off the bay, the steep hills of Oakland and Berkeley are also dotted with residential communities engulfed in dense vegetation. Historically, these hills were once rolling grasslands. As more and more people spilled out from booming San Francisco, the landscape began to change. With increasing development came forests of nonnative eucalyptus and Monterey pine. In 1991 this mixture of dense, ornamental trees, shrubbery, and homes combined under harsh weather conditions to create one of the most destructive fires in California history.

Nearly 2,900 homes were lost in the Oakland Hills Tunnel fire. Across the bay, Marin residents and fire officials immediately recognized that the same conditions existed in their hills. Sure enough, four years later the Vision fire would consume over 12,000 acres of land and 45 homes in northern Marin. In the aftermath of these fires, the FireSafe Marin Council was born.

Once Around the Table

The Golden Gate National Recreation Area's Fire Management Office in Marin County brought me out as part of the same Fire Education Corps program I experienced in the Ozarks. Many projects to reduce hazardous fuels along the park's 40 plus miles of urban interface were already underway. My challenge was to increase communication between the park and neighboring community members concerning fire management activities. I wrote news releases, went door to door, and created web pages in order to accomplish this goal. One of my duties would be to attend the monthly FireSafe Marin meetings. The level of agency coordination I was to witness there surpassed any I had seen before.

The FireSafe Marin Council is an incorporated non-profit organization dedicated to reducing the threat of a destructive wildland fire in Marin. The council is comprised of representatives from local fire departments, the water district, homeowner groups, state and county land agencies, the Marin Conservation Corps, and the National Park Service. Acknowledging that fire does not respect political boundaries, these representatives meet monthly to tackle fire issues that face Marin as a whole. The council has proven effective in increasing fire safety awareness, addressing fuel loading in the wildland-urban interface, and helping provide a means of vegetation disposal following fuel reduction efforts.

The monthly meetings also serve as a forum for coordinating the independent efforts of the agencies and groups represented. Each representative keeps abreast of their neighbor's fire prevention activities through the council. Different agencies, often with disparate objectives and directives, are able to foster cooperative projects. The case of Tamalpais Valley, a small suburb of Marin, is demonstrative of this coordination.

Where Words Become Actions

Much of my outreach focused on the community of Tamalpais Valley. Like many California suburbs, Tamalpais Valley (known locally as "Tam" Valley) is characterized by wood shingle roof homes that line narrow streets. These streets dissolve into 70 acres of highly flammable eucalyptus. Many homes stand just a few paces from public lands, making it impossible for them to create the 30 feet of defensible space required by California code.

In 2003 the National Park Service and Southern Marin fire began a series of projects in Tam Valley with FireSafe Marin serving as the clearinghouse for federal funds. The projects restored two overgrown fire roads that crossed the eucalyptus stand.

My job was to alert park visitors and community members to the full breadth of the projects before work began. Reactions varied. Past park projects had brought a certain amount of backlash from the community. Certainly when the government shows up unannounced with chainsaws, history has given sufficient cause for alarm. However, most citizens approved of the work after learning that this wasn't to be an arbitrary clear-cut, but a well-planned and multi-dimensional project. Not only did fire agencies work together on the project, but park Natural Resources staff followed the cutting with native plant restoration. Still, in canvassing the neighborhoods I encountered some resistance and discovered that the "it couldn't happen here" mentality persisted despite the fires of '91 and '95.

Then, less than a year after these projects took place, an early season fire broke out in the middle of that same eucalyptus stand. I got to take off my outreach hat and put on my firefighting helmet as part of a hand crew. Constant bucket drops spared us from a crowning conflagration but fire still crawled right up the sides of the eucalyptus using the shredding ribbons of bark as a ladder. One of us would often have to break from the fireline and catch a spot fire behind us caused by the constant eucalyptus embers floating by. It was easy to see how homes are lost without even being in the fire's direct path.

The Tam fire came within 30 meters of homes but no structures were lost or damaged. This would prove to be a rare case of a "good" fire. It served to alert the community of the very real threat without real losses. It also proved that agency efforts were on the right track. With the restored fire roads in place after the 2003 projects, emergency crews were able to access the fire safely and without delay.

That same week I went back into the Tam community to distribute information about the fire and defensible space. This time around the reaction was uniformly positive. In fact, whereas just a few months ago some individuals petitioned their county supervisor to stop the cutting of eucalyptus, people now were asking when all 70 acres could be removed.

The Path Ahead

Compared to the Ozarks, Marin is rich in equipment, organizational structures like Fire Safe councils, and, of course, funds. Though Marin fire departments have far superior equipment than their country counterparts, they have a far higher housing density to contend with. In a large wildfire incident Marin fire crews would be stretched just as thin as Ozark crews in their less populated jurisdiction. On scale, the two locales face many of the same issues and require similar coordination with the communities.

Protecting homes and lives from wildland fire is everyone's responsibility. From the homeowner who creates defensible space to the frontline firefighter battling the blaze, it's the combined efforts that truly make us fire safe. Done in isolation, these efforts are rendered nearly futile. With coordination we can efficiently mitigate the hazards that face us.

I've seen cooperative fire prevention efforts with and without money to back them up. The results look very much the same. The key factor seems to be participation. Protecting homes from wildland fire, therefore, is truly an opportunity for everyone to be a hero. Web slinging and a spandex costume are optional.

1. Mixed chaparral on mountainside above Temecula, Riverside County.

2. Vegetation variation due to slope exposure. Chaparral on left, north facing slope. Coastal sage scrub on right, south facing slope.

3. Type conversion, Mission Trails Regional Park, San Diego. Due to repeated burning and grazing, this area has been converted from chaparral and coastal sage scrub cover to non-native, weedy grassland.

4. Red shanks chaparral.

5. Chamise chaparral.

6. Ceanothus chaparral.

7. Manzanita chaparral.

8. Scrub oak chaparral.

9. Coastal sage scrub.

10. Dimorphic leaves on black sage as a drought adaptation.

11. Type conversion. Three-year-old recovering chaparral on left from the 2001 Viejas fire. On right, a portion of the Viejas burn scar reburned in the Cedar fire, 2003, converting to weedy grassland. Thirty-year old growth upper left.

12. Bare zone around purple sage showing results of fencing. Santa Ynez Valley, Santa Barbara County. Originally appeared in Halsey (2004).
Photo supplied by Jon E. Keeley.

13. Cedar fire stopping point. Shows where fire stopped despite available fuel due to favorable weather conditions. Site above the Inaja Memorial near Santa Isabel.

14. Post fire scene near Del Dios, Escondido, San Diego County. March 1991.

15. May 1991.

16. June 1992.

17. June 1995.

18. August 2004.

19. The Cedar fire about to cross Interstate 8 near Harbison Canyon. Taken from the backyard of house in picture 21. Photo by Bob Krause.

20. Similar view post-fire as seen in photo 19 showing structure of neighborhood. Green mulch sprayed on freeway roadbed can be seen in the background.

21. Remains of house after Cedar fire. This home was similar to homes in photo 20: tile roof, no exterior wood surfaces. House possibly burned due to embers entering through seams under roofing tiles. Photo by Bob Krause.

22. The Conniry/Beasley home that survived the Cedar fire. Under-eave misters and thinning of surrounding brush saved this home from the fire front as it moved through Wildcat Canyon.

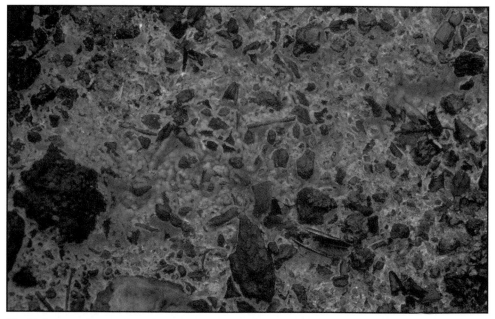

23. Unknown fungus found growing at several locations after the Cedar fire.

24. Fuel driven fire moving downslope. Rancho Penasquitos, San Diego, August 27, 1995.

25. Pine Ridge Trail. One year after the Cedar fire looking east on the Pine Ridge Trail, Green Valley Falls in Cuyamaca State Park, October 2004.

26. Aerial support. Tanker is dropping fire retardant ahead of the fire front in an attempt to reduce the combustibility of the vegetation. Source USFS.

27. Huge pyrocumulus cloud of smoke above a wildfire. Note aircraft for perspective. Source USFS.

28. Remains of homes in Scripps Ranch, San Diego County after the Cedar fire.

29. Taking responsibility. Realizing their townhouse was poorly design to resist wild-fires, the owners purchased fire-fighting equipment. The homeowner's association demanded the equipment be removed due to liability issues. After understanding their own legal liability regarding the building's high fire-risk design, the association permitted the equipment to remain. Owner demonstrating use of fire hose. Source Geoffrey D. Smith.

30. Hydromulched freeway cut showing effect of mild rains. Highway 52, San Diego County.

31. Mulch strips on Viejas Mountain, San Diego County. Although the effectiveness of mulching to control erosion was questionable, this backcountry landscape was treated nonetheless. Numerous sensitive species live on the site.

32. Similar areas in Malibu Canyon, Santa Monica Mountains, demonstrating how native chaparral (left) can be type converted to a laurel sumac weedy grassland (right) after short fire return intervals. Fires burned area on right in 1985, 1993, and 1996. Photos by Stephen Davis, Pepperdine University.

33. Cheatgrass invasion of a recently burned forest in the San Bernardino Mountains. Photo by J.E. Keeley.

34. Vernal Pool in San Diego County.

35. Wilderness in a box? This vernal pool is all that remains after development destroyed the rest of the complex of 67 pools. It is surrounded by a rod-iron fence within the Legacy apartment project and posted with a plaque.

36. Connecting with the natural world. Author with sons observing one of the few vernal pools left in San Diego County.

4

Getting Ready for the Next One

Like California, much of southern Australia has a fire-prone Mediterranean climate. Instead of chaparral, its brushlands are called kwongan and mallee. Home developments are typically built in clusters surrounded by circular roadways that act as protective buffers against wildfire. When the fires come, the homes are designed to provide "shelter in place", whereby able-bodied homeowners are not evacuated. Instead, they remain home to help defend the structures. Only children and the elderly are taken to safer ground. Homeowners can stay not only because the structures are defensible, but also because understanding fire and knowing what to do when the fire comes are basic skills in Australia.

In contrast, many developments in California have homes situated at the end of quiet cul-de-sacs or along narrow streets fingering into wild, open space. Backyard patios and bedroom windows often face into chaparral rather than buffer zones . When fires come, homeowners evacuate and depend on a small force of firefighters to save their homes. When huge wind-driven fires come, some homeowners don't have time to evacuate. Their wooden homes catch fire, one-way access routes to their neighborhoods become blocked with burning trees, and emergency personnel are forced to frantically engage in search and rescue efforts. In Australian fire response model communities are designed to withstand the flames and citizens are trained to know what to do when the fire comes. This is much more economical than funding large fire suppression efforts and retrofitting older structures because fire safety is built into the system from the very beginning.

Due to new building codes, some developments in California are starting to reflect this principle and are much safer than those built in the past. From an evolutionary perspective, wildfires are eliminating many of the maladapted, readily combustible homes and newer, fire savvy structures are replacing them. However, this does not replace the continual need for fire education and the constant maintenance required for managing vegetation fuels around the home.

Survivable Space

One of the most crucial steps a homeowner can take to reduce risk of structural ignition is to create what is commonly called defensible space. This refers to a managed area around a structure with all flammable materials removed, providing a safety zone for firefighters to operate. However, the term does not take into account circumstances occurring during wind-driven firestorms. The reality is that firefighters will not be available to defend most structures. Therefore, a better term to use would be "survivable space," the area necessary to allow a structure to survive on its own without the presence of fire personnel (K. Schasker 2004, personal communication).

Unfortunately creating survivable space is often referred to as "clearing" which leads one to think of taking everything down to bare ground. Worse, homeowners often obtain conflicting interpretations of "clearance" ordinances as they apply to their property. Consequently, there is a significant amount of confusion over what exactly vegetation fuel management is, how much is enough, and what is the best way to accomplish it.

The basic principle behind clearing is to increase the distance of a structure from potentially flammable materials to prevent ignition by radiation or convection. Since chaparral is definitely composed of flammable material, it makes sense to maintain a safe distance between it and a home. Determining how much distance is crucial because too much will create problems that can be extremely difficult to correct, specifically the replacement of drought tolerant native vegetation by nonnative, weedy annuals. In addition to environmental concerns such as loss of valuable watershed, increased erosion, and habitat loss, weedy annuals provide flashy fuels that ignite more readily than native shrubbery.

Jack Cohen (2000) at the Fire Sciences Lab in Missoula, Montana, performed an interesting investigation to determine the distance a house needs to be from a fire to prevent ignition. Three wooden walls were built and set up in a clearing 10, 20, and 30 meters downwind of a 40 foot tall pine forest. The forest was then set on fire and the results were collected. When the flames got close to, but did not touch the wall 10 meters away, the wood was only scorched. But when the flames made contact, the wall began to burn. When flames extended past 10 meters, the wall 20 meters away was scorched, but did not ignite. The wall 30 meters away was neither scorched nor ignited during the entire test. Based on this data and case studies concerning structural loss in numerous wildfires, it has been concluded that when a house with a nonflammable roof is between 10-30 meters away from wildfire fueled by trees, it has more than 90% chance of *not* igniting. Since 10 meters is approximately 30 feet, this has supported the primary 30 foot clearance zone around a house. The extended 100 foot clearance zone supports the 30 meter experimental distance. In related tests, single-pane windows were shown to fail at 20 meters, but double-pane windows survived.

Obviously, a raging forest fire consuming 40 foot trees is radically different from a California brush fire. In addition, the typical California stucco home has a higher heat resistance than bare wood. But the burning wooden wall model provides a standard of measurement to help set approximate clearance distances in order to prevent ignition by radiation and convection under normal weather conditions.

To develop a more accurate estimate of ignition potential for chaparral, it is important to remember not all stands are alike. An assumption often made about chaparral is that as a stand ages, so does the amount of fuel; especially the dead kind. Although this appears intuitively correct, it is based on an overly simplistic model that does not take into account variation within the environment. For example, a hillside of ceanothus chaparral has the capacity of accumulating more potential biomass (all organic matter) in less than 20 years than an expanse of chamise chaparral does in 60 years (Regelbrugge 2000). In addition, chaparral on north facing slopes may have more biomass accumulation in 10 years than drier, south-facing slopes do at 80 years (Black 1987).

The ratio of dead to living material in a chaparral stand is equally complex, with amounts accumulated being determined by multiple environmental factors including prior fire history, direction of slope, and severity of drought periods. Extensive studies by numerous investigators have found similar 30% dead to living ratios across a range of 20 to 60 year old stands without any significant relationship to age (Paysen and Cohen 1990, Regelbruggee 2000). So automatically assuming an older stand of chaparral is always filled with dead fuel ready to burn is not supported by actual field research.

There is no doubt all concentrated sources of fuel need to be eliminated from the 30 foot zone around a structure. The question that remains, however, concerns the next 70 feet. If every chaparral or coastal sage scrub stand has potentially different levels of fuel accumulation, and the negative consequences of blindly clearing everything can be significant, then it seems prudent to treat each vegetation management project individually. Unfortunately, when responding to the most recent firestorm disasters, some regulatory agencies and private citizens have overreacted and view all native vegetation as dangerous and in immediate need of removal. The outcome of such an action ultimately produces less than desired results.

A Contractor's Perspective
Kurt Schasker

Brush clearance is a lonely, mind numbing way to make a living. After you put on a dust mask, face shield, hat, and hearing protection, your world quickly diminishes to what is immediately in front of you: your line trimmer, your feet, the slope, and the heat. That's it. This leaves one with lots of time to think about any number of things. Including dust. Dust inside the house. Dust in the air. Dust in the air conditioning, the lungs, and the car. Oh, and the heat.

Sometimes I ask myself, "How did I get here?"

Clear Your Lot

Brush clearance is the activity of creating firebreaks very near structures in order to protect that "target" structure in the case of an encroaching wildland fire. The concept seemed simple enough, so I started a brush clearing service in the Los Angeles area in 1990 and named it Lotklear. Initially, the company had just one employee, myself. As these things occur, however, Lotklear grew. By 1999 there were 13 seasonal employees. What began as a way to make some extra money turned into a business grossing several hundred thousand dollars per year.

Along the way, however, something happened and perspectives changed. What first seemed like a valuable disaster preparedness service began to appear more and more like a costly and shortsighted response by government pressured into providing an immediate fix to a complicated problem.

Initially, of course, Lotklear cleared brush exactly as prescribed by the various fire authorities. We cut and removed all shrubs, brush, and weeds, while leaving "specimen" shrubs every 20-30 feet. We cleared like this for 100 feet from every structure, and 10 feet from all roadways. Subsequent to the disastrous 1993 fire season, which included the Altadena and Laguna Hills fires, this distance was increased to 200 feet.

In 1999 a Lotklear crewmember started a fire while clearing brush. The fire consumed about a half acre of weeds before being extinguished by firefighters. There was no wind or structural damage. We were very lucky. I remember thinking how impressed I was with the actions of the L.A. County Fire Department in managing it all. Within minutes, several engines and a helicopter were on scene to help fight the fire.

The fire burned right over previously cleared weeds approximately 3 inches high and producing 6 foot flame lengths as it moved up slope. Interestingly, none of the specimen shrubs in the burned clearance area ignited. These included pruned chaparral species such as scrub oak, laurel sumac, and coffeeberry.

Virtually every ignition in L.A. County is caused by human actions. We do not know, however, how many are caused by brush clearance activity. When we started that fire, on-scene firefighters related to me several similar instances where other brush clearance providers had ignited wildland fires. More recently, in mid-August, 2004, a lawnmower ignited a fire near Lake Shasta, California where 70 structures were lost. Additionally, although the cause remains in question, a fast-moving grass fire destroyed a home and burned about 250 acres in Martinez, California in June 2004.

In the wildland-urban interface, weeds can act as both an ignition source and a latent fire hazard. Weeds can not only bring wildland fire directly to structures, they can also bring ignition to wildland fuel. This is important to consider because when shrubs are removed or severely pruned open ground is created. This is called "opening the canopy." Healthy chaparral forest has an intact, or closed canopy. This closed canopy prevents nonnative weedy annuals from obtaining a toehold. Once that canopy is opened up, weeds will invade. Any brush modification that requires the removal of native shrubs without some sort of re-vegetation plan is an excellent format for weed growth. It seems important, therefore, to try and find a way to modify brush in such a manner that does not open the canopy yet also protects the target structure from encroaching fire (photo 22).

How do we create this "closed canopy firebreak?" First of all we need to select a plant palette. There exists numerous "fire-safe plant" lists, but unfortunately no consensus exists as to the definition of "fire-safe" and little if any research exists on a species-specific basis. Current "fire-safe plant" lists typically note that volatile or aromatic plants are more fire prone. Yet this conclusion has not been scientifically substantiated. Finally, nothing exists in the literature accurately differentiating fire risk between native vs. nonnative plants and irrigated vs. non-irrigated landscapes regarding "fire-safe plants." No plant is fireproof. All will burn in an intense fire.

Keeping in mind that live fuel may not be a fire hazard, and in fact can act as a fire retardant, it only remains to identify those plants easiest to maintain free of dead material. Once we identify these plant species, we may actually have the beginnings of a working list. Let's consider some criteria for a fire-safe plant list. The plant *should*

- Have easily distinguished dead vs. living material
- Require only minimal bending over or ladder work to maintain
- Have an open, accessible growth habit to allow easy pruning without damaging the plant
- Have a slow to moderate growth pattern to minimize the frequency of maintenance
- Have a robust root system to help prevent erosion
- Be long lived

The plant *should not*

- Have thorns
- Retain dead leaves within its canopy
- Have small leaves that stay on the plant once desiccated or dead (sages, buckwheat, chamise)
- Accumulate dead parts difficult to isolate (many ice plants, rabbit bush)
- Produce large amounts of hanging or dropping leaf litter (fan palms, pines, Eucalyptus)

Imagine a buffer zone around communities and isolated structures populated by native shrubs, properly irrigated to prevent desiccation and annually pruned to remove fuel build up. The shrubs would act as the first line of defense when fire approaches. Weedy annuals would have difficulty establishing themselves, thus eliminating the need for frequent maintenance with equipment that may cause ignitions or discs that disturb the soil. In addition, such a fuelbreak would still provide wildlife habitat, erosion control, and aesthetic benefits.

Experiments have shown that clearance beyond 100 feet is not particularly meaningful in terms of reducing structural ignition (Cohen 1999). However, vegetation management inside of 100 feet is incredibly important. This is where our current inspection process fails. Inspectors today focus on native brush, while typically ignoring cultivated landscape plants next to structures. Landscape plants, native or not, are allowed to build up considerable dead fuel loads, increasing the chance of ignition and eventual structural loss. This is the important space. 200 foot brush clearance as required by Los Angeles County code diverts attention away from the truly important 100 foot zone around the target structure. Meticulous, consistent, and careful vegetation management near the home can be the most important factor in the structure survival equation.

Inspections

Inspectors are overworked and have a dangerous, thankless, frequently confrontational job. They cannot reward compliance, only penalize non-compliance. Despite added authority provided by the 1992 Bates bill (AB 337) that requires identification of "Very High Fire Hazard Severity Zones," many communities within these zones have row upon row of houses with dangerous landscape plants growing right underneath the eaves. A significant number of houses in La Canada, Monrovia, Sylmar, and Granada Hills have at least one clear violation of the code. It only takes one place where weeds are too close, a cubby for embers to lodge, or a wooden fence under the eaves for a house to ignite during a wildfire. The risk is often not appreciated by those who are required to correct the problem.

In the summer of 1998 I was acting as an enforcement agent for the county of Los Angeles, designated to clear private property. Due to the remoteness of one particular job and the long drive to get there I decided to do it by myself. The county would pay for the cost of the work, and an offset fee would appear on the property owner's tax bill, including a considerable mark-up for the government agency. Rarely would I meet the property owners while clearing due to the fact that most of the property I worked was vacant, unimproved land. On this nice summer day, however, the owner was on site.

In times like this, I usually pretended to not know what was going on, and simply leave. But the property owner seemed cordial, and we chatted. I told him what was really going on so he could take charge of the rest of the clearing himself. The next thing I know he is sticking a knife in one of my tires and pointing a gun at me. Fortunately I managed to extricate myself from the situation. An informal survey of my fellow contractors showed this kind of incident was not unique.

Most of the property owners subject to involuntary clearance orders were unaware of the situation for a variety of reasons. This can be an expensive mistake, costing perhaps thousands to tens of thousands in "up" charges that only covers the regulating authority intervention, not the contracting fee. Not only are service providers like Lotklear at risk of injury and violence, property owners are frequently caught in the middle of a problem they know nothing about. The wildland-urban interface structure loss equation is, at its root, a problem of dollars and common sense. The most logical way to handle the inspection process is through the private sector.

Homeowner insurance companies have a vested interest in requiring adequate brush clearance in homes identified as being in hazardous locations. In fact, Lotklear responded several times to property owners requests to clear brush at the behest of the insurance company. For example, California FAIR plan homeowners are often required to clear their property to be eligible for coverage. California FAIR (Fair Access to Insurance Requirements) was created by the state legislature in 1968, "after the brush fires and riots of the 1960s made it difficult for some people to purchase fire insurance due to hazards beyond their control" (www.insurance.ca.gov). FAIR is an assigned risk program that provides coverage of last resort for homeowners. The wisdom of state law supporting construction in high fire risk locations is another matter.

Through insurance premiums, the property owner has a clear economic incentive to "fire safe" his or her property. Insurance companies have both economic leverage and motivation to require enforcement. If Bates bill communities were to be subject to insurance company inspection, then governmental regulating authorities would return to their primary task of regulation rather than enforcement.

Confusion

The staff of Lotklear worked closely with inspectors from several regulating authorities. In the city of Los Angeles, there are at least three different bureaus that inspect for brush clearance: Lot Cleaning, Forestry, and Fire Department. On the county side: Weed Abatement, Forestry, and Fire Department have inspection authority.

In addition, each of the 20 odd cities in brush areas also have inspection processes. Conflicts abound.

In 1995, Los Angeles County passed two fire safety code changes specifically relating to clearance requirements. One stated that if a thirty-foot firebreak around a structure is not sufficient fire officials "may notify all owners of property affected that they must clear all flammable vegetation and other combustible growth or reduce the amount of fuel content for a distance greater than thirty feet, but not to exceed two hundred feet" (Ord. 95-0063 § 70). The other stated that every fuel modification plan "shall also be reviewed and approved by the forestry division of the fire department for reasonable fire safety" (Ord. 2002-0080 § 55, 2002: Ord. 95-0063 § 70). In response to these code changes, the Forestry Division passed a set of directions for 200 foot clearance in the 1998 Fuel Modification Plan (www.lacofd.org/Forestry_folder/pdf/fmpg.pdf).

The Forestry Fuel Modification Plan specifically prohibits the practice of "clear-cutting" all vegetation in the 200 foot clearance zone. Instead, it outlines clear rules on how to preserve as much of the canopy as possible. Unfortunately, it has been my experience that Los Angeles County does not enforce, follow, or even pay attention to this component of the Fuel Modification Plan. Depending on the inspector, the county generally requires all clearance out to 200 feet to be of the clear cut variety, meaning cut and remove everything except for specimens 20 feet apart. This policy is partially articulated on the Los Angeles County Fire Department website whereby trees and shrubs should be spaced "a minimum of 15 feet or three times their diameter from other shrubs. Trees should be spaced to allow a minimum of 30 feet between canopies at maturity (www.lacofd.org/Forestry_folder/brushclearance.htm). This type of clearing removes about 90-95% of the shrub canopy. However, on the same site, another clearance regime is presented where all the brush is simply pruned and left alive and standing (www.lacofd.org/Forestry_folder/pdf/fmpg.pdf). These are two completely different approaches and create a tremendous amount of confusion in the field.

No More

In the summer of 1999 I cleared a parcel in the Santa Monica Mountains precisely according to Los Angeles County's Fuel Modification, not the brush "clearance" regime; a clearing method fairly gentle on the land. This particular project consisted of clearing brush only in the 100-200 foot zone with respect to a nearby target structure. After clearing the parcel according to the fuel modification specifications, I remember meeting the inspector on site, where he carefully explained to me, "This is not how we clear." He required that I clear-cut the parcel instead, leaving shrubs spaced 20-30 feet apart. I remember this as a seminal moment in my experience in clearing brush. Despite the County's own document distinctly discouraging a clear-cut approach to firebreak installation, I was instructed to do just that. The property owner only wanted this project to pass inspection; he was not interested in any discrepancies between my interpretation of the code and the inspector's interpretation. I went back and cut down two acres of scrub oak and ceanothus.

Today, that parcel is a weed lot with essentially no native brush on it at all. Roughly 30 yards of soil have since eroded along one side of nearby Latigo Canyon Road as a direct result of the actions required by the county inspector. It was the last brush clearance job I ever did.

Preparing for a Wildfire
Klaus H. Radtke

After having lived in highly fireprone watershed areas for almost 30 years, I realize it takes knowledge as well as timely preparation to prevent becoming a home loss statistic, a victim, and a burden to society. The location of my home – the last house in the subdivision – abutted a sea of mature 12 foot tall chaparral at the top of long, steep, easterly facing slopes. The lack of proper brush clearance by adjacent absentee developers and poor enforcement of even minimal clearance requirements in the 1970s almost doomed our home in the 1978 Mandeville Canyon fire.

Upon purchasing the property a year earlier I immediately embarked on extensive watershed rehabilitation to control the velocity and direct the flow of rainwater. Previous developers had precariously undercut steep hillsides for haul roads and slopes were left partially devoid of soil-anchoring vegetation. My work included extensive pipe and board emergency erosion control measures that created a mini-dam system that would intercept and slow down the overland flow of water allowing it to infiltrate into the ground. This provided additional moisture for the extensive plantings within these mini-dams. Being aware of the extensive vegetative fuel loads and the fire history of the area I also carried out an extensive fuel modification program on my own and surrounding vacant properties up until the all-too-predictable wildland fire conflagration came a year later (Radtke 1981).

The Myths of Fire Protection

My wife and I knew that if a fire should start on a weekday, which it ultimately did, I would be too far away to help. Therefore, we realized she would have to assume the responsibility of taking care of what needed to be done. We both accepted that for a house abutting steep slopes, even in a generally fire-safe area such as ours, firemen would not be available to protect our home during a large-scale fire. She would have to become a knowledgeable firefighter. We knew it would be a challenging experience. Water would probably be unavailable for firefighting despite the 1.2 million gallon water tank across the street as it would be drained by fearful, downhill neighbors. In addition, electricity would likely be cut off and police would force residents to evacuate, preventing them from returning and protecting their homes. Hopefully, my wife would be able to outsmart the traffic and roadblocks to get to our home in time from her job 15 miles away. When the moment arrived, she performed as calmly as could be expected and was instrumental in saving the home.

Wherever I turn today, there is still great denial, even resistance to implement fire safety in timely and cost-effective ways. After regularly recurring and predictable "fire disasters," homeowners and agencies' fire investigation teams are generally rediscovering, or again reluctantly acknowledging, that home fire prevention efforts are generally minimal and nature does not differentiate between wildland, landscape, or structural fuels. Fire evaluation reports generally fall back on the myth of fire-resistant plants, the need for more firefighting forces, or even greater clearance distances. This is done in an apparent attempt to deflect the wrath of the public, reduce liability, and continue development in high fire danger areas that are indefensible from wildland fire. And, if defensible, carried out with a high cost to society. Despite all the losses, politics usually dictate how we attempt to carry out community fire protection while largely ignoring long-term, cohesive fire and watershed protection planning efforts.

It is generally not acknowledged that a critical factor in protecting a relatively fire-safe home in a wildland fire is that someone should attend it as the fire moves through the area. This leads to the logical conclusion that the fire safety equation must include knowledgeable homeowners as volunteer fire personnel. They are often a key component in reducing wildland fire losses as there will never be enough fire personnel to protect every single home. It was gratifying to see that after the many public safety seminars held in the 1980s by our National Foundation for Environmental Safety, none of the active participants lost their homes in the fires that followed. After more than 30 years attempting to make neighborhoods in flammable watershed areas more fire-safe, I wonder if we have learned our lessons. Today, rather than including property owners in the equation of effective fire protection, every attempt is seemingly being made to take them out during the most critical time period.

Dr. Jerry Partain, Director of the California Department of Forestry and Fire during the 1980's, succinctly addressed the fire problem from an agency's viewpoint in his timely keynote address at the conference Living in the Chaparral of Southern California sponsored in 1985 by the National Foundation for Environmental Safety and the National Park Service. In an abstract of his speech titled "A Cooperative Approach to Public Safety" he addressed the importance of citizen commitment to fire safety:

> *Living in the chaparral of southern California is somewhat like watching the steam from Mt. Saint Helens out of your living room window, wondering when it will blow! The combination of highly resinous plants, extreme weather conditions, rugged terrain, and urban expansion work together to create some of the most explosive fire conditions in the state of California.*
>
> *Although the danger can never be removed, we can greatly improve the odds to our favor with planning. To beat the odds, there are three basic areas you must seriously plan: personal circumstances (your home), fuel modification, and interagency cooperation.*
>
> *The many agencies in southern California are committed to this cooperation, but to make the odds livable, so must you be!*

As program organizer, I summarized the conference by explaining that living and working more safely in disaster-prone environs such as the chaparral regions of California starts at the planning process. California statutes mandate that each county or city adopt a comprehensive long-term general plan for physical development. The plan must identify and propose measures to reduce loss of life, injuries, damage to property, economic dislocation, and social disruptions.

When subjects such as landslides, fires, floods, soil erosion, earthquakes, and other hazards are properly addressed as part of an integrated review process and land management plan, possible future disasters can be identified, predicted, mitigated, even prevented.

Many disasters have illustrated that the effective planning process was circumvented or that the safety elements were not properly evaluated and their interactions little understood.

A cooperative approach to public safety recognizes the importance of close cooperation among the professionals, the agencies, and the public both at the planning process, the long-term management phase, and during emergencies. Residents in disaster-prone areas have a right to expect such an approach to public safety and their participation is important to make sure that the process is properly carried out. Education and preparation are the tools that allow people to cope more readily with sudden disasters.

The hope was, 20 years later, we could expect that if everyone had done their part, wildland fires would be seen as naturally occurring events, having only minimal impacts on our communities. Because we would be properly prepared, wildfires would no longer turn into the disasters they had been in the past. Unfortunately, catastrophic firestorms have continued as development has expanded further into wildland areas and lessons from the past have been largely ignored. As always, education and preparation remains the key.

The Role of Homeowners

The public should be properly educated and made more responsible for effective fire prevention around their homes and not disenfranchised from protecting defensible homes during wildland fire emergencies. Experience has shown that as a fire moves through an area, homes that are attended, whether by knowledgeable residents/owners or professional firefighters, have a much higher probability of survival than non-attended homes (photo 29).

For example, during the 1993 Topanga-Malibu fire, a colleague and I helped protect numerous homes during the night without the availability of water by using shovels. As we saved several homes by extinguishing embers from ones burning nearby, we watched helplessly throughout the night as other homes slowly ignited and burned even after the fire front had long passed. After quick hit-and-run attacks to initially protect some homes, the majority of firefighting personnel left to deal with the moving fire front.

A post-fire survey indicated that it was largely homeowners who had protected most at-risk homes that survived in such hot spots as the Rambla Pacifico area. Homes that ignited and burned throughout the night, long after the fire front had passed, were largely unprotected. Again, none of the homes burned in areas where National Foundation for Environmental Safety volunteers had helped homeowners understand that effective watershed management and comprehensive fire protection is not just limited to "brush clearance" (Radtke 1985).

Mandatory evacuation in areas that could provide safe "shelter in place" locations for able, fire-literate homeowners squanders a valuable resource. In addition, fire safety related decisions are often made without public input, further disenfranchising the citizens they are designed to protect. For example, after the 1993 fire conflagrations in southern California, Los Angeles County increased clearance requirements around structures in unincorporated watershed areas from 100 to 200 feet without public hearings, disclosing the costs and adequately examining the efficacy of the change or its potential environmental impacts. These new requirements dramatically impacted parks and the budgets of park agencies. Budgets had to be revised and funds reallocated to pay for extensive "brush clearance" and the year-round maintenance subsequently required on steep slopes surrounding the parks. There was also no funding for legal costs for such efforts and contingencies for potential slope failures and their repairs.

There continues to be a tendency to blame home losses on excessive native plant fuel loads and propose additional clearance distances around structures in excess of 200 feet. Common sense dictates that flammable structural fuels should not be intermingled with flammable landscape or native vegetation fuels. Clearance beyond 200 feet is unnecessary if these basic principles are adhered to and flammable homes are not built in highly flammable watershed areas.

Society will never have the budget, the fire services, the time, or the manpower to outrun an advancing fire front and place fire personnel at homes before or immediately after the fire front has passed through. In areas where trained homeowners are not permitted to protect their own homes from wildfire because it is too dangerous, we must ask ourselves what were the underlying fire politics that allowed such subdivisions to be built in the first place?

Owning a Fire-safe Home

The fire safety of a home depends on the continuity and loading of the fuels around it, the location of the home with respect to topography, the design and structural materials of the house, and access and exit points for firefighters. Additionally, it depends on the safety of, and proximity to, neighboring homes as blowing embers can ignite homes blocks away (Radtke 1982, 1983).

Here's how to make a fire-safe home.

1. **Legal Brush Clearance Requirements:** California Resources Code 4219 requires clearance of flammable vegetation (that can be instrumental in spreading a fire) for a minimum distance of 30 to 100 feet around any structure located in a fire hazardous area. The clearance distance is subject to local enforcement, and in extremely hazardous areas, local fire authorities may require clearance beyond 100 feet. However, the intent of the code is readily defeated if basic fire safety principles are not carried into home-site selection, home design, and building materials.

2. **Fire Topography:** The relationship between topography and fire behavior is a factor over which the homeowner has little control. He should, however, be aware of the relationship as it relates specifically to his property.

Homes located in "natural chimneys," such as narrow canyons and saddles, are especially fire-prone because winds are funneled into these canyons and eddies are created (fig. 4-1). Studies have shown that homes located where a canyon meets a ridge are more likely to burn than other ridge-top homes. In very steep and narrow canyons, radiating heat may also be a major factor in fire spread and home losses. Homes without adequate setbacks on narrow ridges are often lost because flames and convection heat impact the home directly (fig. 4-2). Homes located along slopes, especially stilt and cantilevered homes, are particularly vulnerable in this respect.

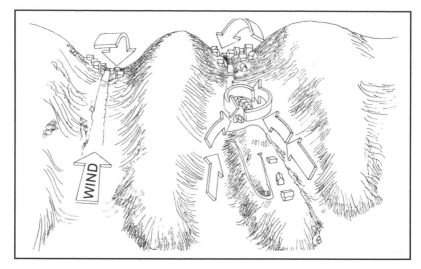

Fig. 4-1 Natural Chimneys. *Winds tend to channel through natural chimneys, making narrow canyons and saddles particularly fine-prone.*

Fig. 4-2 Ridgelines. *On narrow ridges, homes without adequate setbacks are particularly vulnerable to fire.*

3. Building Design & Building Materials: Building density, design, and building materials are important safety considerations because a burning home can ignite adjacent homes.

The roof is the most vulnerable part of a home because it is exposed to airborne embers. The wood shingle roof has been the single most important element in home losses during wildland fires. It is also a major source of airborne firebrands (embers) capable of igniting nearby structures. Studies of structural losses during wild-fires in southern California have shown that with 100 feet of brush clearance, a home with a wooden roof has an approximately 21 times greater chance of burning than a home with a non-wood roof. While fire insurance rates are higher for wood than for non-wood roofs, they do not reflect the greater risk factor and could therefore be viewed as a public subsidy.

Exterior materials used on homes near wildlands should have a fire-resistance rating of 1 to 2 hours, meaning that they should consist of materials such as stucco, metal siding, brick, concrete block, and rock. This is especially critical for parts of a home exposed to fire convection winds or positioned at the top of a slope. Figures 4-3 and 4-4 graphically summarize the principles of topography, vegetation, and architectural design that can improve the fire safety of a planned or an existing home. Many positive features of home design are shown in figure 4-3. Note that reduced overhangs or boxed eaves protect the house from ignition and heat or flame entrapment. Under-eave vents should be located near the roofline rather than near the wall. Exterior attic and under-floor vents should not face possible fire corridors and should be covered with wire screen (not to exceed 1/4 inch mesh). Picture windows and sliding glass doors should be made only of thick, tempered safety glass with other windows made of double-pane glass. Where facing fire winds or possible convection heat sources, windows should be protected with nonflammable shutters. This is especially important if there is only limited slope setback. Stone walls can act as very effective heat shields and deflect the flames. Swimming pools and non-wood decks and patios can be used to create a setback safety zone.

Properly placed rooftop sprinklers or misters under the eaves are extremely helpful in preventing ignition by all sources. Note however, that sprinklers placed on a wooden roof generally provide only limited fire safety if you have your own water supply source pumped by an independent power source. But don't depend on these factors; change the roof!

4. Your Pool as a Water Source: Pools can provide a convenient, as well as home-saving, water source both before and during a fire. Fire engines should be able to get within 10 feet horizontally of the pool so water can be pumped out for use. If this is not possible, the pool should be equipped with a bottom drain and pipe system that terminates with a 2-1/2 inch valved standpipe equipped with a fire hydrant with national standard thread. A floating pool pump or portable gasoline pump with a suction hose that can reach the bottom of the pool can assure a usable water source for homeowners even when water pressure and electricity fail. You will also need a fire hose and nozzle.

Fabric fire hoses are fine for use with pool pumps that are designed for fire-fighting, but should not be used on home faucets because they readily kink as water pressure drops. All outdoor faucets should be equipped with strong 5/8 inch rubber hoses that will not burst when the nozzle is closed. A ladder should be available to reach the roof.

Double pane and tempered safety glass used as appropriate.

On extremely steep slopes in high fire danger areas, fire safety can be increased by the removal of the most flammable plant materials to twice (200 feet) the legal minimum. However, retaining thinned, deep-rooted native plants is crucial to maintaining slope stability as well as helping control the invasion of weedy annuals. Maintenance of thinned shrubbery is extremely important because dead, woody vegetation quickly accumulates again in non-watered zones.

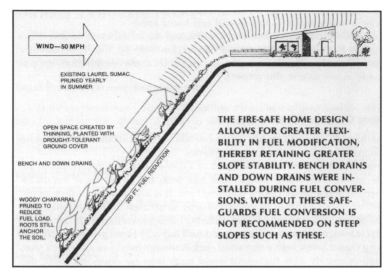

Fig. 4-3 Reducing Fire Risk When Designing a New Home.

New home features to reduce fire risk include:

- Class A fire-resistant roof such as tile with seams and joints between tiles sealed.
- No exposed wood surfaces but stucco or other nonflammable siding of a least 1 hour fire-resistant rating.
- Reduced overhang preferably with closed eaves.
- Roof slanted to accommodate convection heat.
- Safety zone and slope setback of approximately 30 feet for a single story home and vegetation properly thinned within the next 70 feet.
- Pool or other hardscapes used to create buffer zone between house and slope or potential flame sources.
- Shrubs and trees not directly adjacent to home nor overhanging the roof.
- Decks constructed of materials of at least 1 hour fire-resistant rating.
- Adequate filtering or screening on vents to prevent entrance of embers.

Landscaping for Fire and Watershed Safety

The key to landscaping in fire-prone watershed areas is to selectively replace highly flammable plants with lower-growing, less flammable plants of equal root depth and root strength. In reality, optimum rooting depth and fuel volume generally work at odds with one another. That is, low-growing plants usually have relatively shallow root systems and tall plants have relatively deep and broad lateral root systems. Landscaping requires a compromise between minimizing fuel volume and maximizing root depth.

The key to effective low maintenance landscaping is to use the right plant in the right place. Native plants should generally only be planted on the slope aspects they

Fire, Chaparral, and Survival in Southern California

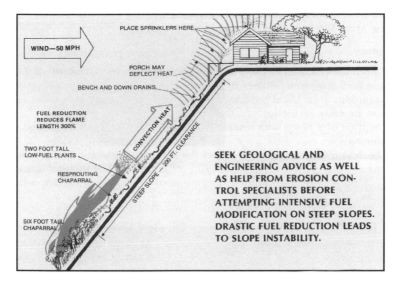

Fig. 4-4 Retrofitting an Existing Structure to Reduce Fire Risks.

NEGATIVE FEATURES OF EXISTING HOUSE	POSITIVE FEATURES OR POSSIBLE RETROFITS
Wood shingle roof	Fire resistant roof
Wood siding	Non-flammable siding
Large overhang (open eaves)	Reduced overhang (closed or boxed eaves)
High gable roof	Lower sloped roof (redesign expensive)
No safety zone (no slope setback)	Setback with non-wooden deck
Large picture window	Install non-flammable shutters
Tree crown overhanging roof	Trees pruned or removed
Steep slope	Increased fuel modification zone (maintained)

occupy naturally or areas that are not subject to over-watering. Water-demanding ornamental plants should generally be planted in more shaded locations, not on harsher southern exposures with thin soils.

There are two important criteria in selecting plants for a fire-safe landscape design.

1. Rooting Depth and Fuel Volume: As a rule, non-woody ground covers have an effective root depth of less than 3 feet and can be labeled "shallow rooted" for use in steep terrain. Grasses also belong in this category. Shallow-rooted plants should not be used as permanent cover on steep slopes unless they are interplanted at approximately 10 foot centers with taller shrubs and approximately 20 foot centers with smaller trees or tree-like shrubs. Such interplanting is required to stabilize fill slopes as well.

Woody ground cover shrubs generally are moderately deep rooted, with roots ranging from 3 to 6 feet in depth, and can be effectively used on slopes in conjunction with taller shrubs and trees. Most plant species found in the coastal sage community fall into this root depth category. Plants with roots ranging from 6 to 15 feet or more in depth include many woody shrubs in the chaparral plant community as well as small, drought-tolerant landscape trees. Very few commercially available woody ground covers, with the exception perhaps of prostrate (twin peak) coyote brush and prostrate acacia, have an effective root depth greater than 6 feet. Plants with roots in excess of 15 feet include some native shrubs such as scrub oak, laurel sumac, and manzanita.

Laurel sumac and scrub oak are two of the most watershed effective, deep-rooted hillside anchoring plants within the chaparral plant community and their systematic removal often leads to soil slippage and slides on steeper slopes. Laurel sumac has been misrepresented as being highly dangerous because of its generally high oil content. However, it has the highest moisture content of any tall-growing woody chaparral plant tested, does not contain or readily accumulate fine, dead fuels when compared to sages and *Ceanothus* species, and can be easily maintained. It takes tremendous heat energy to drive the moisture out of laurel sumac leaves and dry them to the ignition point. This quality makes the plant quite "fire-resistant" when properly maintained.

2. Drought Tolerance and Sprouting Ability: Drought tolerance and sprouting ability are also important considerations when selecting plants. Water will be an increasingly sparse and expensive resource in the future. The plant's ability to survive on little water as well as to resprout after a fire can mean savings over the years on water bills, maintenance costs, replanting costs, and hillside repairs.

Many native plants resprout, and some native shrubs such as sugarbush *(Rhus ovata)*, scrub oak *(Quercus berberidifolia)*, *Ceanothus* species, and holly-leafed cherry *(Prunus ilicifolia)* can be nurtured into short-trunked trees. At spacings of about 25 feet, these species can be kept relatively fire retardant through occasional pruning. *Ceanothus* species will require slightly more maintenance.

Resprouting broad-leaved, evergreen trees such as oaks (*Quercus* species), Catalina cherry *(Prunus lyonii),* and Catalina ironwood *(Lyonothamnus floribundus asplenifolius)* can be effectively blended into the landscape setting. The hardy southern California black walnut *(Juglans californica)* offers an excellent deciduous option. For fire safety, trees must be pruned regularly and limited to the number necessary to provide shade and slope stability.

The use of herbicides and pre-emergent chemicals must be closely monitored in hillside landscaping. Overuse can kill landscape plants and sterilize soils. Fortunately, the deepest rooted chaparral shrubs are also the hardest to kill with herbicides. Since these shrubs serve the dual function of anchoring the soil to the bedrock and pumping water out of the ground, soil slippage is almost never observed where they are present. Mortality of such plants often results in slippage 5 to 10 years later after the roots have rotted away. The original cause of such delayed slippage is seldom recognized.

Maintenance for Fire and Watershed Safety

Landscape maintenance is necessary to keep man-made structures separated from surrounding vegetative fuels; to keep the amount of vegetative fuels at a safe level;

to create a safety zone for residents, firefighters, and fire equipment; and to assure that water flow from the property is channeled properly. Giving correct priorities to maintenance needs and carrying out maintenance and safety inspections on a regular basis is the key to minimizing the effects of "natural" disasters.

For fire and watershed maintenance, the area around the home should be divided into three perimeters of defense:

1. A 0 to 30 foot safety zone: year-round maintenance.
2. A 30 to 100 foot greenbelt area: seasonal maintenance.
3. A greenbelt extension past 100 feet: yearly inspections, periodic maintenance.

1. 0 to 30 foot safety zone (no flammable structural, vegetative components): The area within 30 feet of the home is most critical for fire and watershed safety. Maintenance of nonflammable landscaping such as lawns, border plantings, flower gardens, and structures such as pools, concrete decks, and recreation areas help reduce fire hazards close to the home. This area should not be located on slopes and all water from it should drain toward the street. Rain gutters, pipes, and drainage devices should be cleaned out on a regular basis. Additionally, all leaves should be removed from the roof and roof gutters before the fire season begins. Foundation shrubs and trees are a necessary part of the landscaping. However, these plants often grow into an "urban forest" fuel problem, so that landscape plants rather than surrounding native plants become the primary cause of fire loss. Year-round maintenance should consist of pruning and regular watering of individual plants. Together, these measures decrease plant volume, increase plant moisture content, and reduce or eliminate dead fuels. Unnecessary watering of drought-tolerant landscape plants, however, may cause root rot of native plants nearby.

Trees must receive the same regular maintenance as foundation shrubs, and potentially flammable trees in fire areas should not be planted within 30 feet of homes (think about the expanding crown at maturity). The shaded interior crowns of trees such as coast live oak, usually contain a high amount of dead twigs and branchlets and are exposed to higher wind speeds than exist at ground level. These conditions can produce large flames that are readily bent onto the roofs of nearby structures. Many eucalyptus and pine species are also notorious for their tendency to quickly accumulate fine dead fuels and spread fire.

2. 30 to 100-foot greenbelt area: Seasonal fire maintenance in the 30 to 100-foot greenbelt zone around the home should consist of removing dead woody plants, periodic pruning of trees and shrubs to eliminate fine dead fuel and fuel volume, and eradication of weedy species. Native plants can be thinned out to form an effective greenbelt zone that is easily maintained. To maintain healthy plants and strong root systems, pruning of most native plants should be done during the summer when they are not actively growing. Ground cover shrubs may also need to be thinned out periodically. In thinning and pruning, care must be taken not to expose the surface to a greater degree than can be safely covered by surrounding plants before the rainy season. If this is not possible, the area should be covered with jute netting. Well-pruned, healthy shrubs require several years to build up an excess of flammable live and dead fuel. Therefore, a complete maintenance job can last for several years.

Soil disturbance caused by bulldozing or other radical clearing and discing procedures will ultimately encourage the growth of nonnative grasses and other weedy annuals. These fast growing plants create flashy fuels during the dry season that can easily ignite and quickly spread fire into more concentrated fuels.

3.   **A greenbelt extension past 100 feet:** The intensity of fire maintenance beyond 100 feet from the home is dictated by topography and the structure itself. Minimum maintenance for a home designed with fire safety in mind should consist of reducing the amount and continuity of the vegetation as well as thinning out the most flammable species. Selective maintenance can be done in areas where topography is favorable and geology stable (gentle slopes, rock outcroppings, etc.) every 5 years or less without causing any accelerated soil erosion. Such "feathering out" of more flammable vegetation within portions of a watershed, in favor of plants with a greatly reduced dead-to-live fuel ratio, lowers the possibility and effect of major wildfires.

Learning the Lessons: Caught in a Wildfire

When the 1978 Mandeville fire approached our home, stacks of cut logs from the removal of pines and other miscellaneous flammable items were still closely stacked near the wood siding of the house. My wife, after returning home from work just ahead of the fire, immediately removed these and all other flammable fuels from around the house and threw them into the pool. She also placed gunnysacks for beating out sparks and flames into water-filled trash cans surrounding the house and made sure all the windows as well as the chimney damper were closed. She unlatched the garage door opener, backed the car into the garage, and loaded our pets into it just in case she had to evacuate.

Inside the house she quickly removed the most flammable items from around the windows. With every strong wind gust the downslope-facing windows would danger-ously buckle as the windows were not protected by fire shutters. Because the glass could blow out at any time, rather than staying in the house and checking the exterior after the firestorm had passed, my wife decided to evacuate as the firestorm roared across the canyon. My neighbor, who was safely situated on the other side of the 46 foot wide street and sidewalk, stated afterwards that the firestorm totally engulfed our house for a few seconds, and then suddenly died back. To his amazement, the house reappeared out of the dying flames and was not on fire.

Since we had not yet completed all the necessary fire safety improvements to our home, I was well aware it remained exposed to extreme fire danger. The chaparral on our slopes had not burned in approximately 40 years, our house had wood siding, and the Class B asphalt shingle roof was rated only for moderate heat exposure. I therefore had carried out and had almost completed a native plant fuelbreak around the house. This was accomplished through cutting off near ground level the most flammable vegetation such as buckwheat and black sage, and meticulously removing all dead fuels from larger chaparral plants such as greenbark ceanothus, toyon, sugarbush, and laurel sumac. The result was a still largely closed overstory canopy with almost no flammable fuels that could carry a wildland fire. After the firestorm had roared over the house, taller shrubs below the house remained largely intact with their leaves just heavily scorched. However, on adjacent slopes where I had yet to finish vegetation modification, the fire was so hot it burned everything to the ground.

Many factors contributed to our one-story home surviving the uphill firestorm and the wrap-around flames, but the most important included the fuel break I created and the building's slightly slanting roof facing downslope. The roof's low angle somewhat minimized its exposure to the convection heat sources originating from the downhill slope (fig. 4-3). After the fire I added a 6 foot high stone wall along our uphill northern property boundary approximately 20 feet from the house to act as a convection and radiation heat shield. When we finally remodeled, I replaced the wood siding on the house with stucco, replaced the Class B asphalt shingle roof with a Class A tile roof, changed the single pane windows to dual pane, and provided a further slope setback for a second story addition.

After the fire, a local newspaper quoted one of the fire victims who lost his home as saying, "There was no warning. The flames came up over that ridge and raced down toward us. There were sparks flying everywhere. That's when we left."

The warning signs are with us summer and winter when we live in highly flammable watersheds.

The next time a fires races across the canyon towards our slopes, it will stop near the bottom of the hill because it will have run out of flammable fuels; fuels that could have carried the flames to our house.

A Wake Up Call for Homeowners
Candysse Miller

The 2003 southern California wildfires resulted in nearly 20,000 insurance claims that are expected to cost upwards of $2.03 billion, making it one of the costliest natural disasters in U.S. history. As a spokesperson for the insurance industry, I sometimes feel that I can rattle off statistics and risk avoidance advice in my sleep. These fires, however, were eyeopening.

To a degree, my job is to fight complacency, to remind Californians that if we're going to live with brush fires, earthquakes, landslides, windstorms, and the occasional El Nino, then we must prepare our homes, our families and even our finances to withstand them. The lessons served me well as the Grand Prix fire – one of several major brushfires that simultaneously charred southern California – rushed south from Devore toward the suburban foothill community of Rancho Cucamonga.

The fire had already been burning for days – close enough to see the orange glow of the flames from my yard, but far enough way, it would seem, to feel safe. But Santa Ana winds can be both strong and fickle, and proved dangerously unpredictable that day. Sitting in my Los Angeles office that Friday morning – 50 miles from home – I struggled to catch my breath and grab my car keys as local news reported that the freeway exit closest to my home had been shut down as flames approached, and briefly jumped, the 210 Freeway.

By the time I got home, ash and embers rained down on our street. The high school down the street had been converted into a busy Red Cross evacuation center, and was filled with families, pets, and television crews.

There is a certain feeling of hopelessness when 50 foot high flames are clearly visible from your front yard, but the echo of "Be Prepared" served me well. I pulled a copy of my homeowners insurance policy from its file (I also keep a copy in another location away from my home, just in case) and printed a copy of my home inventory list. But, like many homeowners who inventory their possessions, I had not updated the list recently enough to include some of the gadgets and gizmos I had accumulated in the year or two since I wrote it.

The solution was on a Smart Media card. I pulled out my digital camera and went room-to-room taking photographs: the computer equipment, the appliances, the messy closet full of clothes, the garage, the garden, the furniture, the jewelry, even the vacuum cleaner. The list and photos were quickly placed on CD and, along with the insurance policy, placed on the front seat of my car, where they remained as a talisman against fire for the next several weeks.

The Grand Prix fire charred our local foothill communities for several days and claimed homes in Devore, Lytle Creek, Rancho Cucamonga, Upland, and Claremont before merging with another fire that swept into the San Bernardino Mountains toward Lake Arrowhead. It spared our neighborhood, but when the smoke lifted we found that it had burned up tp 1/2 mile from my home.

Fire danger should come as no surprise to Californians. From north to south, no region of our vast and ecologically diverse state is safe from the perils of wildfire. Even California's famous suburban sprawl has been subject to catastrophic brushfire. The Laguna Beach fire of 1993 claimed 441 homes. Days later, 323 homes burned in the Topanga-Malibu fire. Another 641 homes were destroyed in the 1990 Santa Barbara fire. And then there's Oakland Hills, where a firestorm claimed 2,900 homes and 26 lives in 1991. To this day, it remains the costliest brushfire in U.S. history. None of these areas can be confused for remote mountain hamlets. Though they are developed into hillsides and seaside vistas, they are often densely developed.

Knowing that California's always dangerous fall fire season would only be heightened by years of drought and, in mountain communities, by massive tree die-off, the Insurance Information Network of California worked for months with the California Department of Forestry to track and analyze firefighters' take on brushfire risk across California. We wanted to know exactly how many homes firefighters considered at high risk for wildfire, and what it could cost our state. In a state with such a dramatic history of catastrophic brushfire, the results should not have surprised us. But they did.

We found that firefighters believe more than half of California's 12.5 million homes to be at high or extreme risk of brushfire danger, and that it poses a financial risk conservatively estimated at more than $106 billion. When you live on a suburban cul-de-sac where you can sit in your front yard and watch a wall of flame, those results shouldn't be surprising. But they should nonetheless be a wake up call.

If you're a Californian, the chances are 50/50 that firefighters think you may lose your home to a wildfire. So get prepared. Make a home inventory and store it in cyber space or a bank box. Prepare a family evacuation plan. Review your insurance policy with your agent annually and make sure it keeps pace with the gadgets, the gizmos and the home improvement projects.

And, if your community hasn't done so yet, start a local FireSafe Council where homeowners, firefighters, and anyone else with an interest in keeping your neighborhood safe from fire can work together to be prepared.

5

After the Fire

Shortly after the 2003 fires cooled in southern California, the Burned Area Emergency Response (BAER) team arrived. This is an assemblage of scientists, foresters, and representatives from various government agencies such as the USFS, Bureau of Indian Affairs, and the Fish and Wildlife Service, who are charged with examining burns and recommending mitigation they feel is necessary to protect communities and resources from post-fire effects and to help the land heal. They come after every fire. The majority of the specialists fly in from other parts of the country and may or may not have knowledge of the local environment. They typically list a series of treatments such as mulching, seeding, sediment deflectors, channel clearing, and wattles (rolls of hay held together with plastic netting) to control erosion. Significant resources and huge numbers of personnel are employed to carry out the recommendations. Rolls of wattle are strung across gullies and hillsides, mulch is dropped from helicopters, and chain saws ring out as burned trees are removed. In addition, county agencies and the California Department of Transportation (CalTrans) perform similar assessments and apply the same types of treatments.

By mid-January 2004, huge fleets of hydroseeding trucks arrived across southern California, filled with a gooey combination of wood fiber mulch that looks like papier-mâché, a sticky substance known as tackifier to make the fibers hold together, seed, and green dye. They began spraying roadcuts, hillsides around communities, and burned chaparral near homes until the landscape was artificially bright green again.

Does it do any good? Post fire mitigation is a huge business. It also provides immediate, visible evidence that the government is doing something to help victims of the fire. Although companies involved will provide their own research supporting the need for their services, independent investigations measuring the actual effectiveness of most of the treatments used are seriously lacking. Information regarding the effect of seeding burned areas, however, indicates the practice can cause severe environmental damage.

Forty-three thousand pounds of nonnative rye grass seed *(Lolium multiflorum)* were donated and distributed throughout San Diego County after the Cedar fire. Studies of seeded vs. non-seeded plots in southern California have shown "no evidence that the seeding of ryegrass significantly reduced the amount of surface erosion in the post-fire environment" (Conrad 1993). In addition, "*Lolium* success was at the expense of native cover and this negative effect was greatest on the 'fire annuals'" (Keeley, et al. 1981). Others have made similar conclusions as well (Taskey et al. 1988, Nadkarni and Odion 1985). Griffin (1982) found the use of ryegrass was associated with high mortality of ceanothus shrub seedlings. Ryegrass seeding was also responsible for spreading the 1980 fire on Otay Mountain in San Diego County that lead to the elimination of chaparral on the site (Zedler et al. 1983).

Data relating to mulching with or with out a native seed mix is not complete enough to make any definite conclusions at this point. However, it appears likely any addition of seed or other materials on post-burn sites previously covered with undisturbed chaparral will be neutral at best. The seed mixed used by contractors after the Cedar fire appears to have a full assortment of native species, but closer examination of the actual percentage reveals a different story. Most of the mix remains grass seed. The largest portion (30%) consists of a native wild ryegrass *(Elymus glaucus)*, and 13% *Vulpia microstachys*, a native typically found in disturbed areas, not chaparral. Claims by contractors that mulch does not inhibit the regrowth of native plants are not supported by independent research. The effectiveness of mulching and seed on controlling erosion remains unresolved.

A more serious question relating to post-fire seeding relates to the introduction of exotics. Although seed companies guarantee their mixes, in practice it has proven impossible to eliminate contamination by exotic, weedy annuals. For example, 800,000 pounds of grass seed was purchased and applied over more than 13,400 acres through aerial seeding by a BAER effort on the Cerro Grande fire scar. This was the 2000 fire in Los Alamos, New Mexico that eventually consumed over 47,000 acres and 350 homes. Later it was discovered that an estimated 1 billion cheatgrass *(Bromus tectorum)* seeds contaminated the seed mix (C. Allen, personal communication 2004). Cheatgrass is an invasive nonnative that is creating significant ecological damage throughout many western forests.

Post-fire Recovery: Nature's Way or Our Way?
Wayne Spencer and Richard W. Halsey[1]

Five months after the October firestorms, the hills are greening again in San Diego County. Rains came and the land held firm. Chaparral shrubs are resprouting from their bases or emerging from the blackened ground as tiny seedlings. Native wildflowers not seen in years will soon color the backcountry like floral phoenixes. And wildlife

[1] First appeared in the San Diego Union-Tribune, April 1, 2004.

populations displaced by the fires are gradually recolonizing these renewing habitats, following a natural ecological process that has repeated itself uncounted times since before human memory.

So, were the millions of dollars spent to hydromulch the hillsides, broadcast seeds, plant trees, or feed the deer money well spent? Did these interventions make a difference, or would we be better off just letting nature recover on its own?

The answers aren't simple and will require more time and data to answer fully, but in most cases available facts and scientific reason indicate that these well-intentioned actions were largely unnecessary, and some may be doing more harm than good.

It's essential to understand that fire and the erosion that naturally follows are ecological processes, like water cycles and nutrient cycles – like birth and death.

Science shows that wildland fires, including fires larger than those of last October, have periodically recurred in southern California, long before humans arrived to witness them. If chaparral has burned and recovered countless times before, why does it need our help now? Didn't deer and other wild species endure numerous fires before we arrived on the scene? If erosion carved our canyons and deposited our sandy beaches, why try to stop it? Isn't the wisest course of action after a fire, "hands off, let Mother Nature do her thing?"

Not entirely, of course. To advocate a total hands-off approach to the ecological recovery following fire would be to ignore our own presence and the myriad changes we humans already have made to the environment. We've built in floodplains and on land-slide-prone hills; we've dammed rivers, creating traps for silts and sands that previously washed out to sea, thus forming our estuaries and beaches; we've introduced countless alien weeds, now poised to invade fire-denuded landscapes; and we've fragmented habitats with houses and roads, impeding the natural recolonization process for wildlife displaced by fires.

Because of these changes, there are circumstances where management intervention is necessary to protect human life and property following fire, or to protect our native ecosystem from further degradation. Unfortunately, under the post-fire pressure to "just do something," it appears precious management dollars may have been wasted where intervention is neither necessary nor helpful.

For example, broadcast seeding of either native or especially nonnative species, like ryegrass, in hopes of reducing erosion, has been widely debunked by scientific studies. Such actions are at best a waste of money as most broadcast seed washes away before even germinating or is devoured by rodents and birds. At worst, broadcast seeding may actually increase erosion by hindering recovery of deeper-rooted native plants that are more effective at stabilizing soils. And successfully establishing a cover of nonnative annuals – referred to by firefighters as "flash fuels" – can increase fire ignition rates. Even if done with native seed mixes, the efficacy of the wholesale hydroseed mulching of Wildcat Canyon, Scripps Ranch and other areas is questionable, at best.

Soil erosion naturally increases after fire, exposing mineral soils and frequently increasing opportunities for seed germination. However, landslides and mudslides, like the Waterman Canyon disaster in San Bernardino County, are highly localized phenomena that depend on specific geological conditions. More than $1.25 million was spent laying down strips of mulch on Viejas Mountain near Alpine, ostensibly to control erosion and prevent landslides. However, Viejas Mountain is composed of gabbro-type soils that are not prone to landslides.

So why mulch Viejas or other open-space areas?

The U.S. Forest Service and other government agencies were under tremendous political pressure to recommend hydroseeding and mulching – to "just do something." Off the record, several Forest Service employees have stated, their words supported by previous Forest Service research, that these actions were largely cosmetic, with little hope of actually reducing erosion hazards or aiding ecological recovery.

What about caring for injured, displaced, or starving wildlife?

Efforts to rescue hungry deer by feeding them alfalfa or hay can lead to digestive ailments, bloating, and dehydration. These unnaturally rich feeds are often dumped near roads, increasing road kill risks for the animals attracted to them. And even if supplemental feeding does tide over starving deer in the short term, the artificially sustained population may exceed the capacity of the recovering landscape to support it, thus putting more pressure on the young vegetative growth, prolonging habitat recovery, and increasing erosion potential.

After the human losses, San Diegans grieve for the apparent destruction of our beloved natural environments. Images of the blackened landscape, the torched trees, and the dead and displaced wildlife naturally raise fears that "nature has been destroyed," and "nature needs our help."

But nature is resilient. Repeated fires helped shape southern California's native landscape, and it will rebound again on its own, except where changes we have made interfere with this natural process. In such cases, only carefully reasoned intervention, based on best available science rather than political expediency, should be applied. Otherwise, we should enjoy watching our natural environment quietly heal itself, as it has many times before.

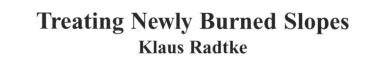

Treating Newly Burned Slopes
Klaus Radtke

As a young forester fresh out of college I was introduced to the all-too-predictable fire-flood cycle on a massive scale. In the winter of 1968/69 I found myself in the Glendora foothills assisting with supervising crews that erected wooden deflector barriers to protect a new subdivision from further advancing mudflows while bulldozers frantically dug mudflow channels and threw up earth berms in preparation for the next winter storm. Where it was not possible to redirect mudflows around homes, they were directed through the houses by removing back doors and front doors and cutting holes through the walls if necessary.

In the fall of 1979 I found myself again in a fire-flood conundrum on a much smaller, but nevertheless still dramatic scale on the Laurel Canyon burn within the foothills of the city of Los Angeles. Approximately 23 homes had burned in a small 30 acre fire on steep hillsides characterized by very limited access and densely packed with mostly wooden homes without, or very limited, slope setbacks. There was no time to argue with irate homeowners about the perceived lack of timely fire response and fire protection. The looming disaster could best be mitigated by quick education and the cooperation of the homeowners themselves. While public agencies prefer to broadcast-seed annual ryegrass over burned watersheds as an emergency "band-aid" measure, seeding by helicopter was ruled out in this case because of the potential danger to the homes. I was therefore called in to evaluate the situation on a property-by-property basis and initiate the most effective emergency erosion control measures feasible in close cooperation with public agencies and affected homeowners.

The steep slopes looking down on narrow streets and homes were covered with a thin layer of highly erosive, well-drained soil developed from the underlying decomposed granite parent material. Before the fire, a mixture of weedy annual grasses, ornamental plants, and remnants of native vegetation had largely protected the slopes from excessive erosion. After a well-attended public meeting held to get everyone involved, wooden deflector barriers were erected in key locations with materials largely bought by homeowners. These were designed to keep the expected mudflows confined within the paved streets while Flood Control personnel made sure that the storm drains and debris basins were cleaned out. Along steep slopes directly below homes, annual ryegrass was broadcast-seeded and watered-in by homeowners in order to quickly establish patches of green vegetation before the winter rains. Along moderately steep slopes where it was feasible to walk safely, pre-germinated barley was seeded in contour rows and homeowners were encouraged to keep it watered in order to get it quickly established. By the time the winter rains came critical slope areas already provided an emergency vegetative cover, mudflows were minimized, and structural damage due to mudflows was avoided.

Most emergency watershed rehabilitation measures carried out by public agencies after wildfires can be characterized as broad "band-aid" measures. They are generally not very meaningful or cost-effective if their goals are to effectively reduce soil erosion and protect watersheds by biological means, like broadcast seeding. Such measures generally do not acknowledge their limited success in timely mitigating post-fire erosional processes nor address possible short or long-term detrimental impacts on the native ecosystem. However, if their goals are to attempt temporary protection of roads and structural improvements to reduce or slow the post-fire peak storm flow and velocity (rarely successful) and redirect expected mudflows (occasionally successful), such measures can be meaningful. At the same time, a soothing pro-active image is conveyed to the general public during a time of crisis irrespective of future results.

Annual Ryegrass

Commercial annual ryegrass *(Lolium multiflorum)* has been used extensively since the 1950s for emergency revegetation of burned watersheds. Information concerning its usefulness had been based on the more limited seeding of watersheds burned by wildfires during the 1930s and 1940s, and of range improvement seedings and type conversions of native vegetation to grasslands. Prior to the extensive use of annual ryegrass, mustard *(Brassica* species) was seeded following wildfires to control erosion. However, the objections of agriculturists and range specialists who considered it a noxious weed caused its use to be discontinued (Bentley et al. 1956). As early as 1963, professional watershed managers carrying out studies on ryegrass-erosion relationships, concluded that ryegrass is largely unsuited to southern California soils and climate (Rice et al.

1963, Rice 1973). Seeded ryegrass had almost no effect on flood peaks but may have occasionally helped reduce the accumulation of debris. The authors concluded that ryegrass seeding is still a low cost alternative, but does not have great promise to the land manager. Subsequently fire ecologists warned about the accumulative detrimental effects of ryegrass on resprouting native vegetation because of its competitiveness. The native herbaceous flora, nature's own "band-aid" erosion control measure, provides the beautiful array of postfire wildflowers whose seeds remain viable in the soil and will be stimulated to germinate by future fires. If this post-fire flora is reduced or eliminated through competition or partial type conversion, erosion may increase after future fires, and fire frequencies will increase because of the more flammable type-converted vegetation.

In the 1970s emergency seeding of burned watersheds with exotic grasses had already become a political and emotional issue. Post-burn seeding ran the gamut from excessive measures on one end of the scale, generally in watersheds affecting more populated urban-wildland interface areas where fire politics demanded immediate action, to "no action" decisions in generally less populated areas. An interagency task force was therefore formed in 1980 to produce an "Interagency Field Guide for Vegetative Emergency Burn Rehabilitation" for southern California. The task force, subsequently divided into three groups – the Social/Administrative, the Physical, and the Biological – and set out to produce a draft copy of the field guide. The core of this document has been used, with some changes, to the present day by interagency burn rehabilitation teams.

As chairperson of the Biological Group and as both a fire ecologist and a watershed manager, I was also a member of the other two groups. I attempted to reduce the pressure on the Biological Group to formulate political and social acceptable conclusions while observing with apprehension the all too willingly accepted "marching orders" by some members of the other groups. Their agencies were much too eager to accept generally preconceived notions that the seeding of burned watersheds with ryegrass was the only politically and socially acceptable thing to do. The perception of what people wanted was apparently the overriding consideration. The political structure was not receptive to a change in the management approach to place more responsibility on the affected individuals. This was often a career-enhancing decision. But out of fairness to public agencies it must be said that they have a duty to protect themselves and the public from the culture of litigation. Being perceived as proactive through emergency seeding of burned watersheds and subsequent expanded "burn rehabilitation" measures frequently takes the edge off this concern. However, the actual results of recommendedations do not always turn out as planned.

During informal burn rehabilitation field inspections in Los Angeles County, I witnessed ryegrass seeding by helicopter in excess of 3 times the recommended maximum rate of 8 pounds/acre (32 seeds per square foot) in immediate urban-interface areas. The homeowners were not aware, of course, that such seeding rates could turn their backyards into high fire hazard areas the following spring. In addition, the possible type-conversion to grassland could significantly interfere with or eliminate their ornamental landscaping unless ryegrass competition is controlled.

Findings by the 1981 Biological Group relating to re-seeding burned areas made careful distinctions between the two distinct shrubland types found in southern California: coastal sage scrub and chaparral.

Coastal sage scrub is dominated by evergreen or deciduous soft shrubs mostly less than 1.5 meters tall. Shrub crown cover ranges from 25-80%, often with grasses and forbs co-dominant. After 5-10 years of growth, many coastal sage scrubs have reached their structural potential. Most shrub species resprout after a fire, but resprouting may be delayed for up to one year following an intense fire – except during severe drought conditions the herbaceous layer always makes a significant response during the first year following fire. Many herbaceous species continue to be present throughout the entire successional cycle into the mature phase. Others are present for a relatively short period of time following fire such as deerweed *(Lotus scoparius)*.

Since the natural response for a burned site is to become almost fully occupied with native fire followers and resprouting shrubs during the first post-fire year, little can be contributed through adding grass seed as a post-burn treatment. Indeed, if introduced grasses are successfully established, they can produce adverse effects on the ultimate structure and species composition of the mature phase. Reseeding every burn can be expected to produce a loss of stabilizing overstory shrubs and thus increase the potential for landslides and increased erosion over time.

Chaparral is dominated by evergreen and sclerophyllous shrubs, mostly less than 10 feet tall. The shrub crown cover at maturity is often close to 100%, although exceptions exist on steep or poor sites. The horizontal arrangement of species groups in mature chaparral can be highly diverse, with different shrub species responding to topographic and microsite changes, or with a single species dominating many square miles of land.

Because of the programmed response of chaparral succession to fire, it is unnecessary, from the biological point of view, to introduce a grass species after fire. The natural successional response of chaparral includes an early herbaceous plant stage and advances through a mature shrub stage repeatedly and within a relatively short time span. Furthermore, the dynamics of chaparral systems, particularly relative to shrub species diversity, may be adversely affected by introducing a highly competitive grass species on a burn. The first 2 post-burn years are the most critical for establishing the complement of species which will exist in a mature chaparral stand. It is also the time when an introduced grass species seeded after a fire will compete most vigorously with chaparral seedlings for nutrients and moisture. A treatment being applied with very good intentions to achieve what may be perceived as short-term erosion control benefits has a high potential for producing adverse effects in the long-term stability of the chaparral watershed. The adverse effects are greatly intensified when a repeated high fire frequency is followed by successful post-burn reseeding treatments. A permanent change in the chaparral structure and species composition of a chaparral stand will result. A critical concern is the change this produces in overall fuel characteristics, and the attendant potential to accelerate fire frequency, increase opportunity for mass wasting, accelerate erosion rates over time, and produce significantly adverse effects (social/economic effects) downstream from where the vegetation changes are occurring.

Re-seeding of any kind has consequently become more of an emotional issue than a scientific one. Action is demanded by the public after disasters such as wildfires, and annual ryegrass seeding is generally the cheapest way to show action and reap the benefit of any cover, ryegrass or not, that is established. Ryegrass seeding, if successful, is also aesthetically very pleasing as it turns the hillsides green and is visible from far away. In the eyes of public agencies not much is lost if a green cover is not established since resprouting and germinating native plant seeds will soon heal the fire scars on their own.

Hydroseeding

After the 1993 Old Topanga/Malibu fire I watched in disbelief as hydroseeding was carried out in the city of Malibu during the first week of March 1994 after the season's rainfall was practically over (Radtke 1994). Areas where I had established extensive and much more successful erosion control measures with area homeowners through contour barleying of highly erosive slopes were hydroseeded as well as areas where native coastal sage scrub and chaparral was reestablishing itself from seeds and sprouts. Even areas dominated before the fire by weedy annual grasses and had already started to turn the hillsides green were hydroseeded. On the 1993 Altadena burn I was even more dismayed when I found areas dominated by oak woodland covered with hydroseeded mulch fibers that made some of the trees look like swamp cypresses. Sadly, these are not isolated instances but a continued waste of taxpayers' money that can now be observed during almost every burn rehabilitation effort. So much money seems to be continuously spent for so few positive results. There is seemingly little accountability in an apparent attempt to show the public that something, anything, is being done.

Wattles and Hay

Hay wattles, long rolls of hay wrapped with plastic netting, and straw bales are used as emergency erosion control measures on slopes and as check dams in minor drainages. They can slow the flow of mud and water during low-to-moderate rainfall episodes, provided however, runoff does not concentrate initiating rill and gully erosion, and drainages are not already partially clogged with pre-fire debris. Such measures are more effectively used within drainages of watersheds partially covered with degraded native vegetation characterized by a high percentage of weedy grasses. Hay bales or wattles should not be used in small drainages pointing directly at homes as they often fail when loaded with debris on their uphill side and will suddenly send a wall of mud towards the house.

Homeowners Guide to Post Fire Emergency Rehabilitation

After brush fires, erosion from burned watersheds once covered with natural vegetation may be more than 20 times greater than from unburned watersheds, although it is normally much less. Fire intensity, steepness and length of slope, soil type and parent material, intensity, duration, and frequency of winter rains all affect the amount of erosion. In any event, immediate action by the homeowner is imperative to reduce property damage from the winter rains immediately after a burn. In addition to the eight potential mitigation strategies provided below, the appropriate County Flood Control office should be able to offer assistance.

The steps to be taken in emergency rehabilitation of a watershed such as slopes above or below structures after a fire depends on the location, the time of year, the intensity of the fire, the erosion potential, and the kinds of plants present.

If the fire occurs in midsummer and the burned watershed cover consists primarily of landscape plants with a large proportion of resprouting ground covers and shrubs, all that may be necessary for rehabilitation is to periodically irrigate and fertilize. Postfire management of native plants is similar. Plants should be allowed to resprout and establish themselves from seed. Light thinning of seedlings, as well as removal of dead stems and branches, can begin the following spring after the rainy season is over.

Timing becomes critical when a hot fire occurs in late fall. In neighborhoods where steep, long slopes overlook canyons and endanger the lives and property of canyon residents, neighbors should work together to quickly establish an emergency vegetation cover before heavy winter rains begin.

Eight Basic Steps to Rehabilitate Burned Areas Around the Home

1. **Hand-seeding Annual Ryegrass:** Ryegrass should be viewed by the home-owner as a management tool for temporary emergency surface erosion control of bare slopes during the immediate rainy season. Eradicating the ryegrass plants on landscape slopes towards the end of the rainy season, before they go to seed, and replanting the areas to deep-rooted low-fuel plants can be an effective method for reducing topsoil erosion. The temporary treatment with ryegrass can greatly reduce surface erosion if the seeds are watered in but it can also compete heavily with the deeper-rooted woody plants. During late spring to early summer annual grasses will become dry, weedy flash fuels. New seeds germinate year after year as long as the soil is disturbed. Perennial ryegrass should not be used, as it can become a weedy pest.

Homeowners should avoid broadcast seeding or contour seeding grasses on recent slippage areas or actively sliding hillsides. The additional infiltration of water into the soil due to the shallow-rooted grasses may cause local soil liquefaction and further slippage and mudflow. Plastic sheets should be spread over these areas until a proper slope-engineering job can be accomplished.

The homeowner must be careful in landscaping a hillside after fire. Planting of woody plants, such as shrubs and trees, as is often done immediately after a fire, is not effective as an emergency erosion control measure during the first few rainy seasons after a fire, as herbaceous cover is needed to immediately reduce surface erosion. Deep-rooted plants are needed to minimize slip-outs on steeper slopes during subsequent years. Shrubs and trees can be replanted if the burned woody plants do not resprout.

Steep hillsides converted from chaparral to less deep-rooted low-fuel plants often show little subsurface instability in the first few years. However, after high intensity rains 5 to 10 years later, slips and slides frequently occur and are seldom attributed to earlier mistakes.

2. **Barley Contouring:** Hand planting barley in contours spaced about 3 feet apart has proven to be one of the most effective post-fire erosion control measures on steeper slopes. The ridges and trenches of the barley contours form a series of miniature check dams that allow water to infiltrate the soil. This lasts for several years if the barley is cut back as stubble and increases plant growth, reduces runoff, conserves soil moisture, and prevents soil loss. On slopes with lower infiltration rates, such as steep, long slopes and hillsides with finer, less coarse soils, contours should be spaced more closely than on watersheds with high infiltration rates. Similarly, contours should be closer in areas where the runoff problems are critical, such as areas near homes at the base of the slopes.

Strip cropping could also be practiced by interplanting the barley rows with rows of low-fuel ground covers in catching and holding water and soil. This method allows for reestablishment of ground covers while at the same time greatly reducing postfire soil erosion. Several years can therefore be saved in re-landscaping of fire-prone hillsides. Quick cover and healthy plants are produced through saving the topsoil that is so valuable for plant growth.

For seeding barley in contour rows, recommended rates are about 150 pounds of barley per acre. Barley is readily available from feed stores and can be ordered immediately after a fire. Care should be taken to order only recleaned barley, since rolled barley (used for feed) will not germinate. Recleaned barley may be cheaper than ryegrass when the demand for it is low.

For quick establishment, barley seeds should be pre-germinated no longer than 1 day and should be covered with soil to a depth not exceeding 2 inches. Seeds lightly covered with soil germinate with the first winter rains, while seeds lying on the soil surface, such as ryegrass, need an extended period of moist weather for effective germination. Compared with ryegrass, barley germinates and grows more vigorously in cooler weather. Even after the barley plant dies, the strong roots and above-ground stubble can hold the surface soil for several years. When reseeding is not desired, the plants should be cut in the spring before they go to seed. Barley, like post-fire seeded ryegrass, is an annual plant and becomes a flashy fuel after it dies in late spring or early summer.

3. **Check Damns, Chain Link Fences, and Boards:** To alter or prevent the movement of rocks or large amounts of soil, check damns, chain link fences, and boards can be utilized effectively. The object of check dams is to hold back rocks, brush, and other debris, and to slow down the flow of water in canyons or large gullies (Fig. 5-1). Where falling rocks endanger life and property, chain link fencing can be useful as barriers. Chain link is flexible enough to catch even large boulders (Fig. 5-2).

Boards are the homeowner's emergency soil engineering tools to reduce the effective length and steepness of hillsides by dividing a larger watershed into smaller sections (Fig. 5-3). When using boards to reduce erosion and slippage, spacing is important. Unless the boards are used as terraces, there should be 1 or 2 feet of clearance between horizontally placed boards. Boards minimize slippage during heavy rains when both soil and excess water can ooze out between them. Remember that a supersaturated slope will slip.

Localized slope instability may result if the pipes that hold the boards are hammered into highly fractured and weak bedrock, especially in areas where such rock layering parallels the slope. Pipes may also fail to hold the boards, especially on steep slopes with thin soils if much new soil is placed behind the boards to establish a foothold for new plants.

4. **Using Jute Netting in Conjunction with Planting:** Netting made from natural fibers can be bought in carpet-like rolls. It is unrolled over the slope and anchored with pins in areas where heavy erosion is expected. Every square of the netting acts as a miniature check dam and effectively catches soil particles. The netting eventually decomposes but holds long enough for plantings to become established. Information on how to use the netting is obtainable from nurseries. Potato sacks (gunny sacks) can be effectively used for both erosion control and weed control of smaller areas.

5. **Maintaining Drains:** Concrete bench and downhill drains reduce the effect of topography on erosion. They reduce runoff and erosion by dividing a portion of a large watershed into smaller watersheds and by removing excess water safely from a

Fig. 5-1 Establishing Check Dams. *The object of check dams is to hold back rocks, brush, and other debris, and to slow down the flow of water in canyons or large gullies. Reseeding and replanting should go hand in hand with temporary erosion control measures. Check dams should be repeated about every 50 feet. Small mesh fencing will act to impede water flow. Additional information may be obtained from local flood control officials.*

Fig. 5-2 Evaluating the Use of Chain Link Fences. *Where falling rocks endanger life and property, chain link fencing can be useful barriers. The chain link is flexible enough to catch even large boulders. Steel posts or telephone poles should be installed to anchor the fence, but not 4-by-4 wooden posts (rock has a better chance of glancing off a round than a square object without breaking it). Telephone poles should be buried at least 3 feet deep. Professional help is advisable when designing a chain link fence system.*

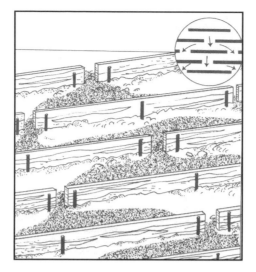

Fig. 5-3 Placing Boards. Redwood boards as thin as 1 inch can be used to temporarily stabilize slopes before planting and to keep existing soil slips from getting worse. The boards reduce the effective length and steepness of hillsides by dividing a larger watershed into smaller sections. Boards can be very effective if well engineered and supported by a proper plant cover, but should not be looked upon as a substitute for permanent soil engineering methods.

Boards should not be placed closer than 5 feet vertical distance and should be held by old pipes or rebars at least 4 feet long by 1 inch or more thick. Pack soil firmly after rebars have been hammered into ground. A board 10 feet long and 1 foot high should be held by a minimum of three rebars.

slope. Every year before the rains return, all drains in the neighborhood should be inspected and cleared of debris. Clogged drains are a major cause of flood damage and hillside slippage. All drains should be re-inspected before sandbags are placed in position and after every heavy rain, especially the first few years after a fire.

6.   Placing Sandbags and Deflector Barriers: Sandbags can be effectively used to direct the flow of mud and water to areas where they will do less harm such as a berm at the top of a slope to prevent water from running downhill. Channeling water down the slope causes supersaturated soil and slippage. Care must be taken, however, to insure the flow of mud is not directed toward another home.

After major fires, fire protection agencies and flood control districts may supply a limited number of sandbags. The sandbags should be filled halfway with sand or soil and the flaps tied and folded under, pointing toward the direction of water flow. When one layer of bags is in place bags should be stomped on to eliminate spaces between them. The next layer of bags should be staggered. Sandbags should never be more than three layers high unless they form a pyramid or a structure is used as backing.

Wooden deflector barricades can be effectively used as well to divert mudflows in critical areas. They serve the same purpose as sandbags but are semi-permanent. The local flood control district office can also provide expert advice regarding these diversion devices.

7. **Building Dry Walls:** Where slippage has occurred or is imminent, dry walls can be effectively installed, provided they have a firm foundation like the base of a slope. Dry walls can be made from unwanted concrete pieces from patios or driveways and natural stones. Such materials are usually free, and the wall can then be put up piece by piece without cement. Such a wall may last a lifetime and may be more effective than a block wall during an earthquake. If the wall is more than several feet tall, it should be sloped slightly toward the hill as new layers are added. Dry walling against a fill slope leads to slope failure (mudflow) during intense rains unless the fill is well compacted, anchored by plants, and only a few feet high. Lateral drains inserted 20 feet or more horizontally into the slope will lessen the chance of slope slippage by draining the excess water out of the slope.

8. **Covering Slopes with Plastic Sheeting:** Plastic sheeting can keep a slope relatively dry during heavy rains and prevent surface erosion especially after a fire in late fall. After a slippage it will prevent further saturation and movement of the soil. The entire slope or slope area should be covered with the plastic so that water is not channeled from one part of the slope to another. The flow of water at the base of the plastic must be controlled to avoid damage to homes below. Improperly placed sheets that concentrate runoff in selected areas or that cover only portions of a hillside are a leading cause of slope failures. Therefore plastic spread on hillsides must be properly tied down or con-stantly maintained throughout the rainy season. Broken pieces should be replaced and windblown sections retied. The thicker 6-mil (0.006-inch) plastic is preferred because it rips less easily and covers the slope better, thereby reducing maintenance problems. Sandbags partially filled with soil are often used to anchor the plastic. On steeper slopes, sandbags should be tied to ropes that are anchored at the top of the slope. Rocks or stakes should not be used to anchor the plastic because rocks wear through the plastic and stakes are ineffective when winds whip underneath the plastic. Rainstorms bring rain and wind, the plastic sheets must therefore be sealed on all edges and overlaps to prevent them from becoming sails as the wind whips underneath them.

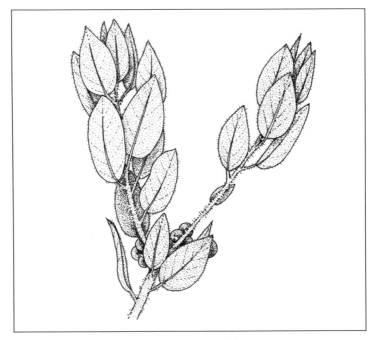

Arctostaphylos glandulosa

Fire, Chaparral, and Survival in Southern California

6

Learning from Fires

It is difficult to read a newspaper article today or listen to a conversation relating to wildfires without encountering some dramatic statement concerning how we have forgotten the important, natural role fire plays in the environment. Smokey Bear is blamed for being too successful in preventing fires, thus causing all wildlands to become overly clogged with vegetation. Humans, supposedly once savvy about how to allow fire to play its natural "cleansing" role, have now forgotten the secrets of nature and only see flames as destroyers. Big fires are our fault and we better do something about it fast before the entire North American continent burns up.

Although accusations and attention-grabbing generalizations such as these create good press, they are not helpful in contributing to sound fire management policy because they oversimplify complicated problems. What needs to be asked is, what does the science show?

One of the more commonly held notions relating to California wildfires is that we have mismanaged our wildlands by preventing nature from creating "mosaics" or mixed-aged stands of chaparral through small, frequent fires. According to this mosaic model, large expanses of old, dense brush have been allowed to form because we have excluded fire from the system through fire suppression. When fires do come, they burn out of control and turn catastrophic due to the unnatural level of fuel accumulation. Intuitively, this is a convincing story; scientifically, it is not supported by a thorough analysis of the data.

Because of southern California's fire-prone climate and vegetation mix, fire prevention and management strategies have had surprisingly little effect in reducing fires in the region despite the tremendous amount of money spent on the effort. The numbers of acres burned per decade has remained relatively constant over the past 100 years for San Diego, Los Angeles, San Bernardino, Ventura, and Santa Barbara Counties (Keeley et al. 1999). For Riverside County, rather than demonstrating successful fire exclusion, the data indicates a tremendous increase in acreage burned since the 1950s. This rise also corresponds with the county's rapid population growth into rural areas (figs. 6-1 and 6-2).

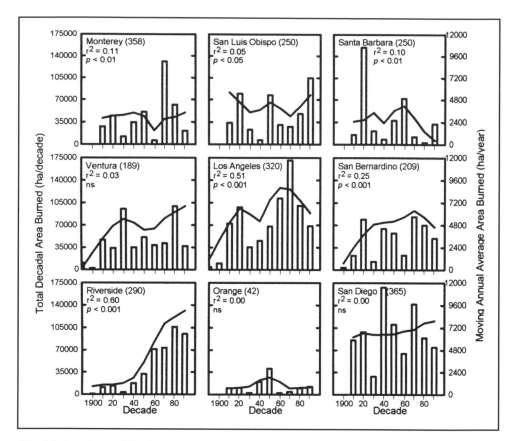

Fig. 6-1 Area Burned Per Decade and 10-Year Running Annual Average During The 20th Century For Nine Counties In Central And Southern California. *Shrubland area in thousands of hectares shown in parentheses following the county name. 1 hectare equals 2.47 acres (adapted from Keeley and Fotheringham 2003).*

The primary cause for faulty conclusions from experimental data rests with poor design of controls allowing more than one variable to affect results. When a variable is ignored, erroneous conclusions are certain to occur. The mosaic model assumes fuel buildup resulting from past land management is the only significant variable in determining fire size. It fails to adequately consider the role of Santa Ana winds and the capacity of younger vegetation to carry fires under extreme weather conditions. The model is attractive, however, because it appears to provide a workable solution to the wildfire problem; carry out large, landscape level prescribed or controlled burns. It also provides someone to blame for wildfire damage: Smokey Bear and land management agencies. After a huge fire roars through a community, it is much easier to point fingers and offer a visible response than to admit failure and say, "These fires are natural events and they are going to happen regardless of what we do." Unfortunately, politics requires immediate and clearly identifiable reactions to problems, effective or not.

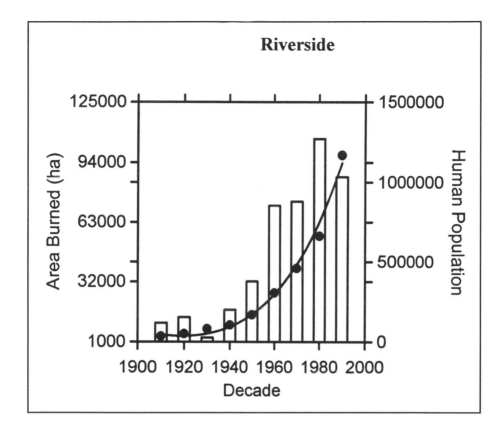

Fig. 6-2 Decadal Variation of Area Burned and Human Population for Riverside County (adapted from Keeley 2004).

The practice of science is no more immune to the influence of personality and politics than any other human endeavor. Sometimes egos become intertwined with scientific debate because of the personal attachment researchers have to their work. The media plays a role in encouraging this because of its tendency to focus on drama and conflict rather than careful analysis, confusing the public with an "expert vs. expert" approach rather than helping to communicate accurate information.

Although personal attachment to one's work is an important motivator, it can interfere with the scientific method because it interjects bias, a variable every scientist tries to avoid. The primary purpose of science is to reveal truth and explain how the universe works by considering a body of evidence and objectively evaluating that evidence. This is a painstaking process requiring time, peer review, and humility. Sometimes, in an effort to prove a favored theory, contrary evidence is ignored and bias unconsciously shapes conclusions.

In a paper read before the Society of Western Naturalists in 1889, Thomas C. Chamberlin (1890) addressed these issues when he wrote, "There is an unconscious selection and magnifying of the phenomena that fall into harmony with the theory and support it, and an unconscious neglect of those that fail of coincidence. There springs up, also, an unconscious pressing of the theory to make it fit the facts, and a pressing of the facts to make them fit the theory."

An example of "pressing of the facts to make them fit" by proponents of the mosaic model involves accounting for why wildfires burn into younger aged stands of chaparral rather than being stopped by them as the model indicates they should. One explanation offered suggests large fires have a kind of momentum that propels them through the younger fuels, causing the flames to burn vegetation that would normally remain unburned if the fire was small. A more thorough examination of fire behavior does not support this explanation. Fire is a dynamic process dependant on three basic elements: heat, fuel, and oxygen. Although fire accelerates gradually, it decelerates instantaneously when one of the elements is removed. Rather than having mass and momentum like a mudflow, fire is transient, depending on localized conditions in order to move forward (Finney 1998). The number of acres already burned is not relevant in determining how a fire front will behave. Santa Ana winds can account for the spread of wildfires through young stands of chaparral without invoking notions of momentum in order to preserve the integrity of the mosaic model.

Propelled by the intellectual excitement and emotional energy that moves knowledge forward, the scientist strives to maintain a delicate balance between desire and truth, knowing one is capable of influencing the other in unconscious, yet dramatic ways. When the balance shifts in favor of emotion, objectivity can suffer and competing ideas are viewed more as threats than legitimate scientific inquiry. This is especially true during periods of change when old paradigms are giving way to new discoveries.

The mosaic model has been the dominant paradigm over the past few decades and has influenced the thinking of not only professional land managers but the general public as well. As data has been collected over the last 10 years calling into question the basic assumptions of the model, ardent proponents have suggested challengers are inexperienced or less than serious researchers. Rather than considering the emerging view that older chaparral is an important resource, some continue to view it pejoratively as "decadent" or "scrub-infested" and favor its elimination. This perspective is neither practical nor scientifically defensible.

The most efficient and effective way to utilize scarce fire management dollars is within the wildland-urban interface, where homes make direct contact with the natural environment, not out in unpopulated, wild space. Attempting to create different aged patches of chaparral in the backcountry through landscape-level prescribed or controlled burning is not only extremely expensive but also potentially damaging to valued natural resources. In contrast, strategically placed burns and other vegetation modification projects around communities can play an important role in lowering fire risk while leaving the backcountry alone. This concept continues to be misunderstood by some land managers and politicians, especially in San Diego County.

Interestingly, the mosaic model has inspired a significant number of studies aimed at investigating its validity. In the process, science demonstrates one of its greatest strengths, advancing knowledge through peer review. "To be sure," Chamberlin continued in his 1889 address, "truth may be brought forth by an investigator dominated by a false ruling idea" because "his very errors may indeed stimulate investigation on the part of others."

Rethinking How We Live With Fire
Max A. Moritz

Fire has been an important and necessary ecological process in much of California for many thousands of years, and it will remain so for many more. Wildfires, like other natural hazards on the landscapes we inhabit, are therefore a phenomena we must learn to live with. After decades of suppressing wildfires, we now struggle to reintroduce them safely. At the most basic level, however, the current "fire problem" exists primarily because we have developed in ways and in locations that are vulnerable to this natural hazard. Fortunately, we have learned enough about floods and earthquakes to start incorporating them into our building guidelines and our urban planning. Unfortunately, we have been slow in making that leap with wildfire. Long-term droughts and changing climates appear even farther off in our collective consciousness, but they too may need to be accommodated eventually. Right now, we need to rethink how we live with fire.

Research about fire behavior and natural fire regimes *should* provide useful information for policy and management decisions. That linkage is part of what makes this line of work interesting. Research questions and findings, however, are typically put in terms of hypotheses and probabilities. Many scientists approach complex systems in terms of gradients, correlations, and mechanisms. These concepts and terms are not always easy for the rest of the world to use in making decisions, but they are necessary for scientific work. In contrast, most people try to understand a situation or problem by categorizing things, by putting names on recognizable patterns or associations. In this attempt to reduce and classify we often end up with simple models of how the world works. We tend toward discrete and "binary" choices (e.g., right versus wrong, us versus them), and we want one-size-fits-all solutions to our problems.

The desire for simple explanations and solutions is one reason for the current debate over whether shrubland fire regimes are fuel-driven or weather-driven systems. This statement itself is an over-simplification, because 1) a fire regime is really a description of a cyclical process with multiple parameters (e.g., fire frequency, intensity, size, season); 2) it can be measured over different periods of time and/or spatial extents; 3) it can involve a statistical characterization (e.g., mean and variance) of parameters and how they interact; and 4) there are other factors, such as topography and ignition patterns, that affect fire regime dynamics. Regardless, by continuing to argue over whether fuel treatments can or cannot solve the "fire problem," we are dooming ourselves to an endless debate without resolution. This is because the terms and underlying assumptions of the argument are not well-defined, and binary causes or outcomes simply do not exist.

Fire spread is a physical process affected by many factors. Different combinations of these factors can produce different fire behaviors and varying rates of propagation across the landscape. As "fire weather" gets worse (i.e., higher temperatures, lower humidity, and greater wind speeds), characteristics of fuels (i.e., amounts and spatial patterns of biomass) become less important in controlling how and where a fire may spread. When winds are so strong that long-range "spotting" occurs, blowing burning embers far ahead of a wildfire, the influence of fuel-related factors is greatly diminished. Thus, there is a natural tradeoff between the importance of fuel characteristics and weather conditions; not surprisingly, a similar tradeoff occurs between topography and varying weather conditions. All of these factors will still impact how a wildfire spreads in a given situation, but their relative importance can vary greatly.

Given an understanding of the different controls on fire spread, we can begin to assess the usefulness of fuel treatments on the landscape, whether through prescribed burning to reduce biomass levels or by some other means. A general conclusion is that the effectiveness of treated patches of vegetation will vary, depending on weather conditions. Under the mildest weather conditions, a fire might reach such a treated area and simply go out, due to a lack of flammable material. In even more hazardous weather conditions, this part of the landscape might still be used by suppression forces, as fire intensities could be low enough to safely work there. Under extreme fire weather conditions, such as the Santa Ana winds that occur each fall, these treatments may only constrain fire spread in a minimal way – if at all – and they are not safe locations for fire suppression forces.

What does the above assessment tell us about the "fuels vs. weather" debate? It means that extreme viewpoints ignore many details that are crucial to pragmatic decision making. This insight may not provide any simple answers, but it should at least allow for a refocused discussion about what we are trying to accomplish.

Landscape-scale fuel treatments must be evaluated according to what the goal is and under what weather conditions this goal can be achieved. These treatments are not cheap, either, so their effectiveness should be weighed against other hazard reduction efforts that could be achieved with the same funds. There can also be negative ecological consequences of vegetation treatments, such as the establishment and spread of non-native invasive species.

Hopefully people will move away from simple models of how the world works and scientific information will eventually be communicated more clearly, despite the fact that fire regimes are inherently complex systems. This shift could be facilitated by considering a fuel treatment's cost in terms of variables and probabilities, such as the following: A given treatment may reduce fire intensity or fire likelihood by $X\%$ under the worst $Y\%$ of fire weather conditions, with $Z\%$ certainty. But is it worth the cost, given this level of risk and the other possible uses of the money? Each of us already thinks somewhat like this in deciding how much insurance coverage we want and what deductible we feel comfortable with, given how unlikely we estimate some catastrophic event to be.

Ultimately, in a world of scarce resources, complicated environmental regulations, and sprawling development, the variable effectiveness of fuel treatments will probably limit them to very strategic locations on the landscape. Such locations may be at or near wildland-urban interfaces, where they can be the last line of defense in suppressing a wildfire. As we further rethink how to live with fire, we will require more retrofits to existing homes and neighborhoods. This will involve alterations to vegetation around structures, updates to certain building materials and designs, and better development of evacuation procedures. These fixes are necessary steps and in the right direction. The general approach, however, may only be as effective as the weakest link in the system. If you live in a fire-prone location and do all of the hazard mitigation you can, but your neighbor does not, what has really been accomplished?

A deeper and more difficult transition is ahead of us because the "fire problem" is truly one of *where* we build, in addition to *how* it is done. There are lessons to be learned from other natural hazards, which have resulted in limited or specialized development in disaster-prone locations. Californians must engage our policy makers and urban planners to create safe and sustainable communities, so that fire can continue to play its inevitable and necessary role on whatever natural landscapes we manage to leave for future generations.

Preserving the Future:
A Case Study in Fire Management and Conservation from the Santa Monica Mountains
Marti Witter and Robert Taylor

The Santa Monica Mountains are coastal mountains that extend west from the city of Los Angeles to the Oxnard plain in Ventura County, and are a major habitat island within one of the world's largest urban areas. The 153,000 acre Santa Monica Mountains National Recreation Area was established as a part of the National Park Service system to protect this area as an important example of a Mediterranean ecosystem; an ecosystem that has a limited worldwide geographic distribution and high biological diversity *(http://www.biodiversityhotspots.org/xp/Hotspots)*. The SMM National Recreation Area is a complex mosaic of federal, state, and private lands. Approximately 70,000 people live within the boundaries of the Recreation Area and 10% of the land area is developed. Millions more live within a short drive of its perimeter. Consequently, the Santa Monica Mountains includes a significant amount of wildland-urban interface where developed lands meet areas of undeveloped natural habitat.

The dominant vegetation in the Santa Monica Mountains is chaparral (55%) and coastal sage scrub (20%) shrublands, which burn in intense, stand-replacing fires. The result of development within this fire prone vegetation type is a long history of large, costly fires (fig. 6-3). Three of California's 20 largest fires for number of structures destroyed occurred in the Santa Monica Mountains: the 1993 Old Topanga, 1978 Kanan, and 1961 Bel Air fires.

As with all of southern California, the most damaging fires in the Santa Monica Mountains are large, wind-driven, autumn fires. The ability to control these fires is limited because of the associated weather conditions of low humidity, high temperatures, and high wind. The speed at which large fires spread means that fires at the wildland-urban interface can do major damage before the majority of firefighting forces have been deployed. The 1978 Kanan fire and the 1993 Old Topanga fire, for example, both started on the inland side of the mountains and spread rapidly downwind to the coast, causing large structural losses. The first fire covered 9 miles in 2 hours, with flame lengths of up to 90 feet reported. The second fire covered 6 miles in 4 hours. During both fires, opportunities for safe and effective direct attack by hand crews were severely limited until the weather moderated. Local fire history is overwhelmingly dominated by these large, extreme fires in terms of total area burned, as well as in terms of structures and lives lost.

The combination of a well-documented fire history, complex wildland-urban interface, and extensive parkland make the Santa Monica Mountains an excellent model for both effective fire management strategies and ecosystem conservation.

YEAR	NAME	AREA (ACRES)
1982	Dayton Canyon	43,043
1993	Green Meadow	38,478
1956	Sherwood/ Zuma	35,217
1970	Wright	28,195
1935	Malibu	28,191
1978	Kanan	25,565
1970	Clampitt	24,650
1967	Devonshire-Parker	23,005
1949	Simi Hills	20,573
1930	Potrero No. 42	20,391
1958	(name unknown)	18,115
1993	Old Topanga Fire	16,462

Fig. 6-3 The Twelve Largest Fires in the Santa Monica Mountains 1928-2001.

Fire Management Strategies

In the Santa Monica Mountains all fires are suppressed as rapidly as possible, so fire management decisions involve those actions that can be taken between major fire events to reduce fire losses. The single most effective action that can be taken in the wildland-urban interface is to create a defensible space by reducing fuel loads in the area around a home or other structure. Vegetation that has been modified and maintained will slow the rate and reduce the intensity of an advancing wildland fire and provide room for firefighters to safely work in and around structures. In combination with fuel modification, property owners need to ensure that their homes are resistant to structural ignition, particularly from flying embers.

While the effectiveness of defensible space is well understood (Cohen and Saveland 1977), the benefits of non-strategic, prescribed burning or other vegetation fuel management projects in backcountry shrublands are not well documented. Fuel reduction efforts are most effective for fire control under slope and fuel-driven fires (i.e., fires occurring under moderate weather conditions). These types of vegetation treatments are also effective at the shoulders of an extreme weather event as normal weather patterns return to the local fire area. This was observed during the October 1993 Kinneloa fire on the Angeles National Forest (Kerr, pers. comm.). The fire was contained on the western flank along the Mount Lowe fuelbreak as the Santa Ana winds slackened. This fuelbreak had been maintained with a prescribed fire in February of 1993.

However, the 10 month old Lake Avenue fuelbreak, which had also been treated in February of 1993, burned over without substantially affecting fire behavior during the height of the Santa Ana winds condition.

In the SMM National Recreation Area the concept of using prescribed burning to create a landscape mosaic of varying aged chaparral stands has been abandoned as a viable or effective fire management strategy. This strategy does not reduce wildfire structural losses because it does not provide direct protection for residences. Treatments are often remote from development because of the danger of prescribed fire escape. Neither does prescribed burning provide effective control of wildfire spread under severe weather conditions because, under these conditions, fires burn through even very young-age classes of vegetation. Physically creating a vegetation age mosaic with prescribed fire in the Santa Monica Mountains would require burning 5,000 acres per year on a 20 year rotation interval and would be impossible to implement because of social and regulatory constraints. Finally, the Santa Monica Mountains already has an extremely high fire frequency and unnaturally short fire return interval of 32 years. Any landscape-level prescribed fire has the potential to eliminate native shrubs from a too-short fire return interval.

The Santa Monica Mountains Plan

A more focused fire management strategy proposed for the Santa Monica Mountains is *strategic fuels treatment*. This is different than the "mosaic" model because strategic fuels treatment tries to identify locations where reducing fuel loads by either prescribed fire or by mechanically removing vegetation would change fire behavior enough to either limit fire spread, allow control of a fire perimeter, or protect specifically identified resources at risk from wildfire (NPS 2004). Strategic fuels treatments are landscape level treatments and do not include the defensible space created by mechanical vegetation fuel modification immediately adjoining individual homes.

To identify areas for strategic fuels treatments that might provide opportunities to either control fire spread (fuel modification strategies) or provide opportunities to contain the fire perimeter (fire containment strategies), a simple geographic information system (GIS) based analysis was developed based on slope, vegetation type, vegetation age, and density of nearby structures. GIS allows the entire landscape to be plotted based on information gathered by satellite and other sources.

A 30 meter digital elevation model was used to calculate slope steepness and identify areas where slopes are moderate enough that opportunities to control wildfire might exist. The thresholds selected were slopes less than 20%(optimum) and slopes between 20-40% (moderately feasible). Slopes steeper than 40% limit tactical firefighting options such as use of mechanized equipment or safe deployment of hand crews, and make aerial support, particularly air tankers, less effective.

The value of fuel modification to reduce fire hazard is strongly dependent on the type and age of the vegetation. Coastal sage scrub and grassland attain only relatively low amounts of fuel at any age, and they exhibit very rapid rates of re-growth. Thus fuel modification projects in these vegetation types produce only relatively small and short-lived benefits to firefighters. Chaparral has the highest fuel loads, generates the most intense and hazardous fire conditions, and takes longer to accumulate maximum fuel loads than other vegetation types in the Santa Monica Mountains. Because total standing biomass in chamise chaparral has been shown to level off after approximately 35 years, chaparral over 35 years in age was selected as the vegetation type that would provide the greatest benefit on fire behavior from fuel modification. A simple overlay of this information produced a map of areas meeting all the necessary criteria (proper slope, vegetation type and age). These sites are areas that may be appropriate for strategic fuel modification projects (fig. 6-4).

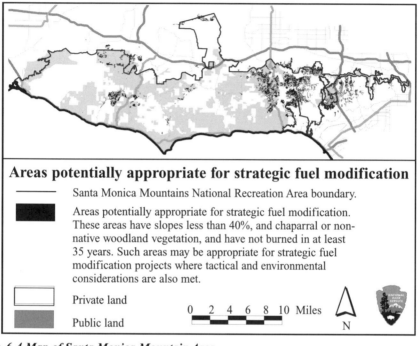

Areas potentially appropriate for strategic fuel modification

———— Santa Monica Mountains National Recreation Area boundary.

Areas potentially appropriate for strategic fuel modification. These areas have slopes less than 40%, and chaparral or non-native woodland vegetation, and have not burned in at least 35 years. Such areas may be appropriate for strategic fuel modification projects where tactical and environmental considerations are also met.

Private land

Public land

0 2 4 6 8 10 Miles

N

Fig. 6-4 Map of Santa Monica Mountain Area.

Given the reality of limited funds to support fuel treatments and the narrow window of opportunity to conduct these treatments under favorable weather and air quality situations, a prioritization process for evaluating potential treatments is required. To identify opportunities for projects that will produce the greatest demonstrable increase in fire safety, we evaluate population density and the ability of proposed treatments to protect residences and other improvements in the vicinity of the proposed treatment. Combining U.S. Census data on housing density with the previous analysis of opportunities for strategic fuel modification projects shows where opportunities for successful fuel modification projects are also close to high densities of structures at risk.

But proximity to high-density population areas cannot be used alone to judge the appropriateness of a strategic fuel treatment location. The ability to provide tactical options to firefighting resources is one of the key elements of many fuel treatments. When strategically located, fuel treatments can provide anchor points for ground-based firefighters to organize firefighting efforts and increase the effectiveness of fire retardant and water delivered by air tankers and helicopters. The reduction in vegetation on treated areas creates lower fire intensities, safer conditions and improved success rates for firefighters. These factors combine to increase the ability to control and extinguish wildfires burning under all but the most extreme weather conditions. Our goal is to assess the relative effectiveness of proposed fuel treatment projects by modeling fire behavior with high quality fuel data under realistic fire weather conditions. This modeling process, when compared with field observations from experienced operations personnel, is expected to provide useful decision-making support in choosing among competing fuel treatment alternatives to produce maximum fire safety with limited public funds.

Decision Criteria for Strategic Fuel Modification Projects

Identifying potential strategic fuel modification locations is only the first step in evaluating fuel treatment projects. Hazard fuel reduction proposals need to be rigorously evaluated to determine if a project will measurably reduce the fire hazard to homes or other resources identified to be at risk from wildfire, and should be evaluated with a formal decision model. The SMM National Recreation Area's Fire Management Plan outlines a decision model (NPS 2004). The use of a decision model ensures that an explicit risk/benefit analysis will be considered. It will make sure changes in fire behavior and potential enhanced protection from wildfire as a result of fuel treatment will be weighed against ecological risk from either subsequent wildfire or cyclic fuel treatments. The effects of fuel treatments are evaluated through the use of fire growth and behavior simulation programs (FARSITE and FlamMap) to determine how the proposed action would affect both fire spread and fireline intensity. The ecological risk is evaluated based on the best available data regarding vegetation and species' response to fire parameters including fire intensity and fire return interval.

Conserving Wildlands for the Future

Although the plant communities of the Santa Monica Mountains are tolerant of wildfire and resilient to a relatively wide variation in the fire return interval, it has been shown that chaparral communities can be degraded by high fire frequencies with a short fire return interval (Keeley and Fotheringham, 2003). The current mean fire return interval in the Santa Monica Mountains is 32 years. Only 1.6%of the vegetation is more than 77 years old. In the high fire frequency environment of the Santa Monica Mountains, no plant communities are considered to be at risk from an excessively long fire-free period. In contrast, short fire return intervals have had a drastic impact on native chaparral in some parts of the mountains. Areas where the fire return interval has been less than 6 years have experienced a significant decline of obligate seeding chaparral shrub species with subsequent type conversion from chaparral to grassland or coastal sage scrub (photo 32) (Jacobsen et al. 2004). With such high fire frequency years, the danger to native plant communities in the Santa Monica Mountains from fire is almost exclusively due to too-short a fire return interval.

Because chaparral is a fire climax community in which vegetation rapidly re-accumulates after fire or thinning, it is important to ask whether the benefits of reduced fire risk from proposed fuel treatments would last long enough to justify their ecological and economic cost. Frequently repeating a fuel treatment is expensive and increases ecological risk of type conversion and exotic species invasion. The trade-off between maintaining fire hazard reduction and limiting ecological risk to a chaparral plant community is illustrated by the graph in figure 6-5. This figure is based on chaparral dominated by *Ceanothus megacarpus,* an obligate seeder species. The fire hazard curve shows that fire hazard is virtually non-existent in the first years following fuel treatment but then gradually increases with regrowth and reaches a threshold value sometime between 25-35 years post-fire. The benefits from treatment with respect to reducing fire hazard are at their maximum in the first years following treatment. Conversely, ecological risk of extinction for an obligately seeding chaparral species is highest in the first years post-treatment when a repeat fire would eliminate the population by killing all seedlings before the seed bank had been replenished. Ecological risk to the community gradually declines until approximately 15 years post-treatment when sufficient seed is available to replace the population in the event of another fire. Similar curves can be generated for any plant community based on its fire/fuel characteristics, the regeneration mode of the dominant species, and its sensitivity to repeated fires.

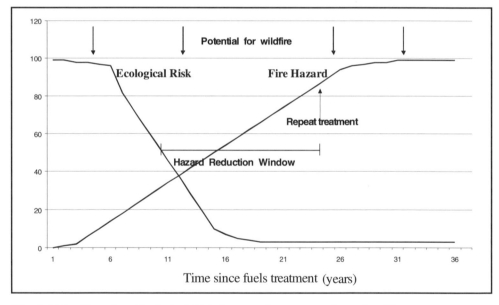

Fig. 6-5 Fire Hazard vs. Ecological Risk. *Line graph estimating the trade-off between maintaining fire hazard reduction and limiting ecological risk to a chaparral plant community.*

Any type of fuel modification project is meant to reduce the risk to communities from wildfire, but their effectiveness depends on when a wildfire occurs along the post-treatment timeline. This is illustrated with the arrows indicating the potential for a wildfire event at various points along the post-treatment timeline in figure 6-6. A wildfire early in the post-treatment timeline will be most effective in providing protection and risk reduction, while a wildfire late in the timeline will be minimally effective. The inherent conflict between fire hazard reduction and resource protection is that fuel treatments that provide the most benefit with an early wildfire also have the greatest potential to seriously degrade native plant communities.

In this example, it is only during the intermediate post-treatment time frame that treatment is both effective at reducing risk and does not adversely impact the plant community. The time between median ecological risk and the time at which re-treatment is necessary is called the "hazard reduction window." The hazard reduction window is the period of time during which wildfire behavior would be successfully modified by the treatment and which would not adversely affect the composition of the native plant community. Obligate seeding species such as *Ceanothus megacarpus* are the most sensitive to short fire-return intervals i.e., they have the longest post-treatment period in which they are subject to ecological risk from fire return. Vegetation dominated by facultative seeder and obligate resprouter species will generally have a shorter post-treatment risk period.

All fire management strategies to reduce wildfire losses by fuel (vegetation) manipulation will degrade the quality of our native habitats because of the need to reduce the fuel load that is characteristic of the vegetation. Even defensible space around homes, while the most effective strategy for reducing structural fire losses, has an enormous cumulative impact on loss of native habitat, spread of nonnative invasive species, and habitat fragmentation.

In the long term, only better land use planning with appropriate zoning and structure siting can stop the parallel processes of habitat degradation and spiraling fire costs. Increased development in the wildland-urban interface has been repeatedly identified as the cause of the escalating public costs of wildland fire suppression. It has been argued that providing public dollars to protect private property in an extreme wildfire environment allowed the development and urbanization of the Santa Monica Mountains (Davis, 1999). At a minimum, development should be limited to defensible sites (e.g., off of ridgelines and set back from steep slopes) and to sites with safe access (e.g., no lengthy or midslope driveways, adequate road capacity for evacuation).

It is impossible to create a fire safe environment for homes in wildland areas of southern California without unavoidable environmental impacts to habitat, wildlife, soil, and geology. In the absence of wise land use that acknowledges the reality of the southern California fire environment, we can only try to reduce the magnitude of the impacts from poor planning with appropriate design, construction materials and landscaping. To minimize the environmental effects of creating a fire safe home, residents in wildland areas should use fuel modification techniques that preserve native species; use appropriate native landscaping; remove serious weed species; avoid nonnative plants that increase fuel load; limit the use of irrigation; preserve slopes; and appropriately site structures to limit the size of the fuel modification zone. Fuel modification zones should be limited to the minimum required to effectively protect structures from ignition due to radiative heat transfer or direct flame impingement. Fire Departments should analyze individual sites and avoid requiring fuel modification beyond 100 feet unless it can be demonstrated by fire modeling that 100 feet would be inadequate to prevent structure loss or inadequate to provide a safe haven for residents and firefighters.

Lessons Learned from the Wildfires of October 2003[1]

Jon E. Keeley and C.J. Fotheringham

The southern California fires of late October 2003 were the largest single fire event in California's recent history (figs. 6-6 and 6-7). These fires burned through a complex mosaic of urban and wildland fragments, as well as across the well-defined and extensive wildland-urban interface, destroying many lives and properties. Understanding the factors leading up to this event and the appropriate human response necessary to reduce the chances of these catastrophic impacts occurring again is the focus of this paper.

These fires burned through diverse plant communities but the amount of different vegetation types burned was not proportional to the media coverage. Thus, outside of southern California there is widespread belief that these were forest fires and this perception may have contributed to the passage of the (Healthy) Forest Restoration Act of 2004 (HR 1904). Media focus on these forest fires was undoubtedly due to the fact that they burned in unnaturally intense and spectacular crown fires in forests with important recreational value and relatively high density housing. However, coniferous forests comprised only about 5% of the total acreage burned (http://frap.cdf.ca.gov/). This is important because the factors leading up to fires and the solutions to reducing fire hazard are distinctly different in forests than in shrublands like those that dominated the bulk of the wildlands burned in the 2003 fires.

How Do Forest Fires Differ From Shrubland Fires?

A century of fire suppression policy has been very effective at excluding fires from forests throughout the western U.S., but not from southern California shrublands. In forests, fire exclusion has been achieved for a number of reasons; mountain climates have a much shorter fire season, ignitions are commonly from lightning, weather conditions are not usually conducive to rapid fire spread, and fires typically spread by surface fuels that produce lower flame lengths. Over much of the 20th century these characteristics have led to a highly successful fire suppression practice that equals fire exclusion. Consequently, there has been an unnatural accumulation of surface fuels, coupled with increased density of young shade tolerant trees. Increased density of young trees is perhaps the most serious problem because these saplings act as ladder fuels that change fire behavior from surface fires to crown fires. As with most of our western forests, southern California conifer forests have been logged one or more times (Dodge 1975, Minnich 1988), and this may have had a greater impact on creation of ladder fuels than fire exclusion, although no one has clearly sorted out the relative contributions. Ladder fuels were certainly a critical factor in determining property damage from these recent forest fires.

Fire suppression policy in the southern California forests may also have had other indirect effects that contributed to increased fire hazard by creating conditions that

---

[1] This is based in part on an article appearing in the September 2004 issue of *Journal of Forestry*.

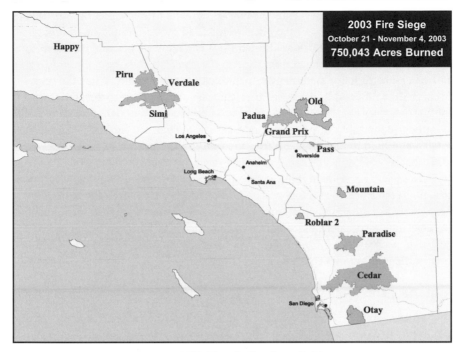

Fig. 6-6 Fire Perimeters for October 2003 Fires in Southern California. *Source: John Craney, California Department of Forestry and Fire Protection (CDF).*

FIRE	COUNTY	ACRES BURNED	START DATE	CAUSE
Roblar 2	San Diego	8,592	Oct. 21	Under investigation
Pass	Riverside	2,387	Oct. 21	Human
Grand Prix/Padua	San Bernardino Los Angeles	69,894	Oct. 21	Human
Piru	Ventura	63,991	Oct. 23	Under investigation
Verdale	Ventura Los Angeles	8,650	Oct. 24	Under investigation
Happy	Santa Barbara	250	Oct. 24	Under investigation
Old	San Bernardino	91,281	Oct. 25	Under investigation
Cedar	San Diego	273,246	Oct. 25	Human
Simi	Ventura Los Angeles	108,204	Oct. 25	Ember caused spot fire from Verdale fire
Paradise	San Diego	56,700	Oct. 26	Human
Mountain	Riverside	10,331	Oct. 26	Under investigation
Otay	San Diego	45,971	Oct. 26	Human
Wellman	Riverside	100	Oct. 26	Under investigation

Fig. 6-7 The 2003 Southern California Firestorm.

greatly increased tree mortality. Estimates for some parts of the southern California San Bernardino Forest are that 3/4 of the pines were killed by a combination of drought followed by subsequent bark beetle infestation. When natural fires are excluded from conifer forests there is an unnatural increase in the density of young trees. This results in intensified competition for water between all trees, young and old. When the region experiences drought conditions, as has been the case during the past several years, mortality of all trees exceeds what would have been predicted under more natural conditions. Extensive mortality of ponderosa pine *(Pinus ponderosa)* in the San Bernardino Mountains appeared to have played very little role in the October 2003 fires only because weather conditions changed and the fire was extinguished by rain.

To reduce fire hazard in these forests there is currently a massive effort directed at extracting dead trees. While this will certainly reduce the chances for destructive wildfires it creates other resource problems. Primarily, removal of such large portions of the forest canopy creates an ecological vacuum that will be filled by aggressive alien species such as cheatgrass *(Bromus tectorum)* that has already infested other forests recently burned in this area (photo33).

Shrubland Fires

Chaparral and related shrublands dominated most of the landscape burned during the October 2003 fires, and there is ongoing debate over whether such massive fires are natural, but infrequent events in the chaparral ecosystem, or are the result of modern fire suppression, as appears to be the case with conifer forests. The 2003 firestorm is relevant to this debate, providing an important case study that we can learn from and use to guide rebuilding efforts and future management activities.

The dominant paradigm governing fire management in southern California shrublands has long been the model that presumes fire suppression has successfully excluded fire and caused an unnatural accumulation of fuels (Minnich 1983; Minnich and Chou 1997). This model assumes that the age and spatial pattern of vegetation are strong constraints on fire spread, even during periods of extreme fire weather. These authors propose that large chaparral wildfires are modern artifacts of fire suppression and they can be eliminated by landscape scale rotational burning (Minnich and Dezzani 1991; Minnich 1998). Fire management plans for USFS national forests in southern California all have incorporated aspects of this model (Conard and Weise 1998).

However, despite heroic efforts by fire fighters during the 20th century, fire suppression policy has not eliminated fires from these landscapes, nor have fuels increased to unnaturally high levels (Conard and Weise 1998; Keeley et al. 1999; Keeley and Fotheringham 2003a; Moritz 2003). In addition there is no evidence that the frequency of large fires has changed over the 20th century (fig. 6-8). However, what has changed on these landscapes is an increase in population density and concomitant increase in fires (fig. 6-9).

An emerging view is that large fires under extreme fire weather conditions are only minimally constrained by the age and spatial patterns of fuels, and this appears to hold over broad regions of central and southern California (Moritz et al. 2004).

Southern California shrublands are an anomaly because, unlike many western U.S. forests, fire suppression policy cannot be equated with fire exclusion. The primary

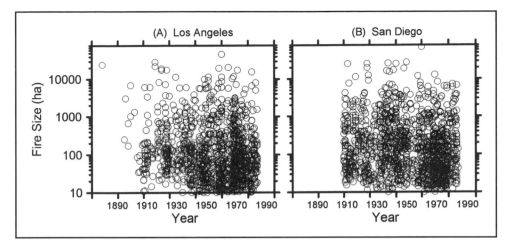

Fig. 6-8 Size of Fires During the 20th Century in Two Southern California Counties. *Hectares (ha) = 2.47 acres. (from Keeley et al. 1999).*

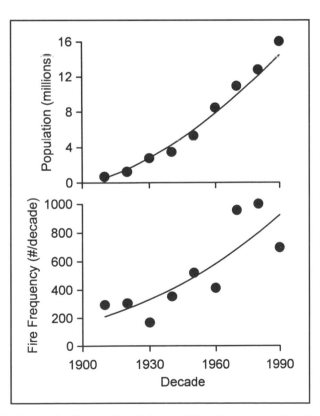

Fig. 6-9 Decadal Changes in Human Population and Fire Frequency in Southern California *(from Keeley and Fotheringham 2003).*

reason is because this region has what fire climatologists have labeled as the worst fire climate in the country (Schroeder et al. 1964). While it is generally true that massive fires anywhere in the West are accompanied by severe fire weather, in southern California these fires typically occur during the autumn Santa Ana winds. These winds reach speeds of 50-60 mph, and occur every autumn at the end of a 6 month drought. Under these conditions fire fighters are forced into defensive actions and can do very little to stop these firestorms.

Illustrative of southern California's uniqueness is the relationship between large fires and drought (Keeley 2004a). Throughout the western U.S., large fires are usually restricted to periods of extreme drought (Westerling et al. 2002). However, in southern California large fires are most likely during the autumn Santa Ana wind season and are not restricted to periods of unusual drought (fig. 6-10). Climate does appear to play a role in that it increases the length of the fire season since large summer fires are restricted to drought conditions.

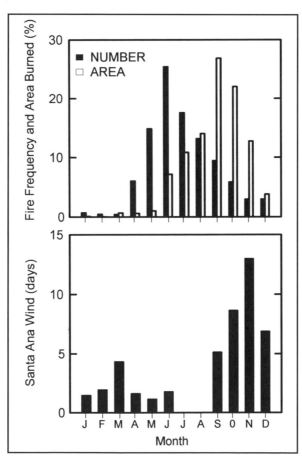

Fig. 6-10 Seasonal Distributions of Fire Occurrence and Area Burned During the 20th Century in Los Angeles County and Seasonal Distribution of Santa Ana Winds (from Keeley and Fotheringham 2003).

Lessons Learned From the October 2003 Fires

Three lessons can be extracted from the 2003 fires:

1. Although these fires were massive, their size was not unprecedented, and thus we can expect similar fire events in the future.
2. The current fire management policy is not effective at preventing these massive fires.
3. Future developments need to plan for these natural fire events much the same way we currently incorporate engineering solutions to earthquakes and other natural catastrophes.

Lesson 1: This 2003 firestorm was a natural event that has been repeated on these landscapes for eons. For example, studies of charcoal deposition extracted from cores off the coast of Santa Barbara have found that the frequency of large fires has not changed in the past 500 years (Mensing et al. 1999). There are even Native American legends in San Diego County that support this conclusion. According to legend, hundreds of years ago there was a mass migration of local tribes due to a massive wildfire (Odens 1972). Although the recent 273,230 acre Cedar fire was the largest in California since official fire records have been kept, there are historical accounts of even larger fire events. For example, during the last week of September 1889, a Santa Ana wind-driven fire east of Santa Ana in Orange County, California reportedly burned 100 miles north and south and 10-18 miles in width (*Los Angeles Times,* September 27, 1889). This event would have been three times larger than the recent Cedar fire. Collectively, September 1889 would have exceeded all of the October 2003 burning since there was another fire that ignited that week near Escondido in San Diego County and in two days the same Santa Ana winds blew it all the way to downtown San Diego (Barrett 1935), a distance roughly equal to the long axis of the recent Cedar fire.

The primary difference between these fires is that California's population has grown about *30 fold* during this period *(http:www.census.gov)* and urban sprawl has placed huge populations adjacent to watersheds of dangerous fuels. Since over 95% of all fires on these landscapes are started by people, there has been a concomitant increase in fire frequency and increased chance of ignitions during Santa Ana wind events (Keeley and Fotheringham 2003).

The important lesson here is that massive fires have occurred at periodic intervals in the past and likely will occur again in the future. It may be more useful from a planning and management perspective to see these events as we currently view 100 year flood events or other such cyclical disasters.

Lesson 2: For the past several decades, southern California shrubland fire management has been based on the philosophy that fuel management practices can control the ultimate size of these massive fire events. This belief stems in large part from the fact that forests such as Southwestern ponderosa pine have had natural fire regimes perturbed by fire exclusion (Cooper 1961, Allen et al. 2001) and there are an increasing number of studies showing that fuel reduction is highly effective at reducing fire hazard. Many researchers have failed to recognize that transferring this model from natural low intensity surface fire regimes typical of forests, to chaparral, may be inappropriate. During the 1970s mathematical models of fire spread demonstrated that if fire suppression was effective at excluding fires then chaparral fires would be expected to increase in size and intensity (Keeley and Fotheringham 2003). Managers accepted this idea and focused on fuel (vegetation) manipulation as a means of preventing large fires. The preferred treatment has long been prescription burning, applied on a rotational basis across the landscape. Theoretically fuel reduction treatments are expected to prevent large wild fires by creating fuel mosaics that include patches of young fuel, which supposedly are expected to act as barriers to fire spread.

However, over the past several decades this management philosophy has proven ineffective and in every decade the region has experienced large-scale catastrophic fires. The extent to which landscape-level fuel treatments are effective is a function of weather conditions during the fire event. Under extreme weather conditions there is overwhelming evidence that young fuels, or even fuelbreaks (fig. 6-11), will not act as a barrier to fire spread. This is quite evident in the October 2003 fires. Crossing nearly the entire width from north to south of the east-west burning Cedar fire were substantial swaths of vegetation that were less than 10 years of age, not just in one but two parts of that fire (Keeley et al. 2004). The Otay fire exhibited the same phenomenon; the fire burned through thousands of acres that were only 7 years of age (fig. 6-12). The primary reason young fuels cannot act as a barrier to fire spread under these severe weather conditions is that if the high winds do not drive the fire through the young age classes, they will spread the fire around them, or jump over them from fire brands that can spread up to a mile or more.

What is the appropriate fire management strategy? Pre-fire fuel manipulations will undoubtedly remain an important part of the southern California fire management arsenal, but their application needs to be carefully considered if they are to be effective

Fig. 6-11 Fuel Break East of Scripps Ranch, San Diego County. During the Cedar fire, fuelbreaks failed to prevent the fire from spreading due to embers blowing far ahead of the fire by Santa Ana winds. Photo: J.E. Keeley

and provide benefits equal to or exceeding their cost. For example, some fires igniting under calm wind conditions have been documented to burn out when the fire encounters young fuels, and the lack of wind limits the likelihood of fire brands jumping these young fuels. These fires, however, seldom present major problems for fire fighting crews and do not pose a major threat to the loss of property and lives. Thus, serious attention needs to be paid to whether or not fuel treatments are cost-effective for these fires.

The key to effective use of pre-fire fuel manipulations in crown-fire ecosystems such as chaparral is their strategic placement. Under severe weather, lower fuel loads will

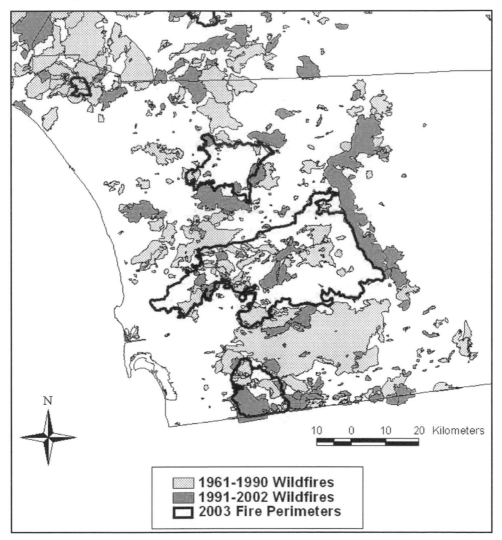

Fig. 6-12 Historical Fire Perimeter Map of San Diego County. Both the Otay fire (lower middle dark outline) and the Cedar (central dark outline) burned through several large patches of young chaparral. This demonstrates the dominating role winds can play over fuel age in spreading fires. Paradise fire upper middle. Map created by Max A. Moritz.

not stop the spread of fire, but they do reduce fire intensity, and thus provide defensible space for fire suppression crews. Thus, the key benefit is to enhance firefighter safety and therefore strategic placement is critical to their success. Much of the southern California shrubland landscape is far too steep to provide defensible space regardless of fuel structure, and thus fuel manipulations in these areas are unlikely to provide economically viable benefits. Fuel manipulations will be most cost-effective when focused on the wildland-urban interface. Often times during severe fire weather homes are lost because fire fighters refuse to enter areas that lack a sufficient buffer zone of reduced fuels to provide defensible space. In terms of management goals, the metric for fuels treatments on these shrubland landscapes needs to change from simply measuring "acres treated" to consideration of their strategic placement, and this change in management philosophy is being recommended by the largest National Park Service unit in southern California (see M. Witter and R. Taylor above in *Preserving the Future: A Case Study in Fire Management and Conservation from the Santa Monica Mountains*).

Fuel manipulations, in particular rotational prescription burning, may have some beneficial impacts on post-fire events since younger fuels are associated with reduced fire severity, and this may affect both vegetation recovery and sediment losses. Extensive studies of post-fire recovery following the 1993 fires in southern California found that the impact of high severity fires was variable, with both positive and negative impacts on post-fire recovery (Keeley 1998a). Thus, it would be premature to at this point conduct expensive fuel treatments with the expectation of producing major changes in post-fire recovery.

Recent studies of sediment loss from chaparral watersheds have shown that rotational burning at 5 year intervals has the potential for greatly decreasing the immediate post-fire sediment loss (Loomis et al. 2003). However, in the long run this may not be cost-effective for several reasons. One critical determinant of sediment loss is the first winter precipitation, high rainfall years being particularly damaging. Prescription burning at 5 year intervals greatly increases the chances of fires being followed by an El Niño year of high rainfall, relative to fires at the normal return interval of 35 years. In addition, the cumulative sediment loss over the long term would be much greater for 5 year burning intervals since there would be multiple peak discharges over the normal 35 year interval. Perhaps most importantly, burning at 5 year intervals will almost certainly effect type-conversion to alien grasslands (Keeley 2004b), which in addition to having negative resource impacts, would greatly increase the chances of slope failure in many of these very steep watersheds.

Lesson 3: Californians need to embrace a different model of how to view fires on these landscapes. Our response needs to be tempered by the realization that these are natural events that cannot be eliminated from the southern California landscape. In this respect we can learn much from the science of earthquake or other natural disaster management. No one pretends they can stop them; rather they engineer infrastructure to minimize impacts.

The primary shortcoming of fire management has been the failure to adequately convey to the public their inability to stop massive Santa Ana wind-driven fires. For much of the past half century public agencies have had a false belief that how or where they allowed new developments was irrelevant to fire safety because of assurances that fire managers could prevent fires from burning across the wildland-urban interface. Undoubtedly there has been substantial pressure on fire managers to convey an overly confident image, and not to highlight their limitations. These recent fires should be recognized as a wake-up call to the fact that there are inherent limitations to containment of Santa Ana wind-driven fires.

Some newspaper accounts have suggested that the conservation planning efforts in southern California contributed to the devastation caused by the fires by allowing the close juxtaposition of developments and natural habitats. While there may have been isolated instances where this was the case, there is evidence that effective preserve design assisted in reducing the loss of human life and structures. The overriding goal of habitat management planning is to create areas large enough to provide contiguous habitats that are not infringed upon by development. This goal is consistent with increasing fire safety for the public. The best example of where this planning process worked well is the Otay fire, which burned a substantial portion of a contiguous habitat management area, yet no structures or lives were lost. Allowing development on an "island" within this preserve would have meant setting structures within indefensible boundaries.

Conclusions

Chaparral is the most extensive vegetation type in California, covering over 8.5 million acres of the most heavily populated state (35 million people) in the union. Massive high intensity wildfires are a normal feature of this ecosystem, creating situations lethal to the expanding human population on these landscapes. Over the past several decades urban sprawl has placed more and more people at risk and added to the human and financial losses at a scale that dwarfs wildfire impacts in other parts of the country. Indeed, since 1970, 12 of the nation's top 15 most destructive wildfires have occurred in California, costing the insurance industry $4.8 billion (Miller 2004).

Unlike western U.S. conifer forests, where fuel reduction projects show promise of reducing the incidence of large wildfires, analysis of the factors leading to catastrophic chaparral fires indicate limited ability of managers to prevent such events. Thus, we need to plan for other massive wildfires on the southern California landscape. Fire management activities cannot prevent these large fires, however, through a combination of buffer zones and better planning, we may be able to engineer an environment that minimizes their impact on property and lives.

There are two important realities to fuel management at the wildland-urban interface that will potentially cause problems in the future. One is the increasing complexity of land ownership and different management goals of neighbors. Fuel clearances necessary to ensure structure survival may not always be possible because of alternative management goals by neighbors. Perhaps a bigger problem is the skyrocketing cost of managing vegetation to reduce fuel loads, illustrated by the recognition that such treatments in many western U.S. forests may need to remove larger commercially valuable timber in order to pay for them. However, extraction of commercial products is not an option for chaparral shrublands, and thus some creative thinking will be required in order to pay for the necessary buffer system needed to protect urban developments. An important area for future research is the use of normal features of development infrastructure as buffers. For example, in southern California many new developments are built around golf courses or recreational parks. However, placing these on the periphery could act as an important barrier to fire spread. Making these designs part of the developers responsibility would have value added in that it would encourage less fingering of developments into dangerous wildland fuels because such configurations would increase the costs of buffer zone construction.

7

The Next 100 Years

Just for a moment, forget your politics, personal tastes, and perspectives on the natural spaces outside your daily life in the world of civilized things. If you find yourself rolling your eyes when you hear yet another person complain about how much habitat for the California gnatcatcher we are losing, put your thoughts aside for now. If you get irritated when an environmental group successfully prevents the expansion of a development or activity you favor, imagine it's not important. If you are too busy enjoying your life and really don't have time to concern yourself with a walk in the chaparral, pretend you're bored stiff.

Now ask yourself, how much wilderness, open space, and natural heritage do we want remaining 100 years from now? Do these things have value? Can they make a positive contribution to your family's quality of life?

In discussing the future, the U.S. Forest Service wrote in its 2004 Draft Environmental Impact Study for the four southern California National Forests, "Projected human population growth throughout all of southern California is expected to bring major increases in pressure upon National Forest resources, including requests to develop and use resources to support community growth (such as water, energy and transportation)."

We obviously don't need the U.S. Forest Service to tell us more people are coming, but they did articulate a phenomenon that is sometimes forgotten among all the shouting between various competing interests. "As the resident population continues to increase, so too will the desire to conserve these remaining vestiges of regional open space and scenic heritage in a natural-appearing intact condition."

Long range planning is notoriously difficult because a significant portion of its benefits occur long after those making the decisions are dead. Politics is the art of the possible. It deals with the here and now; to expect more requires enormous amounts of personal optimism, selfless dedication, and a measure of healthy naiveté over the true motivations behind public policy decisions. But it can happen. It also helps to have a dramatic event to get everyone's attention – an event like the southern California firestorms of 2003.

Despite our technological achievements, humans remain an integral part of nature. Because of our tremendous impact, we can no longer assume natural, wild spaces can function on their own. We have to manage the land to either protect it from our presence or develop plans to maintain its long-term stability in order to continue using it for recreational opportunities. However, when trying to balance competing interests, a fundamental fact needs to be constantly remembered: once disturbed, the pristine value of a resource is gone forever. Dozens of battles can be won to preserve a favored wild space, but all it takes is a single defeat to lose the war. This accounts for some of the emotional intensity and uncompromising nature of preservationists. They know once an area is removed from the inventory of open space, there is no turning back.

Think of how much change has occurred over the past century. Now consider what may happen over the next 100 years. When imagining such things, I often remember one of the scenes in Episode II of the Star Wars movies where an entire planet is a bustle of space age activity; aircraft flying in all directions, buildings covering every available spot, and streets jammed with inhabitants. No trees. No green. No space. While the concept of "multiple use" of southern California's National Forests has merit, we must take great care to make sure our lack of foresight doesn't lead to "multiple degradation."

Still, if you live in a city that provides you with all the things you need or an outlying neighborhood with a wealth of amenities like good schools, nice parks, and nearby shopping facilities, why should you care about natural space, chaparral, or wildfires?

When fire regimes change due to type conversion of chaparral, citizens and community leaders need to have an understanding of the system in order to properly evaluate the negative effects (Brooks et al. 2004). Hillsides covered in grass instead of shrubbery have dramatically different watershed characteristics, allowing greater erosion and lower replenishment of the water table. With the demand for water growing every year, this situation alone is enough to focus intense energy into preserving as much native shrubland as possible. The increase in fire-associated hazards related to invasive weeds needs to be carefully examined. While it is true grass fires are easier to control and do not produce the intense heat chaparral fires do, they ignite easier, move quicker, and under the right conditions can be just as deadly. Degraded chaparral with an understory of grass is much more explosive than chaparral alone. It is not just the fuels themselves, but the arrangement that is important in determining how fires behave (R. Lyle 2004, personal communication). Although mature chaparral is impenetrable, the ubiquitous stickers produced in fields of weedy grass create an inhospitable environment for anyone trying to take a quiet stroll. The potential loss of tourist appeal over such conditions is an issue to seriously consider for a region that depends on visitors for a significant portion of its economy. The replacement of chaparral also seriously alters wildlife habitat. Although the value of such degradation is difficult to measure, it is an important concern to many southern Californians who enjoy the state's natural resources. Which again brings up the question, is preserving chaparral an important goal by itself, without considering other variables?

Chaparral has no value if it is not recognized as being present. In order for anything to be viewed as relevant, it must be identified, have a name, and be understood. This is why it is so important citizens take an interest and make a commitment to learn about their local, native wild places. Without developing familiarity for and appreciation of the surrounding environment, there appears to be no reason to care for it. Although it may be difficult to convince a seasoned urban dweller or someone disinterested in the natural world that understanding chaparral is a worthwhile endeavor, the ability to reconnect to the landscape is within all of us.

Reconnecting

Despite progress made in distancing ourselves from nature in the raw, we remain hardwired to rhythms of wilderness. Our ancestors spent millions of years being intimately connected to seasonal cycles and life around them. A mere 10,000 years of city life is not enough time to forget. Our own personal connection to things wild remains thinly veiled under the artificial constructs of civilization. Making a conscious decision to reconnect to one's natural surroundings can provide significant improvements in the quality of life. It is not just about learning to recognize the call of the wrentit, to be able to identify ceanothus, or understand the value of chaparral as a watershed; in a fire-prone environment like southern California, it is a matter of survival.

By suppressing wild patterns developed over millions of years and replacing them with more sedate, controlled behaviors, *Homo sapiens domesticus* has become alienated from his home. This detachment can manifest itself in a number of ways: increased emotional tension, magnified frustration, a sense of isolation and loneliness. Separation from nature allows pressures, created by trying to survive the demands of civilization, to overwhelm an individual's mindset and magnify minor disappointments into major conflagrations. This is one of the reasons wilderness education programs like Outward Bound are so successful in helping individuals correct self destructive behaviors or establish a more balanced perspective on life. Once removed from the daily rituals of modern society, nature provides an opportunity for catharsis. The wild gives the mind time to reflect upon the essentials of life, to purge the malignant artifacts of civilized living.

> *"Climb the mountains and get their good tidings. Nature's peace will flow into you as sunshine flows into trees. The winds will blow their own freshness into you, and the storms their energy, while cares will drop off like autumn leaves."*
> – John Muir

The urge to "escape into the woods" is a primal urge to return to our roots and find answers we lost along the road to domestication. However, this doesn't mean one has to strap on a backpack and hike 25 miles through the wilderness to feel centered again. All that needs to be done is to recognize our bodies and minds evolved under the requirements of wilderness survival. Our ability to properly measure the natural rhythms around us was critical to our success as a species. Attempting to navigate the stressful conditions of civilization remains an alien behavior to us. The quality of "wildness," a sense of intimacy and belonging to the natural world, developed as we became conscious beings, aware of self and our effects on others. "Wildness" was and remains an innate component of being human. Unfortunately, the structure of civilized society hinders the actualization of "wildness" by filling our lives with tasks and material goods that demand constant attention. There is a tendency to forget who we really are because of the energy required to keep up the civilized pace. Instead of acknowledging the "wildness" within, allowing it to inspire discovery and connectedness, we can be like crippled ships plying unknown seas, destined to remain lost and disorientated.

> *"I went to the woods because I wished to live deliberately, to front*
> *only the essential facts of life, and see if I could not learn what it had*
> *to teach, and not, when I came to die, discover that I had not lived."*
> – Henry David Thoreau

Allowing nature back inside allows us to see the world in a new way. It provides an emotional grounding from which we can derive strength in dealing with the contradictions and frustrations forced upon us by civilization. This is why the message of "wildness" is for all of us, not just those who have the luxury to leave it all behind and live in the backcountry. After all, most of us find our lives within civilization quite rewarding and we enjoy the benefits it provides for our families. Even Thoreau took advantage of nearby Concord during his two-year wilderness experience. Far from being a recluse, he was visited constantly by guests and frequently enjoyed walking into town. Leaving his place in the woods he wrote, "it seemed to me that I had several more lives to live and could not spare any more time for that one." But what he learned during his days with nature changed him forever. His words have been influencing generations ever since.

The intrinsic feature about rediscovering the "wildness" within is in its simplicity and accessibility. Following the teachings of a modern day philosopher is redundant because the knowledge lies within our own minds. A distant trip to some far-off place is unnecessary. As long as we can find a natural place uninterrupted by the rumblings of civilization, the location of one's inspiration is unimportant. For those of us in southern California, the closest and most accessible natural community is the chaparral. Like a coastal tide pool, the desert, or a forest, the chaparral has a unique collection of plant and animal populations intimately connected to its environment and each other. If given the opportunity, these missionaries from nature are willing teachers to help us reconnect with the "wildness" within. By watching them, distinguishing differences between each group, and learning the patterns they display, our senses become attuned again to the rhythms of nature; we become naturalists. As naturalists, our mental gyroscopes attain a new balance that incorporates an understanding of life beyond the confines of human society and reconnects with the wilderness, our original home. After finding our way back, we are grounded again and are able to build the resiliency required to thrive within the outside world of civilization; for indeed, civilization remains an alien place for the progeny of ancient naturalists. However, repudiation of society is unnecessary to return home. All that is required is an appreciation of what the natural world can offer as our true domicile.

When describing his own love of wilderness, John Muir made it clear that it, "was no solemn abjuration of the world," but rather, "I only went out for a walk, and finally concluded to stay out till sundown, for going out, I found, was really going in."

The Value of Vanishing Mud Holes

One of the flash points in efforts to preserve threatened natural resources has been the small, seasonal collections of water called vernal pools. Because of their homely appearance, they provide an excellent example of how the importance of becoming familiar with native open space and efforts to preserve it can violently collide with the desire to develop property by individuals unfamiliar with its value.

To the untrained eye, southern California vernal pools are easily overlooked. They can be anywhere from the size of a car tire to a football field. In San Diego County they are rarely more than 6 inches deep when full. For most of the year, they appear as lifeless bare spots surrounded by chaparral or disturbed coastal sage scrub. In fact, they are relatively unattractive to the average individual unfamiliar with them. During prolonged droughts, their desiccated condition can last several years. When sufficient rainfall does occur and their shallow basins fill, the pools seem naked, out of place. Perched high on mesa tops without feeding rivulets, the water source seems mysterious. The little pools look more like remnants of ancient dinosaur wallows than dynamic, living habitats.

Vernal pools experience an extreme version of the same climatic pressures characteristic of chaparral. The only organisms found in vernal pools are those capable of withstanding both weeks of inundation and months of mummifying aridity. Truly aquatic plants are excluded because pools are not wet long enough. Surrounding terrestrial vegetation is held back because it cannot tolerate the prolonged saturation. In San Diego County, water can remain in the pools for 45 days or more. This has been particularly important for the habitat's persistence since the invasion of exotic weeds. These weeds' intolerance to standing water prevents them from overwhelming pool areas as they have many other open spaces.

Each pool has its own, special combination of plants changing from year to year as environmental conditions vary. A prolific species one year may be absent the next. The pools are ephemeral, as are their patterns. Each spring holds a new surprise. If winter rains fill the pools, sometime in late April or early May standing water disappears. This is when the specialized vernal pool plants produce a flush of growth. Each species' place in the vernal pool assemblage is determined by its own adaptive tolerance to dehydration and ability to obtain required moisture through its roots. One of the most interesting is the diminutive, San Diego mesa mint *(Pogogyne abramsii)*. When in bloom, this tiny plant bursts forth with dozens of snapdragon-like flowers, highlighting the pool bed with what seems like a light purple fog. Its sparkling leaves add to the pageantry by filling the air with a rich, minty fragrance noticeable hundreds of feet away, not unlike breaking open an after dinner mint. This display is truly one of the best-kept secrets of the chaparral. While thousands travel elsewhere to view springtime flower displays, mesa mint and other vernal pool wildflowers quietly celebrate their ever-changing beauty, each pool displaying a different assortment of color and fragrance. The pools animal life is equally impressive with the most obvious representatives being spadefoot toads *(Spea hammondii)* and their favorite food, the San Diego fairy shrimp *(Branchinecta sandiegonensis)*.

San Diego County vernal pools were largely ignored in the early 1900s. The only attention they received was from thirsty livestock and ranchers who filled them in with dirt while attempting to level their land. Edith A. Purer presented one of the first scientific papers fully describing the habitat to the Ecological Society of America in

1937. A science teacher at San Diego's Hoover High School, Purer spent her summers studying the county's natural history and became San Diego's first female professional ecologist. She was also the consummate citizen naturalist.

Purer's survey of San Diego's Linda Vista Mesa described "thousands of pools filling the small depressions of the mesa, intercepted throughout by low, rounded hummocks" (Purer 1939). The key words here are "thousands of pools." Within 40 years of Purer's study none remained, having been filled in and covered over by the burgeoning growth of an expanding city. The remaining collections in the entire county would have disappeared as well if the scientific and environmental communities had not belatedly rediscovered them in the late 1970s and publicly revealed the treasure trove of specialized life forms living there. Half the plant species growing within California's vernal pools are found nowhere else on earth (Thorne 1981). This compares to 24% of all California plants being endemic, a remarkably large number itself.

In a sudden explosion of interest, vernal pools were regarded as deserving protection and endemic species were listed as endangered or sensitive. Unfortunately, a few developers did what they could to avoid the new restrictions by bulldozing pools on their land before the laws took effect. Pools continue to be destroyed today despite their legal protection. The few remaining represent a tiny fragment of a once large network of ephemeral wetlands punctuating the chaparral like liquid sapphires (photo 34).

Before development there were an estimated 28,500 acres of vernal pool habitat in San Diego County. Mesa tops, like the one where San Diego State University now rests, were covered with so many pools that aerial photographs taken back in 1928 look like carpets textured with thousands of tiny, evenly spaced dots. Those are all gone now. When the county was last inventoried in 1986, only 7% of the original vernal pool habitat remained (Bauder 1987). Fewer than 2,400 pools existed in 2001 (CWIS 2002). Of those surviving, some are temporarily protected in restricted areas like the Miramar Air Station or Camp Pendleton, but their futures are still uncertain; others remain vulnerable because they exist on private land.

In December 1999, owners of a protected vernal pool site off Arjons Drive, north of downtown San Diego in Mira Mesa, bulldozed a significant portion of the parcel, scrapping off native vegetation and filling in fragile pool basins. Destruction of a protected vernal pool site is a violation of state and federal Endangered Species Acts and would ordinarily be a clear signal for prosecution. However, in this situation, the city of San Diego issued a grading permit without first checking their files and completing a proper investigation. In response, the U.S. Fish and Wildlife Service and the California Department of Fish and Game co-authored a letter informing the city it violated state and federal regulations in addition to San Diego's own municipal code for issuing permits. The pools were protected in the 1980s by an agreement approved by the Fish and Wildlife Service with the land's former owner and that information was communicated during the sale via a signed letter from both real estate brokers involved (Larson 2000). Responsible parties claimed ignorance and Michael Cafagna, co-owner of the property, denied any wrongdoing. In late 2002, San Diego County prosecutors quietly dropped the case.

"We looked carefully at all the players involved, looked at the liability and decided it didn't meet the standard," said Deputy District Attorney Karen Doty. "It didn't rise to the level of prosecution and provable evidence (McDonald 2002)."

Even under the protection of government sanctioned conservation initiatives, protection of sensitive habitats is not guaranteed. Neither federal nor state Endangered Species Acts provide complete protection of species listed as endangered. Developers are frequently granted permits for the "taking" or killing of protected species. In an attempt to turn over the stewardship of endangered species and habitat preservation to local governments, Habitat Conservation Plans have been implemented. For example, the city of San Diego approved their Multiple Species Conservation Program (MSCP) in 1997 and promoted it as a rational way to balance development with the preservation of the area's remaining wild habitats.

As with many compromises involving competing interests, the MSCP has a significant number of open-ended definitions allowing agencies tremendous flexibility. Specifically, the section applying to vernal pools allows for continued destruction as long as everyone tries to minimize impacts. Section 3.3.3 states, "For vernal pools and narrow endemic species, the jurisdictions and other participants will specify measures in their subarea plans to ensure that impacts to these resources are avoided to the maximum extent possible" (MSCP 1998). The section is open to interpretation as it allows agencies to define the meaning of "maximum extent."

Shortly after the MSCP was approved, a major development was approved in San Diego on Mira Mesa Blvd, next to Interstate 15. On the site were 67 endangered vernal pools recognized by the plan as deserving protection. The developers, however, indicated they could not profitably build unless they were able to use the entire parcel. As a result "maximum extent" was translated into a compromise favoring development over preservation. The consequence was that one vernal pool was salvaged. Today, you can view the remaining pool at the end of a cul-de-sac on Hillery Drive. Under the crowded gaze of multistory homes, surrounded by black asphalt, a stylish rod iron fence encloses the sole remnant of a once dynamic vernal pool complex. The 60 x 40 foot preserve is marked with a plaque and 3 park benches (photo35). The name of the apartment complex that now covers the site where the vernal pool complex once existed is called "Legacy."

Your Home

Can a bare spot in a patch of shrubbery elicit respect and be considered worthy of preservation? It can if we, as southern Californians, become as familiar with the natural world around us as we are with the freeways we drive. Understanding how seasonal patterns shape the landscape, which manzanita species resprouts, and what makes vernal pools so unique, alters forever how we value the chaparral covered hillsides observed on the way home from work. The knowledge gained may very well help save our homes and family during the next wildfire. By recognizing and being able to identify native species and their surrounding environment, we begin to see their habitat as worthy of attention and stewardship. Wild space becomes our space as well. And although economic pressures will continue to shape the future of our wildlands, an educated public armed with the knowledge of what's out there can make sure its preservation, not reduction or mitigation, is the primary consideration. All it requires is a guidebook or two and some time to take a few walks (photo 36).

Recall Mr. Banks in the movie "Mary Poppins." Inspired by Mary's insightful wisdom, Mr. Banks finally rediscovers what is really important in life. After spending a career locked up within the confines of a dusty, old bank and ignoring his family, he resigns in a fit of complete irrationality. As the movie ends he is last seen laughing with his kids in a park while flying a kite. A few of his bank managers are there as well.

Consider the chaparral your Mary Poppins. Stop for a moment and look up at the green hills. Whistle back at a wrentit. Shout *Arctostaphylos* as loud as you can. Better yet, take a quartzite cobble and throw it through your television set. Get outside. Close your eyes and listen. With nature serving as the proper tinder, rekindle your native inquisitiveness for all things wild. Use this book to fan the flames.

The Essential 64 Plants and Animals
of Southern California Chaparral

This chapter is a photo identification guide describing the most common plants and animals a visitor to the chaparral in southern California will most likely observe. Only the red diamond rattlesnake and the mountain mahogany hairstreak are uncommon, but are included because they represent definitive chaparral creatures in their group. The plant selection is based on over thirty years of wandering the backcountry and noting the species most commonly seen. Although the majority of the experiences upon which this list has been developed occurred in San Diego County, most of these organisms will be found throughout the shrublands of southwestern California.

The information in the identification box below each photograph has been obtained through field research and published sources. The "Best Months to Observe Flowering" ranges were established through field observations and crosschecked with "A Flora of San Diego County, California" (Beauchamp 1986).

The plant species have been arranged by family, then by species name. The families are according to the latest taxonomic research as described by the California Native Plant Society (Dean 2004, Kelch 2004, and Olmstead 2004) and therefore differ slightly from the Jepson Manual, "Higher Plants of California" (Hickman 1993).

All the photographs in this guide have been taken by the author except for those listed below. I am indebted to these photographers who were so willing to share their work and help fill in some important gaps:

1. Big-ear woodrat by Scott Tremor
4. Mountain mahogany hairstreak by Michael Klein
29. Silk-tassel bush (both photos) by Gabi McLean
37. Woolly Indian paintbrush by Gabi McLean
46. Delphinium parryi by Gabi McLean
60. Wild hyacinths in field by Gabi McLean

Key to Photo Identification Guide

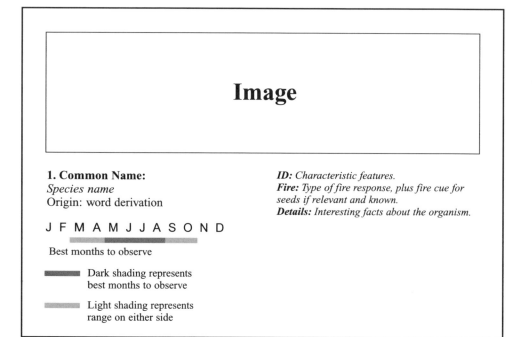

1. Common Name:
Species name
Origin: word derivation

J F M A M J J A S O N D

Best months to observe

▬▬▬▬ Dark shading represents
best months to observe

▬▬▬▬ Light shading represents
range on either side

ID: Characteristic features.
Fire: Type of fire response, plus fire cue for
seeds if relevant and known.
Details: Interesting facts about the organism.

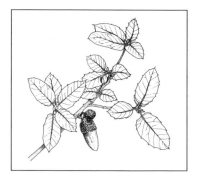

Quercus wislizenii

Definitions/Abbreviations

C/S: Charred wood and smoke as a fire cue.

Dioecious: Plants with separate male and female individuals.

Disciform flower head: For a member of the sunflower family (Asteraceae) which has flower heads with a combination of tiny disk flowers and female pistillate flowers in the same head.

Discoid flower head: For a member of the sunflower family (Asteraceae) which has only disk flowers in its flower head.

Endemic fire follower: Fire dependant annual. Seeds require a fire cue to germinate.

Facultative seeder: Adult plant resprouts after a fire. Seeds germinate post-fire.

Fire dependant: Seeds require a fire cue to germinate.

Fire independent: Plant has no relevant reproductive response to fire.

Frequent fire follower: Annual with germination enhanced by fire.

Heat: fire cue.

Ligulate flower head: For a member of the sunflower family (Asteraceae) which has only a cluster of five-lobed bisexual ray flowers in its flower head.

Monoecious: Plants with separate male and female flowers on the same individual.

Nascent inflorescence: When flower buds form in the late summer, remain dormant, then open late winter or early spring.

Obligate resprouter: Adult plant resprouts after a fire. No germination post-fire.

Obligate seeder: Adult plant dies in the fire. Seeds germinate post-fire.

Opportunistic: Plants that have no particular response to fire, but will colonize open spaces afterwards if given the opportunity.

Polymorphic: Plant produces various types of seeds that have different germination requirements.

Radiate flower head: For a member of the sunflower family (Asteraceae) that has both a central core of disk flowers surrounded by three-lobed ray flowers.

Semi-summer deciduous: Plants that lose most of their leaves during the summer months.

The Essential 64 Plants and Animals of Southern California Chaparral

KEY:
Resp: resprouter
S: Seeder
FF: Fire Follower

Animals

#	COMMON NAME	SPECIES
1	Big-eared woodrat	*Neotoma macrotis*
2	Wrentit	*Chamaea fasciata*
3	Red diamond rattlesnake	*Crotalus exsul*
4	Mt. mahogany hairstreak	*Satyrium tetra*

Plants

#	COMMON NAME	SPECIES	FAMILY	FIRE RESPONSE
5	Laurel sumac	*Malosma laurina*	Anacardiaceae	Facultative S
6	Lemonadeberry	*Rhus integrifolia*	Anacardiaceae	Facultative S
7	Sugar bush	*Rhus ovata*	Anacardiaceae	Facultative S
8	Poison oak	*Toxicodendron diversilobum*	Anacardiaceae	Obligate S
9	Acourtia	*Acourtia microcephala*	Asteraceae	Obligate Resp
10	California Sagebrush	*Artemisia californica*	Asteraceae	Facultative S
11	Everlasting	*Gnaphalium californicum* *Gnaphalium canescens*	Asteraceae	Facultative S
12	Canyon sunflower	*Venegasia carpesioides*	Asteraceae	Facultative S
13	Whispering bells	*Emmenanthe penduliflora*	Boraginaceae	Endemic FF
14	Yerba santa	*Eriodicyton crassifolium*	Boraginaceae	Facultative S
15	Phacelia	*Phacelia brachyloba* *Phacelia cicutaria hispida* *Phacelia grandiflora* *Phacelia parryi*		Endemic and Frequent FF species
16	Popcorn flower	*Cryptantha* species *Plagiobothrys* species	Boraginaceae	Frequent FF some opportunistic
17	Southern honeysuckle	*Lonicera subpicata*	Caprifoliaceae	Obligate Resp
18	Indian pink	*Silene californica*	Caryophyllaceae	Facultative S
19	Yellow rock-rose	*Helianthemum scoparium*	Cistaceae	Obligate S
20	Morning glory	*Calystegia macrostegia*	Convolvulaceae	Facultative S
21	Dodder	*Cuscuta californica*	Convolvulaceae	Obligate S
22	Wild cucumber	*Marah macrocarpus*	Cucurbitaceae	Obligate Resp
23	Manzanita	*Arctostaphylos glandulosa* *Arctostaphylos glauca* *Arctostaphylos pungens*	Ericaceae	Mostly Obligate S some Facultative S
24	Manzanita-like species	*Comarostaphylis diversifolia* *Xylococcus bicolor*	Ericaceae	Obligate Resp
25	Chaparral pea	*Lathyrus vestitus alefeldii*	Fabaceae	Obligate Resp

26	Deerweed	*Lotus scoparius*	Fabaceae	Obligate S
27	Lupine	*Lupinus bicolor*	Fabaceae	Frequent FF mostly
		Lupinus hirsutissimus		
28	Scrub oak	*Quercus berberidifolia*	Fagaceae	Obligate Resp
29	Silk-tassel bush	*Garrya veatchii*	Garryaceae	Facultative S
30	Canchalagua	*Centaurium venustum*	Gentianaceae	Opportunistic
31	Fuchsia-flowered gooseberry	*Ribes speciosum*	Grossulariaceae	Facultative S
32	White flowering current	*Ribes indecorum*	Grossulariaceae	Facultative S
33	Sage	*Salvia apiana*	Lamiaceae	Facultative S
		Salvia mellifera		
34	California fremontia	*Fremontodendron californicum*	Malvaceae	Facultative S
35	Chaparral mallow	*Malacothamnus fasciculatus*	Malvaceae	Facultative S
36	Checkerbloom	*Sidalcea malvaeflora sparsifolia*	Malvaceae	Facultative S?
37	Woolly Indian paintbrush	*Castilleja foliolosa*	Orobanchaceae	Obligate Resp
38	California peony	*Paeonia californica*	Paeoniaceae	Obligate Resp
39	Bush poppy	*Dendromecon rigida*	Papaveraceae	Obligate S
40	Golden eardrops	*Dicentra chrysantha*	Papaveraceae	Endemic FF
41	Fire poppy	*Papaver californicum*	Papaveraceae	Endemic FF
42	Matilija poppy	*Romneya coulteri*	Papaveraceae	Facultative S
43	Bush monkey flower	*Mimulus aurantiacus*	Phrymaceae	Facultative S
44	California buckwheat	*Eriogonum fasciculatum*	Polygonaceae	Facultative S
45	Ropevine	*Clematis pauciflora*	Ranunculaceae	Facultative S
46	Larkspur	*Delphinium parryi*	Ranunculaceae	Facultative S
		Delphinium cardinale		
47	Ceanothus (non-sprout)	*Ceanothus greggii*	Rhamnaceae	Obligate S
		Ceanothus tomentosus		
48	Ceanothus (sprouter)	*Ceanothus leucodermis*	Rhamnaceae	Facultative S
49	Spiny redberry	*Rhamnus crocea*	Rhamnaccac	Obligate Resp
50	Chamise	*Adenostoma fasciculatum*	Rosaceae	Facultative S
51	Mountain-mahogany	*Cercocarpus betuloides*	Rosaceae	Obligate Resp
52	Toyon	*Heteromeles arbutifolia*	Rosaceae	Obligate Resp
53	Bushrue	*Cneoridium dumosum*	Rutaceae	Obligate Resp
54	Snapdragon	*Antirrhinum coulterianum*	Veronicaceae	Frequent FF
		Antirrhinum nuttallianum		
55	Small-flower soap plant	*Chlorogalum parviflorum*	Agavaceae	Obligate Resp
56	Chaparral yucca	*Hesperoyucca whipplei*	Agavaceae	Obligate Resp
57	Mariposa lily	*Calochortus splendens*	Liliaceae	Obligate Resp
		Caolchortus weedii		
58	Fremont's camus	*Zigadenus fremontii*	Melanthiaceae	Obligate Resp
59	Purple needlegrass	*Nassella pulchra*	Poaceae	Obligate Resp
60	Wild hyacinth	*Dichelostemma capitatum*	Themidaceae	Obligate Resp
61	Mustard	*Brassica nigra*	Brassicaceae	Opportunistic
		Herschfeldia incana		
62	Filaree	*Erodium botrys*	Geraniaceae	Opportunistic
		Erodium cicutarium		
		Erodium moschatum		
63	Wild oats	*Avena fatua*	Poaceae	Opportunistic
64	Bromus	*Bromus diandrus*	Poaceae	Opportunisitic
		Bromus madritensis rubens		

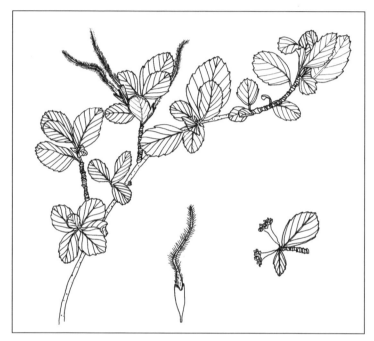

Cercocarpus betuloides

1. Big-eared woodrat: *Neotoma macrotis*

J F M A M J J A S O N D

Best months to observe

ID: Body up to 9" long. Sooty patch on top of feet. Tail with short hairs.
Nest: Up to 6 ft. high pile of sticks. Used by successive generations.
Diet: Specializes on oak leaves, stems.
Details: Normally nocturnal.

2. Wrentit: *Chamaea fasciata*

J F M A M J J A S O N D

Best months to observe

ID: Descending, bouncing ping-pong ball, whistle.
Nest: Cup of bark strips and grass, held together by spider silk.
Diet: Insects, some fruit.
Details: A secretive little bird also known as "the voice of the chaparral." 1-2 acre territories. Mates for life.

3. Red diamond rattlesnake:
Crotalus exsul

J F M A M J J A S O N D

Best months to observe

ID: 2-4 ft. long. Reddish or tan with contrasting black and white rattle at end.
Diet: Rodents, other small mammals, birds.
Details: A federal and state species of special concern. Ranges southern California into Baja. A related species also found in rocky chaparral areas southern pacific rattlesnake (Crotalus viridis).

4. Mountain mahogany hairstreak:
Satyrium tetra

J F M A M J J A S O N D

Best months to observe

ID: Brownish with tiny tails on hindwings.
Diet: Caterpillar eats mountain mahogany. Adults visit California buckwheat flowers.
Details: Overwinters in the egg stage. Pupa is formed in early June and attached to twig by a silken girdle around its midsection.

5. Laurel Sumac: *Malosma laurina*
Origins: *Mal*(L) = apple, *osm*(G) = smell of the leaf when broken open, *laur*(L) = the laurel.

J F M A M J J A S O N D

Best months to observe flowering

ID: Evergreen shrub up to 15ft.
Fire: Facultative seeder. Heat.
Details: The leaves look somewhat like a taco shell by their shape. May cause a mild rash like poison oak. Gummy seed coat must be leached off for germination.

6. Lemonadeberry: *Rhus integrifolia*
Origins: *Rhus*(G) = ancient name for sumac, *integ*(L) = whole, *folia*(L) = leaf.

J F M A M J J A S O N D

Best months to observe flowering

ID: Evergreen shrub up to 10ft.
Fire: Facultative seeder. Heat.
Features: During late summer, each flower produces a flat, reddish-brown drupe Covered with a sour tasting white paste, hence the common name. Leaves are quite thick and may or may not have spiky edges. Common along coast.

7. Sugar bush: *Rhus ovata*
Origins: *Rhus*(G) = ancient for sumac,
ovat(L) = egg shaped for the leaves.

J F M A M J J A S O N D

Best months to observe flowering

ID: Evergreen shrub or tree 6-30 ft.
Fire: Facultative seeder. Heat.
Details: Similar to lemonadeberry, but
generally found at higher elevations and desert
edge. Thick leaves. Excellent landscaping shrub.

8. Poison oak: *Toxicodendron diversilobum*
Origins: *Toxic*(L) = poison, *dendron*(G) =
tree, *diversi*(L) = various, *lob*(G) = lobes.

J F M A M J J A S O N D

Best months to observe flowering

ID: Deciduous, vine-like shrub 4-8 ft. with long
stems twining through shrubs. Greenish-white
flowers.
Fire: Obligate resprouter.
Features: Toxic dermatitis reaction to this plant
is an immune response by the body to oily
chemicals. Relative of cashews. Dioecious.

9. Acourtia: *Acourtia microcephala*
Origins: *Acourt* after amatueur English
botanist Mary A'Court, *micro*(G) = small,
cephal(G) = the head after flower clusters.

J F M A M J J A S O N D

Best months to observe flowering

ID: *Herbaceous perennial, 1-4 ft.*
Fire: *Obligate resprouter.*
Details: *Lavender flwrs are unique. Each
flwr corolla is split in half, one blade with
three lobes, one with two. Represents a
transitional form in Asteraceae evolution.*

10. California Sagebrush: *Artemisia
californica* Origins: *Artemis*(G) = Greek
goddess of the hunt.

J F M A M J J A S O N D

Best months to observe flowering

ID: *A sparse shrub 2-5 ft. tall. Semi-summer
deciduous. COASTAL SAGE SCRUB.*
Fire: *Facultative seeder. C/S.*
Details: *Frothy mass on stems is produced
by nymphs of spittle bugs (right). In the
sunflower family (Asteraceae) so not a true
sage. Sage-like aromatic scent.*

11. Everlasting: *Gnaphalium* species
Origins: *Gnaphal*(G) = lock of wool from the woolly appearance of the leaves in several species.

ID: Annual or perennial 8"-2.5ft tall.
Fire: Facultative seeder (perennials). C/S.
Details: Disciform flower heads surrounded by papery bracts. "Everlasting" refers to how long flowers last. Large genus. G. californicum *(annual or bi-) on left. Most have a woolly covering on their leaves as seen on right with* G. canescens *(perennial).*

G. californicum (L)
J F M A M J J A S O N D

Best months to observe flowering

G. canescens (R)
J F M A M J J A S O N D

Best months to observe flowering

12. Canyon Sunflower: *Venegasia carpesioides* Origins: After Miguel Venegas (1680-1764), a Californian missionary, *Carpesium,* an Eurasian asteraceae species, *oid*(G) = like.

J F M A M J J A S O N D

Best months to observe flowering

ID: Shrub up to 5 ft. tall. Shady, wooded slopes.
Fire: Facultative seeder.
Details: Bright yellow disc and ray flowers bloom atop purplish stems. Only species in genus.

13. Whispering bells: *Emmenanthe penduliflora* Origins: *Emmen*(G) = faithful for how the flwr has a persistent corolla, *pend*(L) = hanging for how the flwrs dangle.

J F M A M J J A S O N D

Best months to observe flowering

ID: Annual. Sticky leaves. 2"-2.5 ft.
Fire: Endemic fire follower. C/S.
Details: Will cover entire hillsides after a fire. Flwrs yellow and make a whispering sound when dry while brushing against each other.

14. Yerba santa: *Eriodictyon crassifolium* Origins: *Erio*(G) = wool, *dictyo*(G) = net after the woolly, soft hairs on the leaves, *crass*(L) = thick, *folium*(L) = leaf.

J F M A M J J A S O N D

Best months to observe flowering

ID: Sparse shrub up to 6 tall with flexible branches, woody base.
Fire: Facultative seeder. C/S/Heat.
Details: Spreads by sprouting from runners. Used as cold remedy by Native Americans, Spanish settlers, early pharmacists.

15. Phacelia: *Phacelia* species Origin: *Phacel*(G) = bundle or cluster for how genus flwrs are in curled clusters (coiled cyme).

ID: Annuals up to 3 ft.
Fire: Some like P. cicutaria *(left) are frequent fire followers, others like P.* brachyloba, P. grandiflora *and P.* parryi *(right) are endemics. C/S.*
Details: Flwrs on many species are on curled, sticky stalks covered with hairs and look like fuzzy caterpillars.

P. cicutaria (L)

J F M A M J J A S O N D

Best months to observe flowering

P. parryi (R)

J F M A M J J A S O N D

Best months to observe flowering

16. Popcorn flowers: *Cryptantha* and *Plagiobothrys* species. Origins: *Crypt*(G) = hidden, *anth*(G) = flower referring to tiny size, *Plagi*(G) = sideways and *bothr*(G) = pit for scar on nutlet (seed).

J F M A M J J A S O N D

Best months to observe flowering

ID: Annual 1"-1.5ft.
Fire: Cyptantha *frequent fire followers.* Plagiobothrys *mostly opportunistic. C/S*
Details: Tiny, abundant bloomers with hairy stems, frequently in groups. Large number of species. Difficult to identify, requiring examination of tiny seeds (nutlets) and hairs with a 20X hand lens.

17. Southern Honeysuckle: *Lonicera subspicata* Origins: After Adam Lonitzer, 16th century German botanist, *sub*(L) = under, *spica*(L) = a spike for some unknown characteristic of the plant.

J F M A M J J A S O N D

Best months to observe flowering

ID: *Evergreen shrub-vine up to 6 ft. Often twinning around other shrubs with long reddish stems.*
Fire: *Obligate resprouter.*
Details: *Reddish or yellow berries appear in the summer. Hard to notice except during the blooming season since its foliage blends into surrounding shrubbery.*

18. Indian Pink: *Silene californica* Origins: *Silene*(G) = intoxicated Greek god who was covered in foam for some species stickiness.

J F M A M J J A S O N D

Best months to observe flowering

ID: *Herbaceous perennial 3"-2 ft.*
Fire: *Facultative seeder.*
Details: *Bright red flowers on long stalks, petals with serrated edges. "Pink" refers to the "pinked" petal edges, not the flower color.*

19. Yellow rock-rose: *Helianthemum scoparium* Origins: *Helia*(G) = the sun, *anthem*(G) = flower, *Scop*(L) = broom and *ari*(G) = much, for the plant's stiff, broom-like appearance.

J F M A M J J A S O N D

Best months to observe flowering

ID: Perennial shrub 12-24". Thin leaves which are lost in drought.
Fire: Obligate seeder. Heat.
Details: Flowers typically open perpendicular to the ground. Lower stamens will bend themselves upward around the ovary to join the others in order to point toward the sun.

20. Morning Glory: *Calystegia macrostegia* Origins: *Caly*(G) = calyx referring to green leaf-like sepals under white blossom, *steg*(G) = covered, *macro*(G) = for large, fused petals.

J F M A M J J A S O N D

Best months to observe flowering

ID: Perennial vine with slender, climbing or trailing stems as long as 12 feet.
Fire: Facultative seeder. Heat.
Details: Six distinct subspecies in southern California. One subspecies found only on the southern Channel Islands. Most intergrade with each other. Resprout from woody caudex.

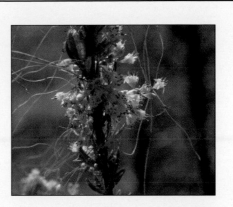

21. Dodder: *Cuscuta californica*
Origins: *Cuscuta*(Arabic) = dodder.
Another common name is witches hair.

J F M A M J J A S O N D

Best months to observe flowering

ID: Annual, leafless, rootless, parasitic herb with thin, orange, twining stems. Common on buckwheat, laurel sumac.
Fire: Obligate seeder.
Details: Does not photosynthesize. Little rounded organs (haustoria) penetrate deeply into the host plants tissues for energy and nutrients.

22. Wild cucumber: *Marah macrocarpus*
Origins: After bitter waters of Marah mentioned in Exodus 15:23 for plant's taste, *macro*(G) = large and *carpus*(G) = a fruit after large, spiny seed pod.

J F M A M J J A S O N D

Best months to observe flowering

ID: Perennial vine with 5-20 ft. twining stems. Separate male and female flowers on the same plant (monoeicious).
Fire: Obligate resprouter.
Details: During drought, plant survives as a huge underground tuber (100 pounds or more). Spiky, tennis ball sized seed pods. Dicot geophyte.

23. Manzanita: *Arctostaphylos* species
Origins: *Arcto*(G) = bear and *staphylo*(G) = bunch of grapes since bears, as well as other animals, enjoy the plant's fruit.

ID: Woody shrub up to 18 ft. with smooth, reddish bark, urn-shaped flwrs.
Fire: Obligate seeders (mostly). C/S.
Details: Alternate, stiff leaves point up to reduce sunlight exposure. Nascent inflorescence. Another common species, A. glandulosa *is similar to* A. glauca *but has fuzzy leaves and is a facultative seeder.*

A. pungens (L)
J F M A M J J A S O N D

Best months to observe flowering

A. glauca (R)
J F M A M J J A S O N D

Best months to observe flowering

24. Manzanita-like species: *Xylococcus* (l) and *Comarostaphylis* (r) species
Origins: *Xylo*(G) = wood, *coccus*(G) = berry for little seed inside fruit, *Com*(L) = together, *staphyl*(G) = cluster for berries.

Size: Woody shrubs. Leaf edges curl under.
Fire: Obligate resprouters. C/S ?
Details: X. bicolor *(left) reddish bark. May be sterile as seedlings have not been observed.* C. diversifolia *(r) shredded gray bark, serrated leaves, red textured berries.*

X. bicolor (L)
J F M A M J J A S O N D

Best months to observe flowering

C. diversifolia (R)
J F M A M J J A S O N D

Best months to observe flowering

25. Chaparral pea: *Lathyrus vestitus ale-feldii* Origins: *Lathyrus*(G) = ancient name, *vest*(L) = coat for ?

J F M A M J J A S O N D

Best months to observe flowering

ID: Herbaceous perennial vine. Thin stems.
Fire: Obligate Resprouter.
Details: Intergrades with other subspecies. Winds through shrubbery.

26. Deerweed: *Lotus scoparius*
(var. *scoparius*) Origin: *Lotus*(G) plant of Greek legend that produced fruit causing dreamy forgetfulness, *scop*(L) = broom for broom like appearance.

J F M A M J J A S O N D

Best months to observe flowering

ID: Subshrub, 1-3 ft.
Fire: Obligate seeder. Heat.
Details: Flowers start yellow, turn orange-red as they age. In late summer, most leaves drop and stems turn golden brown. Polymorphic seeds.

27. Lupine: *Lupinus* species
Origin: *Lupi*(L) = wolf for the mistaken belief these plants robbed nitrogen from soil.

L. bicolor (L)

J F M A M J J A S O N D

Best months to observe flowering

L. hirutissimus (R)

J F M A M J J A S O N D

Best months to observe flowering

ID: *From small 2" annuals to shrubs with flower stalks over 5ft high. Flwrs purple, white, red, or yellow.*
Fire: *Mostly frequent fire followers. Heat?*
Details: *Hand-shaped leaves. L. bicolor on left abundant in open and disturbed areas. Stinging hairs on L. hirutissimus, right. All species add nitrogen to soil.*

28. Scrub oak: *Quercus berberidifolia*
Origin: *Quercus* from two Celtic words: *quer* = fine, *cuez* = tree, *berberi*(L) after a genus in the Berberidaceae family with similar leaves, *folia*(L) = leaf.

J F M A M J J A S O N D

Best months to observe flowering

ID: *Evergreen 3-10 ft. shrub, often becomes tree-like. Separate male and female flowers on the same plant (monoecious).*
Fire: *Obligate resprouter.*
Details: *Red or brown swellings on stems (galls) are caused by a tiny wasp. Native Americans used acorns, but not preferred. Coastal species, Q. dumosa, similar.*

29. Silk-tassel bush: *Garrya veatchii*
Origin: For N. Garry, deputy governor
Hudson's Bay Company and J.A. Veatch of
the California Academy of Science.

J F M A M J J A S O N D

Best months to observe flowering

ID: Shrub up to 6 ft. Opposite leaves.
Fire: Facultative seeder. C/S.
Details: A characteristic chaparral species.
Nascent inflorescence.

30. Canchalagua: *Centaurium venustum*
Origin: *Centaur*(L) = mythical character
who discovered the plant's medicinal uses
and *venust*(L) = charming for the plant's
delicate beauty.

J F M A M J J A S O N D

Best months to observe flowering

ID: Annual usually 4-10", but up to 2 ft.
Variations from dark pink to pure white.
Fire: Opportunistic.
Details: Five anthers twist into wonderful
spirals. Used as fever reducer by early
settlers. Common name "con-cha-log-wah".

31. Fuchsia-flowered gooseberry: *Ribes speciosum* Origins: *Ribes*(Arabic) = for plants of this genus, *specios*(L) = showy.

J F M A M J J A S O N D

Best months to observe flowering

ID: Spiny shrub 3-6 ft. tall. Semi-summer deciduous. Spines on stems.
Fire: *Facultative seeder.*
Details: *Red, bristly berries and round, shiny leaves make the plant quite beautiful. Attracts hummingbirds.*

32. White-flowering currant:
Ribes indecorum Origins: *Ribes*(Arabic) = for plants of this genus.

J F M A M J J A S O N D

Best months to observe flowering

ID: Deciduous shrub up to 10 ft.
Fire: *Facultative seeder.*
Details: *One of the earliest bloomers in the chaparral. Fruit valuable food for birds.*

33. Sage: *Salvia* species   Origins: *Salveo*(L) = "to save" from the ancient medicinal use of a plant by the same name.

J F M A M J J A S O N D

Best months to observe flowering

ID: *Shrubs 3-6 ft. tall with brittle branches. Semi-summer deciduous. Dimorphic (2-sized) leaves.* COASTAL SAGE SCRUB.
Fire: *Facultative seeder. C/S/Heat.*
Details: *Twirl flower stems between your fingers and feel four edges. Left, white sage (S. apiana). Right, black sage (S. mellifera). Rich, minty scent.*

34. California fremontia: *Fremontodendron californicum* Origins: For John C. Fremont, western explorer, *dendro*(G) = tree.

J F M A M J J A S O N D

Best months to observe flowering

ID: *Large shrub up to 15 ft.*
Fire: *Facultative seeder. C/S/Heat.*
Details: *Leaves covered with tiny, stellar shaped hairs (pubescence). One of the most beautiful chaparral flowering shrubs. Good hillside and yard plant.*

35. Chaparral mallow: *Malacothamnus fasciculatus* Origins: *Malac*(G) = soft, *thamn*(G) = shrub, *fasci-cul*(L) = little bundle.

J F M A M J J A S O N D

Best months to observe flowering

ID: Shrub up to 6 ft.
Fire: Facultative seeder. Heat.
Details: Tiny star-like hairs on leaves.
Roots of another mallow, the marsh mallow
(Althaea officinalis), *plus sugar, were used to make the original treat.*

36. Checkerbloom: *Sidalcea malvaeflora* Origins: *Sida*(G), *alcea*(G) = names for mallow, *malv*(L) = mallow, *flor*(L) = flower.

J F M A M J J A S O N D

Best months to observe flowering

ID: Herbaceous perennial with flower stems reaching out up to 2 ft.
Fire: Resprouts. More study needed.
Details: Lower leaves rounded, upper leaves are deeply clefted. Flower styles fan out into delicate curls. Spread by rhizomes.

37. Woolly Indian paintbrush: *Castilleja foliolosa* Origins: Domingo Castillejo was a Spanish botanist in the late 1700's and *foli*(L) = leaf.

J F M A M J J A S O N D

Best months to observe flowering

ID: Perennial or subshrub 1-2 ft tall.
Fire: Obligate resprouter.
Details: Most of the red is not part of the flower, but colored leaf-like bracts. Actual bloom is a narrow tube formed by two lips that open slightly at the top. Look carefully and you'll see the stamen and style. Parasitizes roots of neighboring plants.

38. California peony: *Paeonia californica* Origins: *Paeon*(G) = the mythical physician to the Greek gods.

J F M A M J J A S O N D

Best months to observe flowering

ID: Herbaceous perennial up to 1.5 ft. tall.
Fleshy leaves. Shady areas. Survives drought as fleshy root tuber.
Fire: Obligate resprouter.
Details: Blossom forms on a single stem nods downward. Since maroon petals never really fully open, flower must be lifted up to appreciate. Extremely primitive dicot.

39. Bush poppy: *Dendromecon rigida*
Origins: *Dendro*(L) = tree, *mecon*(G) =
poppy, *rigid*(L) = stiff.

J F M A M J J A S O N D

Best months to observe flowering

ID: Shrub 3-10 ft.
Fire: Obligate seeder. C/S.
Details: Extremely drought tolerate and an
excellent yard plant.

40. Golden eardrops: *Dicentra chrysantha*
Origins: *Di*(G) and *-centr*(L) = two spur for
pointed outer petals, *chrys*(G) = gold.

J F M A M J J A S O N D

Best months to observe flowering

ID: Short-lived herbaceous perennial,1-5 ft.
Fire: Endemic fire follower. C/S.
Details: Seeds must ripen in soil for a year
and then will germinate only if exposed to
smoke/charred wood. Fern-like leaves. Long
taproot. Toxic to livestock.

41. Fire poppy: *Papaver californicum*
Origins: *Papaver*(L) = poppy.

J F M A M J J A S O N D
▬▬

Best months to observe flowering

ID: Annual. Flwr stem 2"-1 ft. tall.
Fire: Endemic fire follower. C/S.
Details: Seeds germinate freely in lab without fire cue. Germination possibly inhibited by factors in the soil.

42. Matilija poppy: *Romneya coulteri*
Origins: T. Romney Robinson, Irish astronomer and friend of Thomas Coulter, the original collector (Coulter was already used as a genus name).

J F M A M J J A S O N D
▬▬▬

Best months to observe flowering

ID: Shrub emerging from single stalks up to 6 ft. tall.
Fire: Facultative seeder. C/S.
Details: Largest California native wildflower. Spreads by creeping rhizomes. Flowers look like sunny-side up fried eggs.

43. Bush monkey flower: *Mimulus aurantiacus* Origins: *Mim*(G) = an actor or little mine for the face-like flower and *aurantiacus*(L) = orange, orange-yellow or orange-red.

J F M A M J J A S O N D

Best months to observe flowering

ID: *Herbaceous subshrub, 1-3 ft. tall.*
Fire: *Facultative seeder. C/S/Heat.*
Details: *Stigma closes upon touch.*
Tremendous color variation from orange to deep red. Several former species have been combined into this one. Many hybridizing, local forms. Further investigation is needed to clarify classification.

44. California buckwheat: *Eriogonum fasciculatum* Origins: *Erio*(G) = wool, *gony*(G) = knee for hairy joints (nodes) on stems of some species, *fascia*(L) = bundle referring to plant's leaf clusters.

J F M A M J J A S O N D

Best months to observe flowering

ID: *Shrub, narrow stems 2-4 ft. high. White flower clusters turn amber during drought.* *COASTAL SAGE SCRUB.*
Fire: *Facultative seeder. C/S/Heat.*
Details: *Large native California genus. Small leaves attached to stem in little bundles. Buckwheat flour is made from the seeds of a cultivated Eriogonum.*

45. Ropevine: *Clematis pauciflora*
Origins: *Clem*(G) = twig, *pauc* (L) = few,
flor(L) = flower.

J F M A M J J A S O N D

Best months to observe flowering

ID: Woody vine climbing into other trees and bushes. Underside of sepals hairy.
Fire: Facultative seeder. C/S.
Details: Flowers have 30-50 stamen each. Tiny fruits with long, hairy tails form shaggy clusters.

46. Larkspur: *Delphinium* species
Origins: *Delphi*(G) = dolphin after the shape of the flower.

D. cardinale (L)
J F M A M J J A S O N D

Best months to observe flowering

D. parryi (R)
J F M A M J J A S O N D

Best months to observe flowering

ID: Herbaceous perennials with flower stems up to 6 ft. high. Survives drought as a fibrous or fleshy root. Many highly toxic.
Fire: Obligate resprouter.
Details: Flowers have a unique structure formed by uppermost sepal stretching into a nectar-filled spur. Attracts hummingbirds. D. cardinale *on left.* D. parryi *on right.*

47. Non-resprouting ceanothus:
Ceanothus species Origins: *Ceanothus*(G) = a thorny plant or thistle after the stiff branches.

ID: Mostly evergreen shrubs 6-12 ft. tall. Flowers white to purple.
Fire: Obligate seeders. About 20 out of 40 ceanothus do not resprout (mostly in the subgenus Cerastes). Heat.
Details: Major chaparral component. Returns nitrogen to the soil. Left, C. greggii. Right, C. tomentosus.

C. greggii (L)

J F M A M J J A S O N D

Best months to observe flowering

C. tomentosus (R)

J F M A M J J A S O N D

Best months to observe flowering

---

48. Resprouting ceanothus (example species): Whitebark or whitethorn ceanothus, *Ceanothus leucodermis* Origins: *leuco*(G) = white, *derm*(G) = skin for pale colored bark.

J F M A M J J A S O N D

Best months to observe flowering

ID: Evergreen shrub up to 12 ft.
Fire: Facultative seeders. About half of 40 ceanothus species resprout (mostly in the subgenus Ceanothus). Heat.
Details: Stiff thorns. Alternate leaves much smoother than most other ceanothus.

49. Spiny redberry: *Rhamnus crocea*
Origins: *Rhamnus*(G) = buckthorn, the
Greek name for a plant in this family,
croc(G) = orange colored for the berries
even though they are red.

J F M A M J J A S O N D

Best months to observe flowering

*ID: Dense, evergreen shrub 3-6 ft. tall. Many
short branches often tipped with thorns.*
Fire: Obligate resprouter.
*Details: Monoeicious. Shiny, red berries best
seen in June. Host plant for Hermes copper
butterfly.*

50. Chamise: *Adenostoma fasciculatum*
Origins: *Adeno*(G) = gland, *stoma*(G) =
mouth for the little glands inside flower
throat, *fasci*(L) = bundle, *cul*(L) = little for
bundles of needle-like leaves.

J F M A M J J A S O N D

Best months to observe flowering

*ID: Evergreen shrub 3-8 ft. tall. Fine leaves.
Tiny creamy flowers.*
Fire: Facultative seeder. C/S.
*Details: Most characteristic chaparral plant.
Extremely flammable due to fineness of
foliage.*

51. Mountain-mahogany: *Cercocarpus betuloides* Origins: *Cerco*(G) - *carpus*(G) = tailed fruit a fruit, *betul*(L) = birch referring to shape of leaves, *oid*(G) = like.

J F M A M J J A S O N D

Best months to observe flowering

ID: Evergreen shrub or tree up to 20 ft. tall.
Fire: Obligate resprouter.
Details: Each flower produces one seed with a fuzzy, curled achene. Food plant for mt. mahogany hairstreak butterfly. Adds nitrogen to the soil.

52. Toyon: *Heteromeles arbutifolia* Origins: *Hetero*(G) = different, *mel*(G) = apple for apple-like fruit, *arbut*(L) = after *Arbutus*, *foli*(L) = leaf for leaves like *Arbutus*.

J F M A M J J A S O N D

Best months to observe flowering

ID: Evergreen shrub less than 15 ft. tall.
Fire: Obligate resprouter.
Details: Sweet, red berry-like fruit in winter eaten by Native Americans and many birds. Another common name is Christmas berry or hollyberry.

53. Bushrue: *Cneoridium dumosum*
Origins: *Cneo*(L) = scratch referring to an
old world genus and *dum*(L) = bramble.

J F M A M J J A S O N D

Best months to observe flowering

ID: Evergreen shrub under 3 ft.
Fire: Obligate resprouter.
Details: Aromatic leaves with large number
of rounded oil glands. May cause allergic
reaction in some. One of three native citrus
plants in California, only one in chaparral.

---

54. Snapdragon: *Antirrhinum* species
Origins: *rhin*(G) = nose like object after the
flower shape.

C. coulterianum

J F M A M J J A S O N D

Best months to observe flowering

C. nuttallianum

J F M A M J J A S O N D

Best months to observe flowering

ID: Annual with a flower stalk 1-4 ft. tall.
Fire: Frequent fire follower. C/S.
Details: Dragon mouth opened by a gentle
finger squeeze on opposite sides of the flower.
Left, A. coulterianum. *Right,* A. nuttallianum.

55. Small-flower soap plant: *Chlorogalum parviflorum* Origins: *Chloro*(G) = green, *gala*(G) = milk for the plant's white sap and *parvi*(L) = small, *flora*(L) = flower.

J F M A M J J A S O N D

Best months to observe flowering

ID: Herbaceous perennial. Sends up a leafless, branching flower stalk 1-4 feet tall.
Fire: Obligate resprouter.
Details: Ground hugging cluster of 1 ft. long, narrow, wavy-margined leaves common after fires. Monocot with bulb.

56. Chaparral yucca: *Hesperoyucca whipplei* Origins: *hesperos*(G) = west, *Yuca*(Haitian) = a native name and after A.W. Whipple (1816-1863) who led the Pacific Railroad Survey in 1853 to Los Angeles.

J F M A M J J A S O N D

Best months to observe flowering

ID: Monocot with stiff, pointed leaves 1.5-3 ft. long radiating from the base. Single flower stalk 5-10 ft. Dies after blooming.
Fire: Obligate resprouter. Charred leaves continue growing from base.
Details: Pollinated by yucca moth. Yucca schidigera similar but has fiberous strings pealing off leaves and blooms repeatedly.

57. Mariposa lily: *Calochortus* species
Origins: *Calo*(G) = beautiful,
chortus(G) = grass.

ID: Herbaceous perennial with branching, bare flower stem 1-3 ft. tall.
Fire: Obligate resprouter.
Details: Nectary surrounded by hairs at base of each petal. Left C. splendens. Right C. weedii. Monocot with bulb.

C. splendens (L)

J F M A M J J A S O N D

Best months to observe flowering

C. weedii (R)

J F M A M J J A S O N D

Best months to observe flowering

---

58. Fremont's camus: *Zigadenus fremontii*
Origins: *zugon*(G) = , yoke, *aden*(G) = gland for bulb. John Fremont, western explorer.

J F M A M J J A S O N D

Best months to observe flowering

ID: Herbaceous perennial. Flwr stem 1-3 ft.
Fire: Obligate resprouter.
Details: Extremely toxic. Genus common name is death camus. Appearance of flwrs nearly exclusively post-fire, often covering entire hillsides. Monocot with bulb.

59. Purple needlegrass: *Nassella pulchra*
Origins: *Nass*(L) = wicker basket, *pulch*(L)
= beautiful.

J F M A M J J A S O N D

Best months to observe flowering

ID: Perennial bunch grass. Stems up to 3 ft.
Fire: Obligate resprouter.
Details: Found in areas with fine soils and
frequently in gaps within chaparral.
Awn 38-100 mm, longest Nassella.
California state grass. Indicator of
original grassland.

60. Wild hyacinth: *Dichelostemma*
capitatum Origins: *Di*-(G) = separate,
chela(G) = claw, *stemma*(G) = garland all
referring to shape of 3 anthers, *capiti*(L) =
head or how flowers are clustered.

J F M A M J J A S O N D

Best months to observe flowering

ID: Herbaceous perennial. Flower stems
1-2 ft. high. Up to 20 flowers per cluster.
Fire: Obligate resprouter.
Details: Slender 1 ft. long leaves are found
at the flower stem base. Monocot with
bulb-like corm.

61. Black mustard: *Brassica nigra*
Origins: *Brassica*(L) = cabbage and
nigra(L) = black for the dark seeds.

J F M A M J J A S O N D

Best months to observe flowering

ID: Annual NON-NATIVE herb 1-8 ft. tall.
Fire: Opportunistic INVASIVE with high fire
frequency.
Details: Relative of the radish, flowers taste
like hot mustard. Smaller Herschfeldia incana
is common along roadsides.

62. Filaree: *Erodium* species
Origin: *Erod*(G) = heron after the long
beaked appearance of the seed clusters.

J F M A M J J A S O N D

Best months to observe flowering

ID: Annual NON-NATIVE herbs. Lays flat on
the ground. Flower stems 1-2 ft.
Fire: Opportunistic INVASIVE with high
fire frequency.
Details: Left, E. moschatum. *Seed photo and*
center, E. botrys. *Right,* E. cicutarium
Corkscrew seeds can drill into soil with
humidity change.

63. Wild oats: *Avena fatua*
Origins: *Avena*(L) = oats, *fatu*(L) = foolish or worthless.

J F M A M J J A S O N D

Best months to observe flowering

ID: Annual NON-NATIVE grass. 1-4 ft.
Fire: Opportunistic INVASIVE with high fire frequency.
Details: 1-1.5" awns aid in seed burial.

64. Bromus: *Bromus* species
Origins: *Bromus*(G) = oats.

J F M A M J J A S O N D

Best months to observe flowering

ID: Annual NON-NATIVE grass. 6"-2 ft.
Fire: Opportunistic INVASIVE with high fire frequency.
Details: Left B. diandrus. Right B. madritensis. Sock stickers! Extremely common in disturbed areas.

Appendix

Nature's Services and Values:
Why and how do we depend on nature?
By Anne S. Fege

Southern California's natural environments provide land for agriculture, water-sheds that collect drinking water, places to hike and find solitude, unique natural beauty, and more. These can be grouped into four types of values: direct economic benefits; indirect benefits (known as ecosystem services); recreational and aesthetic values; and intrinsic, spiritual, and ethical values. Chaparral, in particular, provides essential values of water retention, reduction of erosion, moderation of local climate, scenic beauty, recreational places, and habitats for hundreds of plants and animals.

Direct economic benefits: The tourism industry derives direct economic benefits from nature as recreation-based industries sell more outfitted trips, outdoor clothing, and equipment to hunters, anglers, birdwatchers, hikers, campers, weekend pleasure drivers, and others,

Indirect economic benefits: Natural ecosystems provide clean water, reduce flooding and erosion, moderate weather, and cycle many nutrients and wastes. Most of these services have been "free goods," provided year after year without any cost except the labor or capital involved in bringing the water to consumers or the financial costs of holding property until it is developed.

These natural environments are invaluable for sustaining watershed values, especially the quantity of local drinking water and the quality of that water. For example, about 10% of the water distributed in San Diego in 2003 is local, and requires less treat-ment than imported water. Natural environments also stabilize stream banks, absorb water during storm events and release it slowly, hold the soil and reduce erosion and sediment flow, and provide water, food, and/or shelter for hundreds of species of plants and animals. Removal or disturbance of the natural vegetation creates demonstrable soil erosion, runoff, downstream flow of sediments, and local flooding. When small wildfires remove the natural vegetation, the rapid regrowth minimizes and localizes these effects.

Chaparral, forests, meadows, and riparian areas contribute to the moderation of local and regional weather, including temperature and precipitation, as paved and devel-oped areas absorb and hold heat longer and moisture shorter than natural areas. Natural habitats contribute to the cycling of elements, particularly carbon, nitrogen, oxygen, and sulfur; to the decay of organic matter; and to the biological transformation, detoxifica-tion, and dispersal of wastes. In 2003, the 14,000 acres of trees in the city of San Diego was estimated to remove 4.3 million pounds of pollutants from the air each year, a benefit worth $10.8 million annually. Nature is important for controlling parasites and disease; habitats for bees and other pollinators of crops; and decomposing dead plants and animals.

Natural environments enhance property values, as view lots and land near parks and nature reserves command higher selling prices. Overall, these natural habitats benefit a fortunate few, and the costs are borne by many whose scenic and recreational experiences in nature are diminished. These benefits were free goods, and became monetary benefits to individuals only as land was bought and sold. The public is never compensated for the transfer of these indirect economic benefits of nature to individuals.

Recreational and aesthetic values: Nature excites and quiets our senses, invites us to play, and enhances social bonds. As humans, we are affected by light and dark cycles (both daily and seasonally), and nature returns us to these natural cycles and to the dark sky that we can no longer experience in the city. Noise can both distract and restrict us, and we react to distracting sounds by increased excitement levels, drained energy, and tiredness from unconsciously trying to suppress their effects. Nature can give us silence and natural sounds, and can restore us. As humans, we make cultural, biological and behavioral adaptations to temperature, humidity, rain, wind, and other weather elements; and we can experience the unaltered natural elements in nature.

Humans evolved in small groups and we are affected by social density, trying to maintain "personal space" and creating homes that provide identity, privacy, intimacy and reduced stress. Brain development depends on complex stimuli, and nature provides a much wider range of smell, hearing, and vision stimuli than the indoor space in our homes, schools, and neighborhoods. Nature's change is gradual, periodic, and often predictable, and it can ease the "mental fatigue" that we get from extra stimuli and concentration.

> *Prize the natural spaces most of all, because once they're gone, they're gone. In our bones we need the natural curves of hills, the scent of chaparral, the possibility of wildness. We require these patches of nature for our mental health, our spiritual resilience. And future generations, regardless of whatever recreation or sport is in vogue at the time, will need nature all the more. (Richard Louv, June 22, 2003)*

Intrinsic, spiritual, and ethical values: Many southern Californians have strong attachments to special places in nature, which are often defined by the diverse plants and animals in those places. Many have deeply held ethical and religious values about nature. From these environments, we gain lessons in harmony, wonder, creativity, competition and cooperation, change, birth and death, stability and instability, power and energy, and much more.

> *The intensity of that need has grown. As San Diego's arteries have clogged and its hills have been scraped, many of us have come to understand the growing importance of the forest to the east, and not only because of its rare species . . . The most potent argument for protecting and regenerating the backcountry is the physical, psychological, and spiritual health of future generations of San Diegans, who will need those mountains even more than we did, in ways we're only beginning to understand. (Richard Louv, November 16, 2003).*

Literature Cited

Allen, C. D., M. Savage, D. A. Falk, K. F. Suckling, T. W. Swetnam, T. Schulke, P. B. Stacey, P. Morgan, M. Hoffman, and J. T. Klingel. 2002. Ecological restoration of southwestern ponderosa pine ecosystems: a broad perspective. Ecological Applications 12:1418-1433.

Axelrod, D.A. 1989. Age and origin of chaparral. The California Chaparral: Paradigms Reexamined. Symposium, the Natural History Museum of Los Angeles County.

Barbour, M.G. and R.A. Minnich. 2000. Californian upland forests and woodlands. In North American Terrestrial Vegetation, M.G. Barbour and W.D. Billings (eds.). Cambridge University Press.

Barrett, L. A. 1935. A record of forest and field fires in California from the days of the early explorers to the creation of the forest reserves. San Francisco, CA: USDA Forest Service.

Bartholomew, B. 1970. Bare zone between California shrub and grassland communities: the role of animals. Science 170: 1210-1212.

Bauder, E.T. 1987. San Diego vernal pools: Recent and projected losses; their condition; and threats to their existence, 1979-1990. Report prepared for Endangered Plant Project, California Department of Fish and Game, Sacramento, CA.

Beauchamp, R.M. 1986. A flora of San Diego County, California. Sweetwater Press, National City, California.

Bentley, J.R., et al. 1956. Range Species Recommended for Sowing on Cleared Brushland in California. U.S. Forest Serv. Pacif. S.W. For. & Range Exp. Sta. Res. Note 111. 10 p.

Biswell, H.H., Taber, R.D., Hedrick, D.W. & Schultz, A.M. 1952. Management of chamise brushlands for game in the north coast range of California. California Fish and Game 38: 453-484.

Black, C.H. 1987. Biomass, nitrogen and phosphorus accumulation over a southern California fire cycle chronosequence. In J.D. Tenhunen, F.M. Catarino, O.L. Lange, and W.C. Oechel (eds.), Plant Response to Stress: Functional Analysis in Mediterranean Ecosystems. Berlin: Springer, pp. 445-458.

Bolsinger, C.L. 1989. Shrubs of California chaparral, timberland, and woodland: areas, ownership, and stand characteristics. Resource Bulletin PNW-RB-160. USDA Forest Service, Pacific Northwest Research Station.

Brewer, W. H. 1930. Up and Down California in 1860-1864. Francis P. Farquhar (ed.). Yale University Press.

Brooks, M.L., C.M D'Antonio, D.M. Richardson, J.B. Grace, J.E. Keeley, J.M. Ditomaso, R.J. Hobbs, M.Pellant, and D. Pyke (2004). Effects of invasive alien plants on fire regimes. Bioscience 54: 677-688.

CNPS: California Native Plant Society (2002). E. Dean, R.G. Olmstead, and D.G. Kelch. Fremontia 30: 3-29.

Castellanos, A.E. 1986. PhD thesis. Physiological ecology of *Heteromeles arbutifolia* under sun and shade field conditions. Stanford University. 109 p.

CDF. 1978. Brushland range improvement. Annual report 1974-1977 inclusive. Sacramento, CA.: California Department of Forestry.

CDF: California Department of Forestry and Fire Protection. 2004. California Fire Siege 2003. The Story. October 21-November 4, 2003. *http://www.fire.ca.gov/php/fire_er_siege.php*

Chamberlin, T.C. 1890. The method of multiple working hypotheses. Science: Feb. 7. Also reprinted in 1965. Science 148: 754-759.

Chester, T. 2004. *http://tchester.org/sd/places/agua_tibia.html.*

Chester, T. 2004b. *http://tchester.org/sgm/lists/lion_attacks_ca.html*

Cleland, Robert Glass. 1951. The Cattle on a Thousand Hills: Southern California, 1850-1880.

Cohen, J.D. 1999. Reducing the wildland fire threat to homes: where and how much? USDA Forest Service Gen. Tech. Report PSW-GTR-173, pp 189-195.

Cohen, J.D. 2000. Preventing disaster: home ignitability in the wildland-urban interface. Journal of Forestry 98: 15-21.

Cohen, J. and J. Saveland. 1997. Structure ignition assessment can help reduce fire damages in the W-UI. Fire Mgt. Notes 57:19-23.

Coleman , Ronny J. 1995. Structural Wildland Intermix. In: The Biswell Symposium: Fire Issues and Solutions in the Urban Interface and Wildland Ecosystems, pp. 141-145. USDA Forest Service Gen. Tech. Rept. PSW-GTR-158.

Conard, S. G., and D. R. Weise. 1998. Management of fire regime, fuels, and fire effects in southern California chaparral: lessons from the past and thoughts for the future. Tall Timbers Ecology Conference Proceedings 20:342-350.

Connell, J.H. 1990. Apparent versus "real" competition in plants, p. 9-25. In J.B. Grace, and D. Tilman (eds.), Perspectives on Plant Competition. Academic Press, San Diego.

Conrad, S. 1993. The effects of fire and post-fire rehabilitation measures on surface erosion and vegetation development in California chaparral. Work Plan #8, 1993-94. Fiscal Agreement 8CA53048 (PSW-86-CL-031). Los Padres National Forest Files.

Cooper, C. F. 1960. Changes in vegetation, structure, and growth of southwestern pine forests since white settlement. Ecological Monographs 30:129-164.

Countryman, C.M. 1974. Can southern California wildland conflagrations be stopped? Berkeley: USDA Forest Service, Pacific Southwest Forest and Range Experiment Station, Gen. Tech. Note PSW-7.

Covington, W.W., and M.M. Moore. 1994. Southwestern ponderosa forest structure: changes since Euro-American settlement. Journal of Forestry 92: 39-47.

CWIS, California wetlands information system. 2002. California vernal pool regions. San Diego Region. *http://maphost.dfg.ca.gov/wetlands/vp_asses_rept/san_diego.htm*

Dean, E. 2004. Upcoming changes in flowering plant family names: those pesky taxonomists are at it again. Fremonita 30: 1-12.

DeSimone, D. 1995. California's coastal sage scrub. Fremontia 23: 3-8.

Dodge, J. M. 1975. Vegetational changes associated with land use and fire history in San Diego County. Ph.D. dissertation, University of California, Riverside.

Fabritius, S. and S. D. Davis. 2000. Increased fire frequency promotes vegetation-type conversion in southern California chaparral: a 15-year study. In: Mediterranean-type ecosystems: Past, present and future, p.18. Medecos 2000, Ninth International Conference on Mediteranean-type ecosystems, 11-15 September, Stellenbosch, South Africa. Conference abstracts.

Fenn, M.E. M.A. Poth, P.H. Dunn, and S.C. Barro. 1993. Microbial N and biomass respiration an N mineralization in soils beneath two chaparral species along a fire-induced age gradient. Soil Biol. Biochem. 25:457-466.

Finney, Mark A. 1998 FARSITE: Fire Area Simulator-Model Development and Evaluation. USDA, Forest Service, Rocky Mountain Research Station Research Paper RMRS-RP-4. March 1998. 51 pages.

Flematti, G.R., E.L. Ghisalberti, K.W. Dixon, R.D. Trengove. 2004. A compound from smoke that promotes seed germination. AAAS. Science Express Brevia. July 8.

Fosberg, M.A. 1965. A case study of the Santa Ana winds in the San Gabriel Mountains. Berkeley: USDA Forest Service, Pacific Southwest Forest and Range Experiment Station, Res. Note PSW-78.

Fultz, F. M. 1927. The Elfin Forest. The Times-Mirror Press. Los Angeles, CA.

Green, L.R. 1981. Burning by prescription in chaparral. Berkeley: USDA Forest Service, Pacific Southwest Forest and Range Experiment Station, Gen. Tech. Report PSW-51.

Griffin, J.R. 1982. Pine seedlings, native ground cover, and *Lolium multiflorum* on the Marble Cone burn, Santa Lucia Range, California. Madrono 29: 177-188.

Haidinger, T.L., and J.E. Keeley. 1993. Role of high fire frequency in destruction of mixed chaparral. Madrono 40: 141-147.

Halsey, R.W. 2004. In search of allelopathy: an eco-historical view of the investigation of chemical inhibition in California coastal sage scrub and chamise chaparral. Journal of the Torrey Botanical Society, Issue 4. In press.

Hanes, T. L. 1971. Succession after fire in the chaparral of southern California. Ecol. Monographs 41: 27-52.

Harper, J.L. 1975. Book review of Allelopathy, Physiological Ecology, by Elroy Rice. The Quart. Rev. of Biol. 50: 493-495.

Head, W.S. 1989. The California Chaparral, an Elfin Forest. Naturegraph Publishers, Inc. Happy Camp, CA.

Hickman, J.C. (ed.) 1993. The Jepson Manual: Higher Plants of California. University of California Press.

Hubbard, R.F. 1986. Stand age and growth dynamics in chamise chaparral. Master's thesis, San Diego State University, San Diego, California.

Jacobsen, A.L., S.D. Davis, S. Fabritius. 2004. Vegetation type conversion in response to short fire return intervals in California chaparral. Annual Meeting of the Ecological Society of America, Portland OR. Abstract.

Jones, G., J. Chew, R. Silverstein, C. Stalling, J. Sullivan, J. Troutwine, D. Weise, and D. Garwood. 2003. Spatial analysis of fuel treatment options for chaparral on the Angeles National Forest. In press. USDA Forest Service Gen Tech Rep. PSW-GTR-xxx. 2003: xx-xx.

Jones & Stokes. 1987. Sliding toward extinction: the state of California's natural heritage, 1987. California Nature Conservancy, San Francisco, CA.

Jones, D. 2004. Governor's Blue Ribbon Fire Commission, State of California. Transcript of Proceedings, January 7, 2004.

Keeley, J.E. 1973. The adaptive significant of obligate-seeding shrubs in the chaparral. Master's thesis, California State University, San Diego. 79 p.

Keeley, J.E. 1975. Longevity of nonsprouting *Ceanothus*. American Midland Naturalist 93: 504-507.

Keeley, J.E. 1991a. Resilience to fire does not imply adaptation to fire: an example from the California chaparral. Tall Timbers Fire Ecology Conference, 17th Proceedings, pgs. 113-119.

Keeley, J.E. 1991b. Seed germination and life history syndromes in the California chaparral. The Botanical Review 57: 81-116.

Keeley, J.E. 1992. Demographic structure of California chaparral in the long-term absence of fire. Journal of Vegetation Sci. 3: 79-90.

Keeley, J.E. 1993. Smoke-induced flowering in the fire-lily *Cyrtanthus ventricosus*. S. Afr. J. Bot. 59: 638.

Keeley, J.E. 1995. Future of California floristics and systematics: wildfire threats to the California flora. Madrono 42: 175-179.

Keeley, J. E. 1998a. Postfire ecosystem recovery and management: the October 1993 large fire episode in California. Pages 69-90 in J. M. Moreno, editor. Large forest fires. Backhuys Publishers, Leiden, The Netherlands.

Keeley, J.E. 1998b. Coupling demography, physiology and evolution in chaparral shrubs. Landscape Degradation and Biodiversity of Mediterranean-Type Ecosystems. Ecological Studies, Vol. 136.

Keeley, J.E. 2000. Chaparral. In North American Terrestrial Vegetation, M.G. Barbour and W.D. Billings (eds.). Cambridge University Press.

Keeley, J.E. 2002. Native American impacts on fire regimes of the California coastal ranges. Journal of Biogeography 29: 303-320.

Keeley, J. E. 2004a. Impact of antecedent climate on fire regimes in coastal California. International Journal of Wildland Fire 13:173-182.

Keeley, J.E. 2004b. Invasive plants and fire management in California Mediterranean-climate ecosystems. In M. Arianoutsou (ed) 10th MEDECOS – International Conference on Ecology, Conservation and Management, Rhodes Island, Greece, electronic, no page numbers.

Keeley, J.E. and C.J. Fotheringham. 1998. Smoke-induced seed germination in California chaparral. Ecology 79: 2320-2336.

Keeley, J.E. and C.J. Fotheringham. 2001. Historic fire regime in southern California shrublands. Conservation Biology 15: 1536-1548.

Keeley, J.E., and C.J. Fotheringham. 2003. Impact of past, present, and future fire regimes on North American mediterranean shrublands. Pages 218-262 in T. T. Veblen, W. L. Baker, G. Montenegro, and T. W. Swetnam, (eds). Fire and climatic change in temperate ecosystems of the Western Americas. Springer, New York.

Keeley, J. E., C. J. Fotheringham, and M. Morais. 1999. Reexamining fire suppression impacts on brushland fire regimes. Science 284:1829-1832.

Keeley, J. E., C. J. Fotheringham, and M. Moritz. 2004. Lessons from the 2003 wildfires in southern California. Journal of Forestry 103(9). In Press.

Keeley, S. C., J.E. Keeley, S.M. Hutchinson, A.W. Johnson. 1981. Post fire succession of herbaceous flora in southern California chaparral. Ecology 62: 1608-1621.

Kelch, D.G. 2004. Consider the lilies. Fremontia 30: 23-29.

Kelly, 1990. Population Ecology an Social Organization of Dusky-footed Woodrats, *Neotoma fuscipes*. Ph.D. dissertation, University of California, Berkeley. 191 p.

Kinney, A. 1887. Report on the forests of the counties of Los Angeles, San Bernardino, and San Diego, California. Sacramento: First Biennial Report, California State Board of Forestry.

Kummerow, J. 1981. Structure of roots and root systems. In DiCastri, F., D.W. Goodall, R. L. Specht (eds.), Ecosystems of the World II. Mediterranean-Type Shrublands.

Kummerow, J., Krause, D., and Jow, W. 1977. Root systems of chaparral shrubs. Oecologia 29: 163-177.

Lanner, R.M. 2002. Conifers of California. Cachuma Press, Los Olivos, California. Second printing.

Larigauderie, A., T.W. Hubbard, and J. Kummerow. 1990. Growth dynamics of two chaparral shrub species with time after fire. Madrono 37: 225-236.

Larson, T. 2000. Fairy shrimp, the mayor of poway, and the city of San Diego. San Diego Weekly Reader, page 28, 4/20/2000.

Loomis, J., P. Wohlgemuth, A. Gonzale-Caban, and D. English. 2003. Economic benefits of reducing fire-related sediment in southwestern fire-prone ecosystems. Water Resources Research 39(No 9, WES 3): 1-8.

Marion, L. H. 1943. The distribution of Adenostoma sparsifolium. American Midland Naturalist 29: 106-116.

McDonald, Jeff. 2002. San Diego Union-Tribune. November 30.

McMaster, G.S., P.H. Zedler. 1981. Delayed seed dispersal in *Pinus torreyana* (Torrey pine). Oecologia 51: 62-66.

Mensing, S. A., J. Michaelsen, and R. Byrne. 1999. A 560-year record of Santa Ana fires reconstructed from charcoal deposited in the Santa Barbara Basin, California. Quaternary Research 51:295-305.

Miller, C. 2004. Wildfire underwriting in California. Insurance Information Network of California, Los Angeles, CA.

Minnich, R. A. 1983. Fire mosaics in southern California and northern Baja California. Science 219:1287-1294.

Minnich, R. A. 1988. The biogeography of fire in the San Bernardino Mountains, California. University of California Publications in Botany 28:1-120.

Minnich, R. A. 1998. Landscapes, land-use and fire policy: where do large fires come from? Pages 133-158 in J. M. Moreno, ed. Large Forest Fires. Backhuys Publishers, Leiden, The Netherlands.

Minnich, R. A., and R. J. Dezzani. 1991. Suppression, fire behavior, and fire magnitudes in Californian chaparral at the urban/wildland interface. Pages 67-83 in J. J. DeVries, editor. California watersheds at the urban interface, proceedings of the third biennial watershed conference. University of California, Davis. Water Resources Center, Report No. 75.

Minnich, R. A., and Y. H. Chou. 1997. Wildland fire patch dynamics in the chaparral of southern California and northern Baja California. International Journal of Wildland Fire 7:221.

Minnich, R. A., M. G. Barbour, J. H. Burk, and R. F. Fernau. 1995. Sixty years of change in Californian conifer forests of the San Bernardino Mountains. Conservation Biology 9:902-914.

Mooney, H.A. 1977. Southern coastal scrub. In M.G. Barbour and J. Major (eds.), Terrestrial Vegetation of California. Wiley, New York. Pp. 471-478.

Mooney, H.A. unpublished data from Keeley, J. E., Keeley, S.C. 1988. Chaparral, Ch. 6., North American Terrestrial Vegetation. Edited by M.G. Barbour and W.D. Billings.

Moritz, M. A. 2003. Spatiotemporal analysis of controls on shrubland fire regimes: age dependency and fire hazard. Ecology 84:351-361.

Moritz, M.A., J.E. Keeley, E.A. Johnson, and A.A. Schaffner. 2004. Testing a basic assumption of shrubland fire management: how important is fuel age? Frontiers in Ecology and the Environment 2:67-72.

Multiple Species Conservation Program. 1998. City of San Diego. Page 3.27.

Muller, C.H., R.B. Hunawalt, and J.K. McPherson. 1968. Allelopathic control of herb growth in the fire cycle of California chaparral. Bull. Torrey Bot. Club 95: 225-231.

Muller, C.H., W.H. Muller, and B.L. Haines. 1964. Volatile growth inhibitors produced by aromatic shrubs. Science 143: 471-473.

Nadkarni, N.M. and D.C. Oechel. 1991. Fire intensity effects on germination of shrubs and herbs in southern California chaparral. Ecology 76: 1993-2004.

NPS, United State Department of the Interior, National Park Service. 2004. Environmental Impact Statement Fire Management Plan. Santa Monica Mountains National Recreation Area, CA

Odens, P. 1971. The Indians and I: Visits with Dieguenos, Quechans, Fort Mojaves, Zumis, Hopis, Navajos and Piutes. Imperial Printers, El Centro, CA.

Oechel, W.C. 1982. Carbon balanced studies in chaparral shrubs: implication for biomass production. In C.E. Conrad and W.C. Oechel (eds), Proceedings of the symposium on dynamics and management of Mediterranean-type ecosystems. USDA Forest Service, Pacific Southwest Forest and Range Experiment Station general technical report PSW-58.

Olmstead, R. 2004. What ever happened to the Scrophulariaceae? Fremontia 30: 13-22.

Patric, J.H. and Hanes, T.L. 1964. Chaparral succession in a San Gabriel Mountain area of California. Ecology 68: 434-443.

Payson, T.E., and J.D. Cohen. 1990. Chamise chaparral dead fuel fraction is not reliably predicted by age. Western Journal of Forestry 5:127-131.

Plummer, F. G. 1911. Chaparral, studies in the dwarf forests, or elfin-wood, of southern California. U.S. Department of Agriculture, Forest Service Bulletin 85.

Purer, Edith A. 1939. Ecological study of vernal pools, San Diego County. Ecology 20: 217-229.

Quick, C.R. and A.S. Quick. 1961. Germination of *Ceanothus* seeds. Madrono 16: 23-30.

Radtke, K.W.H. 1982. A Homeowner's Guide to Fire and Watershed Management at the Chaparral/Urban Interface. Pacific Southwest Forest & Range Exp. Station, Forest Service U.S. Department of Agriculture and County of Los Angeles. 36 p.

Radtke, K.W.H. 1983. Living More Safely at the Chaparral-Urban Interface. PSW-67. Berkeley, CA: Pacific Southwest Forest & Range Experiment Station, Forest Service, U.S. Department of Agriculture. 51 p.

Radtke, K.W.H. 1985. Proceedings – Living in the Chaparral of Southern California. K. Radtke, technical coordinator and scientific editor. Focused articles on Fire, Vegetation, Watershed Management; Land Use and Planning; Disaster Prevention, Preparation, and Assistance by Anthony, Partain, Grisselle, Gray, Holtom, Loeher, Paule, Partain, Potter, Radtke, Severynen, Wakimoto, Zinke. Los Angeles County Museum of Natural History, Los Angeles, California; October 20, 1984. National Foundation For Environmental Safety in cooperation with the National Park Service. 72 p.

Radtke, K.W.H. 1994. Postfire Hydroseeding – Damaging or Protecting Wildland Watersheds? (A Waste of Public Funds to the Tune of Millions of Dollars?). Prepared for the National Foundation For Environmental Safety as News Release/Public Information Paper. March 15, 1994. 5 p.

Radtke, K.W.H., A.M. Arndt, and R.H. Wakimoto. 1981. Fire History of the Santa Monica Mountains. In Proceedings of the International Symposium on Dynamics and Management of Mediterranean-type Ecosystems, June 1981: 22-26: San Diego, CA PSW Forest & Range Exp. Sta., USDA Forest Service. Gen Tech. Report PSW-58 1982: 438-443.

Regelbrugge, J.C. 2000. Role of prescribed burning in the management of chaparral ecosystems in southern California. In J.E. Keeley, M.B. Keeley, and C.J. Fotheringham (eds.) 2nd Interface between Ecology and Land Development in California. Sacramento: US Geological Survey Open-File Rep. 00-02, pp. 19-26.

Rhode, D. 2002. Early holocene juniper woodland and chaparral taxa in the central Baja California peninsula, Mexico. Quaternary Research 57: 102-108.

Rice, R. M. 1973. Sowing Ryegrass on Burned Watersheds is a Mistake Unpubl. Rept. 20 p.

Rice, R. M., R. P. Crouse and E.S. Corbett. 1963. Emergency Measures to Control Erosion after a Fire on the San Dimas Experimental Forest. U.S.D.A. Misc. Publ. No 970. 8 p.

Romme, W.H., 1982. Fire and landscape diversity in subalpine forests of Yellowstone National Park. Eco. Monographs 52: 199-221.

Rothermel, R.C. 1993. Mann Gulch fire: a race that couldn't be won. USDA Forest Service, Intermountain Research Station. Gen. Technical Report INT-299.

Rowntree, Lester 1939. Flowering Shrubs of California and Their Value to the Gardener. Stanford University Press. Pg. 20-21 second edition, 1948.

Rundel, P.W. 1981. Structural and chemical components of flammability. In H.A. Mooney, T.M. Bonnicksen, N.L. Christensen, J.E. Lotan, and W.A. Reiners (eds.). Fire regimes and ecosystem properties. General Technical Report QO-26, USDA, Forest Service, Washington D.C.

Sawyer, J.O, and T. Keeler-Wolf. 1995. A Manual of California Vegetation. California Native Plant Society.

Schaffer, J.P. 1993. California's geological history and changing landscapes. In Hickman, J.C. (ed.) The Jepson Manual, Higher Plants of California. University of California Press.

Schimper, A.F.W. 1903. Plant geography on a physiological basis (translated from the 1898 version by W.R. Fisher). Clarendon Press, Oxford.

Schlesinger, W.H, and D.S. Gill. 1978. Demographic studies of the chaparral shrub *Ceanothus megacarpus* in the Santa Ynez Mountains. Ecology 59: 1256-1263.

Schroeder, M.J., et al. 1964. Synoptic weather types associated with critical fire weather. Washington, DC: U.S. Department of Commerce, National Bureau of Standards, Institute for Applied Technology, AD 449-630. 372 p.

Schwilk, D.W. 2002. Plant evolution in fire prone environments. Ph.D. thesis, Stanford University, California.

Simpson, L.B. 1938. California in 1792. The expedition of Jose Longinos Martinez. Henry E. Huntington Library and Art Gallery, San Marino, CA.

Spech, T.L. 1969. A comparison of the sclerophyllous vegetation characteristics of mediterranean type climates in France, California, and southern Australia. I: Structure, morphology and succession. Aust. J. Bot. 17: 227-292.

Storer, T.I. and L.P. Tevis, Jr. 1955. California Grizzly. University of California Press.

Swetnam, T.W. and C.H. Baisan. 1996. Historical fire regime patterns in the southwestern United States since AD 1700. In C.D. Allen (ed.) Fire Effects in Southwestern Forests: Proceedings of the Second La Mesa Fire Symposium, Los Alamos, New Mexico, March 29-31, 1994. USDA. General Technical Report RM-GTR-286.

Taskey, R.D, C.L. Curtis, and J. Stone. 1988. Wildfire, ryegrass seeding, and watershed rehabilitation. In Proceedings of the symposium on fire and watershed management. USDA Forest Service General Technical Report PSW-109.

Thorne, R.F. 1981. Are California's vernal pools unique? Vernal Pools and Intermittent Streams. A symposium sponsored by the Institute of Ecology, University of California, Davis.

Turner, M.G., W.H. Romme, R.H. Gardner, W.W. Hargrove. 1997. Effects of fire size and pattern on early succession in Yellowstone National Park. Ecological Monographs 67: 411-433.

Tyler, C.M. and M.I. Borchert. 2003. Reproduction and growth of the chaparral geophyte, *Zigadenus fremontii* (Liliaceae), in relation to fire. Plant Ecology 165: 11-20.

University of Utah, Department of Meteorology. Normal monthly precipitation, inches. Normals 1961-1990. *http://www.met.utah.edu/jhorel/html/wx/climate/normrain.html*

USDA Forest Service Remote Sensing Lab, Ecosystem Planning. Western Core Table Reports. http://www.fs.fed.us/r5/rsl/publications/westcore/area.shtml

Wells, P.V. 1969. The relation between mode of reproduction and extent of speciation in woody genera of California chaparral. Evolution 23: 264-267.

Westerling AL, Gershunov A, Cayan DR, Barnett TP (2002) Long lead statistical forecasts of area burned in western U.S. wildfires by ecosystem province. International Journal of Wildland Fire 11, 257-266.

Western Region Climate Center. Western U.S. historical summaries by individual stations. *http://www.wrcc.dri.edu/summary/climsmsca.html*

Wicklow, D.T. 1977. Germination response in Emmenanthe penduliflora (Hydrophyllaceae). Ecology 58: 201-205.

Zedler, P.H. 1995. Fire frequency in southern California shrublands: biological effects and management options, pp. 101-112 in J.E. Keeley and T. Scott (eds.), Brushfires in California wildlands: ecology and resource management. International Association of Wildland Fire, Fairfield, Wash.

Zedler, P.H., C.R. Gautier, G.S. McMaster. 1983. Vegetation change in response to extreme events: the effect of a short interval between fires in California chaparral and coastal sage scrub. Ecology 64: 809-818.

Zedler, P.H., and C.A. Zammit. 1989. A population-based critique of concepts of change in the chaparral. In S.C. Keeley (ed.), The California Chaparral: Paradigms Reexamined. The Natural History Museum of Los Angeles County, 1986.

Zedler, P.H., Seiger, L.A. 2000. Age Mosaics and Fire Size in Chaparral: A Simulation Study. In 2nd Interface Between Ecology and Land Development in California. USGS Open-File Report 00-02, pp. 9-18.

Contributors

Melanie Baer-Keeley: horticulturist. Over the last 20 years, Melanie has made a study of the cultivation of California native plants. She conveys her knowledge as well as passion by freelance writing, illustrating, and teaching. She is currently the Restoration Horticulturist at Sequoia and Kings Canyon National Park.

Christopher Blaylock: graduate of UCSB. After a year's study at the University of St. Andrews in Scotland, Chris immediately boarded a plane to China where he taught Kindergarten-12th grade English. Upon returning to the U.S. Chris became a substitute teacher by day and fine dining chef by night before finally entering the world of fire education. Chris enjoys long walks on the fireline.

Susan Conniry: teacher and writer who, with her husband Tom Beasley, runs a non-profit education organization in San Diego that teaches urban preparedness. They have also published a book, First Response Survival. For more information visit their web page at *www.backyardtourist.com.* Email: sconniry@mail.sdccu.net.

Anne S. Fege: Ph.D. Botany Research Associate at the San Diego Natural History Museum. Anne retired on May 15, 2004, as the Forest Supervisor of the Cleveland National Forest. She is widely known as a co-founder of the San Diego Partners for Biodiversity and San Diego Fire Recovery Network, and recently earned a Masters in Business Administration at San Diego State University.

C.J. Fotheringham: Ph.D. in process, Ecology and Evolutionary Biology, UCLA. In the course of her graduate career C.J. has received funding and fellowships from the National Science Foundation Graduate Fellowship and numerous other organizations. Much of her research has focused on evolutionary aspects of seed germination and the impact of altered fire regimes and other human mediated impacts on fire-prone shrublands.

Stephen L. Halsey: licensed landscape architect in California with over 35 years experience. Steve received his Bachelor of Science in Environmental Design and Landscape Architecture from Cal Poly, Pomona and is Principal-in-Charge at his landscape architect firm Halsey Design Group, Inc. He is an advisor to the City of San Diego's Land Use and Housing Commission.

Jim Hart: a rough-edged individualist, former teacher, current naturalist, firefighter, and reluctant poet. Exists only in the minds of people like him who dream, if only occasionally, of leaving the madness behind and heading into the hills for good.

Bill Howell: biologist, teacher, nature photographer. Bill taught biology for 30 years in the San Diego City School District. He received his B.S. in Biology at San Diego State University and his M.S. in Biology at Humboldt State University. For the past 15 years Bill has coordinated and taught two outdoor education programs for volunteer trail guides at the San Diego Natural History Museum and Mission Trails Regional Park.

Jon E. Keeley: Ph.D., Botany and Ecology, University of Georgia. Jon is currently a research ecologist with the U.S. Geological Survey, stationed at Sequoia National Park. Jon also served 1 year in Washington, D.C. as director of the ecology program for the National Science Foundation, was professor of biology at Occidental College for 20 years, and a 1985 Guggenheim Fellowship recipient. He has written over 200 publications.

Michael Klein: San Diego entomologist with a love of butterflies that spans 43 years. He took his avocation to the professional level in 1997 through the encouragement of many friends. Today he is a wildlife biologist with a small company in the area. He enjoys teaching and presenting the fascinating world of insects in public forums. Michael can be reached at keps2@flite-tours.com.

Gabi McLean: naturalist and native plant photographer since 1993 when she was studying to become a volunteer docent naturalist in Pasadena. In 2003, Gabi and her husband Cliff McLean created a Field Guide on CD of Common Plants of Eaton Canyon and the San Gabriel Foothills, with over 700 of Gabi's photos. You can contact Gabi at *www.natureathand.com.*

Candysse Miller: executive Director, Insurance Information Network of California. Candysse earned her B.A. at UC Riverside in Political Science and Journalism and is a former newspaper reporter at several southern California publications. Prior to joining IINC, she served as deputy press secretary for the California Department of Insurance.

Max A. Moritz: Ph.D., Spatial Ecology focusing on relationships between fire, land management, and chaparral vegetation, UCSB. He holds a master's degree in energy & environmental studies from Boston University. Max currently works at UC Berkeley as the Cooperative Extension Specialist in wildland fire for California and as Adjunct Assistant Professor in the Environmental Science, Policy, and Management Department.

Klaus W.H. Radtke: Ph.D., UCB, Wildland Resource Sciences. Author, principle consultant and president of Geo Safety, Inc., a consulting and management firm in Los Angeles, California, specializing in integrated resource and land use management. Klaus is an accomplished fire safety expert and national authority on wildland-urban interface fire management.

Kurt Schasker: studied chemical engineering at California State University, Long Beach. Started a tree service in 1986 which, by 1990, had morphed into a brush clearance business working mostly in the San Fernando Valley. Kurt is currently working in the financial services industry.

Geoffrey D. Smith: a 35 year resident of San Diego, having worked in the software industry for over 20 years. He recently left a dot com for a dot org, and now works for the Desert Protective Council as Imperial County Projects Director, and for the USDA Forest Service Cleveland National Forest as Volunteer Coordinator. He volunteers in many capacities for public lands-based nonprofit advocacy and advisory groups.

Wayne Spencer: Ph.D. in Ecology and Evolutionary Biology at the University of Arizona. Earned his M.S. at UCB studying pine martens in the Sierra Nevada. Wayne currently serves as principal biologist for the Multiple Habitat Conservation Program in San Diego County, principal investigator for recovery research on the Pacific little pocket mouse, and biologist with the Conservation Biology Institute in San Diego, California.

Robert Taylor: Ph.D., Biogeography, UCSB. Fire GIS specialist and biogeographer for the National Park Service's Coast Mediterranean Network. Robert studies vegetation change over time in response to physical factors including land use, fire and other disturbance regimes, and climate.

Scott Tremor: wildlife biologist who specializes in mammals from southern California and Baja California. Scott is a co-investigator for the San Diego County Mammal Atlas project, an Associate Biologist with the Conservation Biology Institute, and a mammalogist for the San Diego Natural History Museum.

Michael Wangler: professor of Geography and coordinator of the Earth Sciences Program with Cuyamaca College in Rancho San Diego. Michael holds a Master of Science degree in Geography with a specialization in fire ecology and remains active in the field as a public speaker and field trip leader throughout San Diego's backcountry.

Marti Witter: Ph.D., Botany, the University of Hawaii. Marti has lived in the Santa Monica Mountains and dealt with fire and land use issues for 20 years. She is currently the fire ecologist for the Mediterranean Coast Network of the National Park Service including Cabrillo National Monument, Channel Islands National Park, and Santa Monica Mountains National Recreation Area.

Zackery Zdinak: lifetime artist of nature in Flagstaff, Arizona. After years in various federal park, forest, and wildlife biologist positions, he founded Life Drawing & Education in 1998, a resource for retail wildlife art, custom interpretive media design and free-lance education programs *(www.lifedraw.com)*. When not working, Zack roams the Arizona chaparral and the western states' backroads, rivers, and skyscapes.

Xylococcus bicolor

Fire, Chaparral, and Survival in Southern California

Acknowledgements

Writing and editing a book is a tumultuous affair. After teaching biology and exploring the chaparral plant community for more than two decades I decided it was time to get my notes published. I was granted some time off from my teaching duties in 1993 through a Christa McAuliffe Fellowship. After nearly eight years of writing and rough drafts, a workable model was finally developed. Then the fires of October 2003 occurred. My phone started ringing off the hook from people calling who wanted to know what this stuff was that was burning all over the place. So instead of waiting to complete the chaparral natural history guide, I decided it might be a good idea to get some information out now with an emphasis on wildfire. That's how this book was born. My work on the natural history guide continues, but I need a break. I had no idea how much energy is required to put this kind of thing together.

Throughout it all, the one person who kept me sane and focused was my wife and best friend, Vicki. She has provided both the emotional and financial support necessary for me to follow my passion over the past 10 years. After hours of working in my basement lab, pounding away at the keyboard, she would arrive at just the right moment to bring me a smile and some snacks. She helped me keep moving toward the finish line when it was difficult to see. This project would have never been completed without her.

My two boys, Nicholas and Jake, provided not only invaluable field assistance when their dad dragged them out on yet another one of his adventures, but they continue to inspire me on a daily basis and remind me that kids are the reason we do what we do. To them and Vicki, I dedicate this book.

The premier naturalist behind it all who has continually challenged my assumptions and encouraged me every step of the way has been my close friend Bill Howell. Bill has accompanied me on so many field research projects and excursions into the chaparral I have lost count. He introduced me to the field of botany as well providing a background in natural history for which I will forever be grateful. Whenever I couldn't figure out a plant species or remember its name, Bill was always there. His interest and assistance in helping to get this publication properly edited and assembled has been truly remarkable.

The scientific rigor and inspiration I needed came from Jon E. Keeley. What began as a brief email exchange turned into a full-blown education project for Jon to help me understand the finer details of fire ecology. I have worked with a lot of scientists over the years, but none of them can match Jon's sincere interest in helping others understand. After you've worked in a discipline long enough and have analyzed hundreds of research papers, it becomes pretty clear who the true scientists are, who is sharp enough to ask the right questions, and who is able to objectively isolate the proper variables. There aren't many. Jon is one of the few.

Now for all the important people who have contributed the infinite details necessary to make sure this book told the story straight. To the guys in the various fire-fighting agencies who shared their valuable experiences and expertise with me, I salute with honor. Randy Lyle and Thomas Porter from the CDF, Clayton Howe from the Bureau of Land Management, and several others from the U.S. Forest Service have all been with me on this project from the get go. I thank them for showing tremendous patience for a guy who has never fought a fire. They have continually pointed me in the right direction when it may have appeared as if I was getting caught in my own backfire. Special thanks to Ray Chaney for providing details of his experiences during the Cedar fire on Wildcat Canyon Road.

Thanks of course to all those who provided chapter contributions. You have added important voices to the story. After repeated requests to change yet another fire perimeter map, Max Moritz not only maintained his humor but his warmth of personality to help make the last few days of production of this book a lot more enjoyable. Without Klaus Radtke's sincere interest in the project and his unwavering commitment to meet very short deadlines, a major portion of this book would not have been completed in time.

All the new friends I have met through the San Diego Fire Recovery Network deserve a measure of gratitude, especially Anne Fege and David Younkman for providing some creative guidance, and Kay Stewart for her perspective on landscape issues. I am also grateful to the many people who shared their stories with me about both survival and loss during the Cedar fire.

And thanks to artists Zack Zdinak, Steve Halsey, Melanie Keeley, and Marianne D. Wallace for adding the needed artistic additions. Melanie drew the dramatic charred laurel sumac at the front of the book. Marianne originally did the plant sketches for the 1994 USFS publication, *Ecological Guide to Southern California Chaparral Plant Series*. And thanks to the photographers who provided those so important missing pictures: Gabi McLean, Scott Tremor, Michael Klein, Geoffrey Smith, and Bob Krause.

I am also indebted to all the folks who helped me edit the previous drafts and provided important commentary especially Bill Howell, Nancy Jordan, and Jon E. Keeley. I have discovered editing is by far the hardest part of a publication and could not have possibly caught the errors without a lot of help. If some snuck through, blame sleep deprivation.

And thanks to my friends at Sunbelt Publications, Lowell and Diana Lindsay for staying with me for so long and being there when I finally had something to print. And thanks to Jennifer Redmond and Jerry Marino for helping get the final product out the door. Jerry, I owe you another pizza.

Apologies to all those who worked hard and sent me materials I was unable to use. Thank you so much for contributing. Your stuff will be around for the next run.

And finally thanks to Allstate Insurance and Klaus Radtke for providing major financial support, permitting this book to sell for such a reasonable price. What you have in your hand should have cost an additional ten bucks. When Bob Daniels from Allstate called me and offered to help get the word out about fire safety it symbolized one of the major goals of this entire effort: cooperation and participation between all those who play a role in wildfire management. There are a large number of competing interests and opinions after large fires that often make it difficult to create the collaborative spirit necessary to get everyone on the same page. With the inclusion of contributions from Allstate Insurance, individuals from local, state, and federal fire fighting agencies, fire scientists, and community leaders, this book represents a significant move in that direction.

Index

Agua Tibia, 8
air mass, 4, 6, 48
allelopathy, 27
anchor point, 57, 108
Anza-Borrego, 5
Arrollado, S., 31, 54
Australia, 65
avoider, 15
BAER, 85, 86
Barona Casino, 52
Barona Mesa, 52
Bates bill, 69
Bell Valley, 31, 32
black sage, 12, 17, 82
Borchert, M., 20, 21
Brewer, W.H., 12
buckwheat, 12, 82
bushrue, 4
California Department of Forestry and
    Fire Protection (CDF), 26, 31, 33, 35, 52
CalTrans, 85
camus, 20
ceanothus, 4, 8, 9, 10, 11, 15, 16, 19, 20, 28, 82
chain link, 94
Chamberlin, T.C., 101
chamise, 8, 9, 10, 16, 23, 24, 26
Chaney, R., 50, 52-54
chaparro, 2,11
charred wood, 22, 24
cheatgrass, 114
check damn, 95
Clayton, B., 50
clearance, 66, 67-75, 81-82
coastal sage scrub, 5, 6, 12, 13, 105, 107
Cohen, J., 66
Coulter pine, 19
creosote bush, 2
Crest, 32, 34, 40
Cuyamaca, 5, 33, 39, 40
deerweed, 23, 24, 91
defensible space, 37, 59, 61, 63, 66, 106, 120
dimorphic, 17
Douglas, C., 58

embers, 36, 58
endemic fire follower, 18, 20, 24
Eucalyptus, 63, 69
facultative seeder, 18, 20, 24
FAIR, 70
FARSITE, 109
fire beetle, 42
fire break, 56
fire exclusion, 114
FireSafe, 34, 62, 84
fire triangle, 50, 51, 55
fireline, 33, 56
frequent fire follower, 18, 20, 24
fuelbreak, 56, 106
fuel-driven, 48, 104
geophyte, 18, 20
GIS, 61, 107
golden eardrops, 23, 24, 45
grizzly bear, 7, 10, 11
Harbison Canyon, 36, 40
Harmony Grove, 49
Harrison Park, 40
Hawkins, R., 34
Hermes copper, 42
Hood, L., 34
Howe, C., 31
Inaja, 34
initial attack, 32
Jones, J., 53
Julian, 40, 47
jute netting, 94
Keeley, J.E., 23
Kniebes, C., 58
knobcone pine, 19
Krause, B., 36
La Jolla, 32, 59
latitude, 4, 5
laurel sumac, 12, 21, 24
lemonadeberry, 12
Malibu, 47, 74, 106
Mandeville fire, 82
Mann Gulch, 47
manzanita, 2, 8, 11, 16, 19, 20

Marin County, 62
maritime, 9, 11
Mediterranean climate, 5, 17, 65, 105
mesic, 10
Mira Mesa, 128-129
mission manzanita, 24
Mission Trails Regional Park, 43, 44
mixed chaparral, 10
mock chaparral, 3
Mojave, 6
montane, 9, 12
mosaic, 25, 99, 100, 102, 105, 112
mountain lion, 14, 33
mountain mahogany, 28
MSCP, 129
mulch, 85, 86, 92
Muller, C.H., 27
multiple use, 124
Mussey Grade, 34
National Fire Plan, 60
Native American, 7, 25, 117
Oakland Hills, 48, 62, 84
obligate resprouter, 18, 19
obligate seeder, 18, 19, 24, 109
Ozarks, 60, 61, 64
Pine Valley, 33
ponderosa pine, 29, 40, 114, 117
pre-adaptation, 21
prescribed burns, 33, 28, 106
Purer, E. A., 127-128
red shanks, 9, 10
retrofit, 60
Rowntree, L., 17
Rucker, S., 47
ryegrass, 86, 89-91, 93
sagebrush, 12, 27
San Diego Board of Supervisors, 33
San Diego County Estates, 52
San Diego fairy shrimp, 127
San Diego mesa mint, 127
Santa Ana winds, 6, 10, 19, 32, 34, 37, 39, 48
Santa Monica Mountains, 71, 105-111
Schimper, A.F.W., 3
sclerophyllous, 3, 12, 16
Scripps Ranch, 35, 40, 54, 87
scrub oak, 9, 11, 28

senescence, 27, 28
shelter in place, 52, 65, 74
smoke, 22, 23, 24
Smokey Bear, 100
serotiny, 19
spadefoot toads, 127
stomata, 15, 16
Student Conservation Association, 60, 61
survivable space, 66
Sweetwater River, 32, 39
Tecate cypress, 19
Torrey pine, 11
toyon, 4, 15, 19, 28, 43
Tyler, C., 20, 21
type conversion, 8, 25, 109
unnatural accumulation, 29
USFS, 88, 123
Valley Center, 50
vernal pools, 127-129
Viejas, 32, 55
Viejas Mountain, 87
Vizcaino Desert, 7
voice of the chaparral, 3, 30
wattle, 85
white sage, 4, 12, 24
Wildcat Canyon, 38, 50, 52, 54, 87
wildland-urban interface, 62, 68, 102, 112
wildness, 43, 126
wind-driven, 48, 50, 51, 104, 121
woodrat, 14
wrentit, 3, 13, 30, 130
Wynola, 47
xeric, 9, 10